BRUGGEN

A Beautiful Fairy Tale

A Beautiful Fairy Tale

The Life of Actress Lois Moran

Richard Buller

Limelight Editions

Published in 2005 by

Limelight Editions
512 Newark Pompton Turnpike
Pompton Plains, New Jersey 07444

For sales, please contact

Limelight Editions
c/o Hal Leonard Corp.
7777 West Bluemound Road
Milwaukee, Wisconsin 53213
Tel. 800-637-2852
Fax 414-774-3259

Website: www.limelighteditions.com

Grateful acknowledgment is made to the following for permission to reprint excerpted material:

Reprinted with permission of Scribner, an imprint of Simon & Schuster Adult Publishing Group, from TENDER IS THE NIGHT by F. Scott Fitzgerald. Copyright 1933, 1934 by Charles Scribner's Sons. Copyright renewed © 1961, 1962 by Frances Scott Fitzgerald Lanahan.

Permissions to quote from other published and unpublished material, as well as photograph and illustration credits, appear on page 337.

Printed in the United States of America

Library of Congress Cataloging-in-Publication Data

Buller, Richard P.
   A beautiful fairy tale : the life of Lois Moran / Richard P. Buller.— 1st
Limelight ed.
      p. cm.
   Includes bibliographical references and index.
   ISBN 0-87910-312-4 (pbk.)
   1. Moran, Lois, 1909-1990. 2. Motion picture actors and actresses—United
States—Biography. I. Title.

PN2287.M699B86 2005
791.4302'8'092—dc22

2004015999

For my parents, Hurley and Billie Joan Buller,
with great love and appreciation

For my friend and mentor Colonel Timothy Marshall Young,
with admiration—and with thanks and gratitude
for his unwavering patience and inspiration

I want to go places and see people. I want my mind to grow.
I want to live where things happen on a big scale.

F. Scott Fitzgerald, "The Ice Palace," 1920

Table of Contents

Foreword
by Col. Timothy M. Young

August 1, 2004

Lois Moran, the actor, the loving mother, the physically beautiful woman with a mind that was composed of both fantasy and intellect.

How does an only son speak of a mother with the God-given talents and compassion that this wonderful human being possessed? You see, I hardly knew Mother. My world was one of caring and love and protection by others.

I came to know Lois Moran, the mother and friend, in her last years of wonderful productivity and love for others. She lived in a world of colorful hues, with a deep, abiding caring for her fellow human beings.

My mother's communication skills never diminished as the years moved forward. She wrote with candor and love on every subject. These would range from her beloved Red Rocks of Sedona to the reviews of plays and performances produced locally by budding young thespians and directors. Mother's inspiration of others from all walks of life will be her legacy.

Mother's life and body of work, so carefully portrayed by Richard Buller, are a living tribute to the wonderment of Lois Moran, the person. Here is a portrait of some eighty years of giving without reservation to the people of this planet.

The author's insightful and diligent research, coupled with some memorable findings in Mother's journals, papers, and photographs, have made this book a true and masterfully constructed literary achievement.

"Of Thee I Sing," Mother.

Your son,
Tim

Acknowledgments

As a college student majoring in literature in the summer of 1985, I first became aware of Lois Moran. I was wild for F. Scott Fitzgerald and adored silent movies, and when a friend informed me that Lois, who appealed strongly to both of my interests, was alive and living in Sedona, Arizona, I found an address for her, began a correspondence that would continue until 1990, the year she died, and set into motion the nearly twenty years of research that have made the present volume possible. Researching the life of Lois has not been an easy task, especially at the beginning, when I could find only the briefest mention of her anywhere, including most of the books about F. Scott Fitzgerald that I read. Lois herself was not as helpful on the matter as she might have been, because she disliked what she called "dwelling on the past." Thus, over the years, I have relied upon a variety of other individuals and institutions that have enabled me to write a biography. In the course of two decades, there are many acknowledgments I wish to make. Alas, to credit everyone would be cumbersome, if not impossible, and if in the present list I have omitted a citation, I apologize. It is my pleasure, though, to publicly offer my most sincere thanks as follows.

First and foremost, I must thank Lois Moran Young herself. One of the most gracious, giving people I have ever encountered, she answered questions I put to her, was always happy to send me a copy of her latest Sedona "Down at the Barn" newspaper column or the newest snapshot of herself, and in the process also offered some pretty wonderful advice about life in general. The subject of an autobiography was much on her mind, but toward the end of our correspondence, she admitted that needed someone else to tell her story and suggested that I might be that person. I feel lucky and grateful to have lived in a time when it was still possible to be in contact with a person such as Lois Moran, and I treasure my personal memories of her.

My parents, Hurley and Billie Joan Buller, have always been my strongest supporters and allies. To them I owe much, because their encouragement of my love for what my mother calls "the old things" has led to a lifetime of pleasure in study and research. Lois herself exchanged a letter or two with my mother, who in turn one Christmas embroidered a beautiful wall hanging that Lois hung in her bedroom.

Col. Timothy M. Young, Lois's son, has been the driving force behind this book, and by allowing me access to his mother's scrapbooks, letters, journals, and photographs, has given me the means to piece together Lois's story. Tim is a clear thinker and one of those rare people who can see all things, including his own family, with a sometimes shocking clarity, as his comments in this book will demonstrate. As was Lois, he is eternally young, and I profoundly thank him for bestowing upon me the honor of setting upon paper the events of Lois's life.

Two friends, John Drennon and Mary Anne Styburski, have contributed generously to this book, both in spirit and in helping me discover facts. In the early 1990s, I thought of us as "The Three Musketeers," as we each had an interest in one particular silent-era actress, he in Priscilla Dean and she in Laura La Plante, and as we each lived in different cities across the country, we were ever on the prowl for material of interest for the group. John is the best-informed silent film historian I have known personally, not to mention one of the nicest people. His knowledge of the subject is prodigious, and he has recommended several excellent books to me that contain mention of Lois. Mary Anne, who regretfully passed away in 1999, helped me in locating elusive photographs of Lois. Like John, she was marvelously well versed in silent films, and it was always a pleasure to receive her many packages containing her newest Lois discoveries, such as photos or magazine and newspaper clippings. Her passing was a saddening event, indeed.

There are other special friends I would like to acknowledge as well. Dena Feldman, editor, English professor, and dear friend, has been a source of constant encouragement and editorial suggestions. Harry Hart-Browne, an actor, writer, and free spirit, has also been enormously supportive of my efforts and has proffered some of the best editorial advice I received while writing the book. Melodie Williamson has been there to offer calming advice and assurance. Lana Madrid has located some amazing Lois research materials for me. Pamela Nagami, M.D., author of *Maneater* and *Bitten*, was the catalyst of my finishing and marketing the book, for she related her own book-publishing experiences to me and educated me in the proper way of acquiring an agent and setting things in motion. I shall never forget her looking at me and pronouncing, "Your book is doable."

The patient, wonderful people who have worked with me since I finished the book deserve my utmost thanks. Andrew J. Whelchel III has proven the finest, most resourceful agent any writer could hope for, not to mention the fact that he is kindhearted and gives his all to a project in which he believes. My publishers at Limelight Editions, John Cerullo and Carol Flannery, have been charming and focused, and because of them I have known without doubt that my book has been in the right hands. Barbara Norton, my editor, admirably streamlined and polished my manuscript, and her talents are nothing short of amazing. Jenna Young, my publicist and jacket designer, possesses shrewdness, astonishing enthusiasm, and fine artistic skill.

Several high-profile individuals have been kind enough to help me in my research. Douglas Fairbanks Jr. was all for the book from the get-go, and I regret that he did not live to see the final product. Diana Serra Cary, a child film star in the 1920s and extraordinary writer presently, has for over a decade encouraged me to follow my dream of completing this book. Film historian Kevin Brownlow has been exceptionally kind, allowing me access to his own personal file on Lois and providing keen feedback on the manuscript. Frances Kroll Ring, F. Scott Fitzgerald's secretary at the time of his death, recalled for me her meeting with Lois at the Ambassador Hotel in the 1980s. Lupita Tovar shared her memories of Lois with me on the telephone, as did Quentin Crisp, who remembered seeing one of Lois's films in London in the early 1930s. Anita Page and her friend the actor and film historian Randal Malone were lovely to me, as was Marian Marsh. Betsy Blair was uncommonly gracious in sharing memories with me about her distant cousin Lois. Luise Rainer, Esther Ralston, Charles "Buddy" Rogers, Frances Dee, and Jane Russell were kind enough to answer Lois-related questions I posed to them at various film-history functions. Ray Bradbury absolutely stunned me when, in response to a letter I wrote him in which I mentioned this book, he wrote back that he had actually danced with Lois in the 1950s. Myrna Loy, Lillian Gish, Billie Dove, Gloria Stuart, Pauline Curley, Colleen Moore, and Cloris Leachman each provided me bits of information in mailed notes. And Arthur Mizener, through his archive of Lois letters and mementos, deserves to be thanked even though he passed away before I could ever have contacted him. The letters that Lois wrote to him in the late 1940s and early 1950s are by far the most vivid and honest resource of information about her relationship with F. Scott Fitzgerald. Professor Mizener has been so great a part of my life during the writing of this book that I feel as if he is now a personal guardian angel.

There are numerous other individuals to whom I would like to give my thanks for their help in my ongoing research on Lois. These include, but are not limited to: Michael Ankerich; Beverly Armstrong; Lawrence Austin, the late owner of the Silent Movie Theatre in Hollywood; Harry Eugene Baldwin; Phil Barragan; Ralph Benner, publisher of the former *Hollywood Studio Magazine*; Denise Brauer; Craig Broadway; the late theatrical agent Alan Brock; Bridget Cavanagh; David Chierichetti; Alfred Chico; Villa Clarkson; Irwin Clyman; Donald Collins; Michael Collins; Kirk Crivello; Linda Daniel;

LaVerne Decker; William M. Drew; Anthony Escalante; Elana Feldman; Milo Garfield; Kyle Husfloen; Al Jacobs; Professor Lesley Johnstone; Don Jolliff and Ed Mehlenbacher; Reverend Larry and Virginia Keene; Bob King, publisher of *Classic Images* and *Films of the Golden Age*; Casey Kramer; Ron Kruger; Mike Lambert; Michael Lizarraga; Barney and Catherine Martin; John McKay; Carl Oberer; Kenneth Parker; Guy Pearson; Lois Peyton; Professor Ruth Prigozy; Stephen Rafael; Denise Ricks; Rita Rosencranz; Rusty Schrader; Kevin Sullivan; Leif Thorsted; Charles Utley; Dale Vandergriff; Gene Vazzana; Mark Vieira; Sivinee Visessmith; Laura Wagner; and the ever helpful staffs of Cinema Collectors bookstore, Larry Edmunds bookstore, Eddie Brandt's Saturday Matinee, Film Favorites photo service, Hollywood Book City, and Baby Jane of Hollywood.

There are, additionally, people at university libraries and research institutions that I wish to thank. The staff of Princeton Library Special Collections, especially Margaret Sherry Rich, AnnaLee Pauls, and Ben Primer, were always friendly and helpful. Professor Matthew J. Bruccoli and Judith S. Baughman of the University of South Carolina were generous in helping to locate a print of the photo reproduced herein of Lois and F. Scott Fitzgerald together. Craig Tenney at Harold Ober Associates kindly aided me in gaining publication rights of Fitzgerald material from Fitzgerald's estate. The staff of Stanford University Special Collections, especially Polly Armstrong and Sean Quimby, were accommodating in providing me access to the Albert Guérard papers upon which I draw briefly in the book. Lydia Zelaya of Simon and Schuster guided me in the process of obtaining rights to quote from Fitzgerald writings, most particularly *Tender Is the Night*. Claire Fortune of Condé Nast Publications helped in gaining permission to reproduce the Ralph Barton illustration. The knowledgeable staff of the Academy of Motion Picture Sciences Library in Beverly Hills helped to clarify several questions for me. The staffs of George Eastman House in Rochester, the University of Wisconsin, and the British Film Institute allowed me to obtain research prints of Lois photographs.

I must also thank my family, aside from my parents. My late grandmother, Opal Vallee, brothers Douglas and Marshall, Aunt Phyllis Farrar and her husband Clarke and daughter Shannon are all in my heart and have always been supportive, if not sometimes a bit bewildered, by my fascination with the past. I am lucky to have these special people in my life. Even my young niece, Skye, and nephews Tyler, Abraham, Jacob, and Adam have been supportive; I hope, in time, they will write books about subjects they love. My late grandfather, Francis McClanahan, who was killed in a bombing raid over Berlin in the Second World War, has always been a beacon to me of the virtues of living for what one believes. My great uncle, Wayne Smith, learned and well-read, has long been an inspiration to me as a person and as a writer.

Additionally, I would like to thank a man who has had perhaps the most profound influence upon my life and the direction it has taken, Professor Lawrence D. Stewart. A Fitzgerald scholar who knew Carl Van Vechten, worked for Ira Gershwin, and co-wrote the first major biography of the Gershwins in 1958, Dr. Stewart was instrumental in attuning my mind when I was in college in the 1980s to the wonders of Jazz Age literature and culture. He has also been my friend. I owe him a great deal.

On a more ethereal note, I must thank, with all my heart, my patron saint, St. Thérèse of Lisieux, "The Little Flower." St. Thérèse effects astonishing things in the lives of those who pray to her, and her acts of goodness are revealed by the unexpected appearance of roses. Whenever I have fretted over the way a chapter was going, or whether I would ever finish the book, or whether it would ever see a publisher's press, St. Thérèse has given me the tenacity and faith to persevere. Indeed, since I began work on this book there have come my way enough rose petals to fill an arboretum.

A Beautiful Fairy Tale

⦵ Book I ⦵

"Eyes Have Appetites"

Of course the Neverland had been make-believe
in those days; but it was real now.

J. M. Barrie, *Peter Pan*, 1906

Another Cinderella has triumphed.

Review of Lois Moran's performance in *Stella Dallas*,
Photoplay, November 1925

Pittsburgh's Own "Billy," Paris in the 1920s, and the Celebration of Fairy Tales

eated high in a balcony at the Apollo Theater in New York City on a windy night in November 1925, sixteen-year-old Lois Moran looked around nervously but tried to conceal her apprehension. She was there for an elaborate film premiere, one of those glittering and exciting spectacles popular at the time, and, ordinarily, attending a movie screening would not have caused her any anxiety. This evening, however, she happened to be one of the stars of the film being shown, a major, much-heralded Samuel Goldwyn production entitled *Stella Dallas*. It also happened to be her first appearance in an American film, and she knew the audience's reaction to her performance would be crucially important to her career. She enacted one of the most complex roles in the picture, that of Laurel, the emotionally conflicted daughter of a broken home. She was aware that advance reaction to *Stella Dallas* had been highly encouraging; nonetheless, she worried this evening about the reception it would be accorded by the opening-night audience.

The casual observer looking up at her in the theater that evening would have been hard pressed to discern that she was an actress in the film at hand; and he would have been astonished to know that by the time it had finished screening she would be a celebrity. At five foot two, weighing about 107 pounds, and endowed with a lithe, boyish figure and features that reflected her Irish heritage, she did not have the glamorous look prized by actresses of the time. Her smile was cordial and pleasing but seemed to suggest warm friendship rather than hot romance. Her hair was golden, sprinkled with just a hint of red, and she often styled it conservatively, in fashions that differed from the austere, short-cut bobs that were then popular with young girls. Her complexion was photogenic but spattered with freckles, which made her appear perpetually freshly scrubbed and prompted her friend the writer Michael Arlen to dub her the "Queen of Ten Thousand Freckles." Only her eyes appeared to conform to the rigors of the film glamour machine. They were a piercing gray-blue. The *Los Angeles Times* had described them recently as "neither a child's nor a woman's but which just belong to Lois."

Seated in the balcony with her mother, Gladys, Lois looked around her at the many cinema personalities, most of them personally invited by Goldwyn, as they poured into the theater. She sensed that she was different from these polished and urbane people, and her tension increased as she noted with amazement their sophisticated personalities and glittering attire. Wearing only a simple green georgette, she was awash in a celebrity-crested sea of silks, furs, and fine jewelry; and although she had much to talk about with her mother, she could not help but be intimidated by the wide range of animated conservation she overheard all around her.

Seized with self-doubt, she began to wonder whether appearing in the movies had been such a good idea after all. It was true that she had spent time in Paris and had appeared in two French films, but she was at heart an unaffected girl, born and raised in Pittsburgh, and felt no sense of belonging here in the glossy trappings of the American film community. But Gladys, unwaveringly confident in her daughter's abilities, assured her that her fears were only butterflies, that when viewers saw her performance the world would be hers. Clutching Lois's hand in silent affirmation that all would be well, Gladys foresaw, even if Lois did not, that this would be the beginning of a bold new journey in both their lives.

Amidst the fanfare, Lois was unsure that any of those present would even bother to notice the film itself. Once the lights were dimmed, however, she began to hear sniffles and sobs, and when her biggest scene appeared on the screen, a sequence in which Laurel is snubbed by her peers at her tenth birthday party, the sounds turned into veritable wailing. When intermission came, the audience applauded vigorously. Looking up toward her in the balcony, people beseeched her to stand and wave. She did so, and to her surprise this seemed to elicit even more admiration. Soon she was asked to blow kisses as well. Amazed and caught utterly off guard, she did as she was asked. Feeling as if she were in a dream and holding back tears, her knees started to buckle, and for a brief moment she felt that she might lose her composure. Gladys, ever strong and ever reassuring, was beside her; and suddenly, as she looked down at the seemingly endless expanse of adoring faces, she began to remember her personal motto, a saying of her stepfather's, Timothy Moran: *nothing is impossible to a Moran*. She felt calm and confident, then; and she knew that, just as her mother had promised, everything would turn out all right.

Lois Moran experienced her first encounter with film stardom that evening, and, as her friend F. Scott Fitzgerald described it in a 1935 letter to her, she began to "galvanically" ascend the Hollywood hierarchy of motion picture actresses. Her rise from orphan to movie star was nothing short of a modern fairy tale.

Before the disillusionment brought on by World War I made films so important to the masses who sought to escape reality—indeed, even before films had really arrived at all—Lois Moran was born Lois Darlington Dowling, of Irish and German descent, on March 1, 1909, in Pittsburgh, then a city of roughly a million inhabitants, to Roger Dowling and Gladys Evans Dowling. Her middle name honored her maternal great-aunt, Edith Darlington Ammon. Lois's father, a loving man who, like his father, had succeeded at the Jones and Laughlin Steel Company, died in an automobile accident in his thirties, when she was only one year old; but his daughter had been born embodying the better aspects of his character and personality. In a 1931 *New Movie* magazine article, Franklin A. Ammon, a Pittsburgh attorney, offered that Lois had inherited from Roger a sense of physical dexterity and natural rhythm, attributes that would be vital to her future work as a dancer: "Her father was no mean acrobat himself."

Lois's mother, a strong and dynamic personality, had no intention of spending the rest of her life a grieving widow, and a few years after Roger's death she remarried. Her second husband was Dr. Timothy Moran, an Irishman employed as an oculist for the Carnegie Steel Company and, as Roger had been, a caring man who adored Lois. He looked after her as he would have his own daughter, took her to Saturday afternoon vaudeville shows, and formed a strong bond with her. Mindful parents, he and Gladys enrolled the child in Seton Hill Academy, a quiet Catholic girls' school (but not, as would later be popularly believed, a convent) in Greensburg, near Pittsburgh. Life proceeded happily until Timothy, too, died, of influenza, Gladys by his side, at Camp Oglethorpe, where he was waiting to be sent overseas during World War I. Nine-year-old Lois felt this new loss acutely. "I cried and cried," she wrote in the 1970s in a series of notes she prepared for an intended autobiography. "He was my dad, my dearest person in the world next to mother."

In spite of the setback, at Seton Hill Lois displayed personality and character extraordinary for her age. She took to playing on the steps of the Carnegie Library; at school, she was popular and well liked, by both her peers and the sisters; and she grew into a tomboy deserving of the pert nickname bestowed upon her by Gladys, "Billy." The 1931 *New Movie* article also included an interview with one of Lois's classmates of the time, Mary Harris, the daughter of John P. Harris, a Pennsylvania state senator and cofounder of the first nickelodeon theater. Harris recalled that "Billy" was a "sweet girl" who demonstrated an intense interest in the theater, took leading roles in school plays, and danced gracefully. She noted, too, that when Seton Hill screened movies for its students, Lois took only an "ordinary" interest in them, even then evincing that her ambitions were directed more toward the theater than the cinema.

Perhaps because of the shared tragedies of the loss of first Roger and then Timothy, Gladys and Lois were an extremely close and devoted pair, not just mother and daughter but also best friends. Unquestionably, Gladys had a profound impact on Lois's formative years, a fact that Lois was careful to point out in interviews she gave at the time of *Stella Dallas*. "It's funny about people, isn't it?" she said to one reporter. "I do like them so much and I wonder what they think about and why they do the things they do, but no one satisfies me really, but mother." When Gladys, determined that her daughter develop an appreciation of theater, encouraged Lois's interest by taking her to plays, operas, and dance recitals that came to Pittsburgh, the child responded with enthusiasm. It was also in those early Pittsburgh days that she developed her passion for dancing.

Gladys also introduced Lois to the world of reading. "Somehow I could never play games with children and amuse them that way," she explained to the *New York American* in November 1925, "so I taught Lois to amuse herself with a book." Lois's grandparents the Dowlings were also instrumental in kindling her affection for the written word, and Lois would speak fondly, in later years, of her days as "Billy" when she would beat up every boy her size in the neighborhood, only to later retire to her grandparents' cozy den, where her grandfather would read, her grandmother would crochet, and she would explore the many volumes in their library. "It was wonderful to have a fine library," she said in her notes. "Grandpa gave me *carte blanche*." In that parlor in Pittsburgh, she read works by, among others, Sir Walter Scott, Edgar Allan Poe, and Charles Dickens. Her early exposure to the written word helped shape the curiosity and appreciation of literature that would prove invaluable to the sensibilities she would later develop both as a person and as an actress and would influence the friendships she would choose to cultivate with various intellectuals in Paris, Hollywood, and New York.

After the death of Timothy Moran, Gladys came to regard Pittsburgh as an unhappy, lonely place and believed that a change in environment would be beneficial to herself and Lois. Aware of her daughter's achievement in dance at Seton Hill, she resolved, in the bold, thunder-and-lightning decision-making process for which she would increasingly become known, that they would move to Paris. Lois would commence ballet lessons there, so as to acquire the best possible cultural and intellectual education. Lois explained to the columnist Dorothy Donnell in a 1927 film magazine interview that Gladys "used to say that if anything ever happened to her she wanted to be sure that I had seen all sides of life." Gladys was also concerned that the Dowlings' strict Catholic beliefs would hinder the breadth of Lois's education were she to remain in Pittsburgh. "[Gladys] was about fifty years ahead of her time," observed the actress Betsy Blair, Lois's distant cousin, in her 2003 autobiography, *The Memory of All That: Love and Politics in New York, Hollywood, and Paris.*

The money left her by the deaths of two husbands was insufficient to finance Gladys's ambitious relocation, but Lois's wealthy name-sake took a keen interest in her upbringing. In a 1928 *Modern Screen* profile, Lois remembered her great-aunt Edith as inhabiting a large Victorian house, collecting rose leaves and cloves in a potpourri jar, and devoting hours to her love of petit point. Beyond her domestic hobbies, Edith was a woman of strength and determination who possessed both the means and the desire to finance Lois's education abroad. Without hesitation, she wrote Gladys a check. First-class sailing accommodations were arranged, and the Morans' dream of Paris began turning to reality.

In 1921, Gladys and Lois, aged twelve, embarked for the City of Light, a move that changed both their lives forever. But France was not the only country to play a part in Lois's life at this time. Once settled in Paris, Gladys ran into an old friend from her own school days, Mary Martin, a meeting that yielded interesting results. Martin was a niece of Alexander Moore, a Pittsburgh newspaper publisher, the widower of Lillian Russell, and the current ambassador to Spain. She invited Gladys and Lois to Madrid, where she was serving as hostess at the embassy for her uncle. There Moore gave a tea dance in honor of Lois, who responded by dancing for the guests. In the audience was a Spanish film director who was at the time working on a biblical epic and in search of an actress to play a vestal virgin who is thrown to the lions. Upon seeing Lois, he was heard to exclaim, "The face of a vestal virgin! The girl for my picture!" Although the Spanish film did not materialize, on the horizon were two French productions.

Lois remained fond of Moore, whom she called "Uncle Alec," and from 1920 to 1924 she and Gladys visited him often in San Sebastian. Lois described these visits in her notes as "Really Something. All the boys went for me because I was very blonde then, really a tow-head. The other little girls were very much dark-haired." The Spanish court also summered in San Sebastian, and during one visit there Lois danced for the Spanish queen mother.

Gladys's decision to leave their hometown to sail for Europe was a bold and courageous break with tradition. As Lois's son, Timothy M. Young, has observed, "Gladys was a force, and she knew exactly what she wanted." Certainly, the dramatic alteration of lifestyle that she set in motion proved refreshing and invigorating for Lois. Before actually taking up residence in Paris, Gladys settled with her briefly in nearby Tours, and from their home there, Lois penned a letter to family back in Pittsburgh in September 1921 in which she spoke of how much she had enjoyed sailing to Europe and of how "I am having the loveliest time over here." She and Gladys had visited Paris and had become tourists, and the girl's starry-eyed description of the sites they visited reflects not only the city as it was at the time, shortly after the bitter conclusion of World War I, but also her initial reactions to it, which differed from the more studied and polished accounts of her impressions she would convey to the press in later years. "We went to the top of the Eiffel Tower & oh, you can see for miles around!" she exclaimed. "We went to see the Panorama of the War. There is a big circular platform all around, a little distance away is a great big picture of the War. It has all of the important people etc. & all the countries and you would think that some of them were standing right there, they look so real!" In Tours, Lois also attended school and applied herself assiduously to mastering the French language.

Lois differed from the other girls in Tours, however. "The girls at the Tours school weren't planning for careers," she commented in her interview with Dorothy Donnell. "They expected to be married and keep house." Lois had more ambitious aspirations, and, not surprisingly, after six happy but staid months in the city, she could no longer contain her eagerness to begin dancing. Gladys, mindful that Timothy Moran had wanted Lois to wait until she was twelve to begin lessons, realized that the time was right to look into dancing as a serious possibility. She and Lois journeyed to Paris.

They took lodgings at the Hotel Fleurus, a stimulating residence, for James Joyce resided there—they glimpsed the nearly blind writer almost daily—and it was near one of the most celebrated addresses in the city, 27 rue Fleurus, the home of the American expatriate writer Gertrude Stein, whose no-nonsense approach to life and blazing intelligence appealed to Gladys and whose famous art-lined salon she visited. Living at the Hotel Fleurus also allowed Gladys and Lois to make the acquaintance of the avant-garde writer Jean Cocteau and the photographer Man Ray, who took Lois's photograph in 1922, when she was thirteen. Gladys had chosen in Paris a city and a home of considerable color and personality. There she and Lois rejuvenated their wounded spirits, emerging centered and happy.

At the time of Gladys and Lois's residence in Paris, the city glowed brightly as the center of a miniature artistic and literary high renaissance, the place, in Stein's estimation, where twentieth century culture "was." Within its streets, cafés, and salons thrived an eclectic variety of gifted people, including writers such as Stein, Joyce, Ernest Hemingway, Sherwood Anderson, and Ford Madox Ford; artists such as Pablo Picasso, Henri Matisse, and Juan Gris; internationally known movie actors such as the serial star Pearl White; and, of particular interest to Lois, ballet stars such as Vera Trefilova and Anton Dolin, whose unique and disciplined techniques fueled and inspired her own desire to dance.

The postwar flowering of Paris, was, alas, brief. In his 1931 short story "Babylon Revisited," F. Scott Fitzgerald, who also inhabited Paris during the 1920s but at different times than Lois did, described it all as having had a "sort of magic" that "was nice while it lasted." Lois lived there at an ideal time, however, and the city could not have been a better location for her. As Gladys had hoped, she liked her new life there, matured, and took considerable strides in healing the suppurating emotional wounds that had been left by the deaths of Roger and most particularly of Timothy. As appealing as she found her new Parisian surroundings, however, she did not lose sight of the fact that her purpose for being there was to become a dancer.

In hope of finding a dance instructor, she visited the Paris Opéra, an aged, rambling, dark stone building in the heart of the city. What resulted was highly unusual. She began taking classes at and dancing with the Opéra itself, a rare achievement for one so young. In a 1925 interview she gave to the *New York Chronicle Telegraph*, she explained the process by which she entered the ballet. "I wanted to study under the very best instruction I could get," she began, "so we [she and Gladys] applied to the mistress of the ballet at the opera. I was given a tryout and accepted." She added, "You know, they take you there if you agree to remain two years. The first year is devoted to study and the second year you take a place in the ballet."

At the Opéra, Lois, deemed too old to begin the study of classical ballet, was assigned to the Jaques Dalcroze eurhythmics school, which held that all elements of music could be expressed through movement. In her study of eurhythmics, she performed Russian and

French ballet, even dancing with Trefilova, as well as barefoot dancing. Such creativity helped to expel the demons of her losses and, in fact, did much to make this period one of the most carefree of her life. The combination of Paris and dancing made for a cultural confectionery that was liberating and irresistible to a talented child such as Lois. It aided her in focusing her attentions upon culture, beauty, and self-knowledge, subjects she had contemplated comfortably in the confines of her grandparents' library in Pittsburgh and that now in Europe helped powerfully to define and develop her burgeoning personality.

By devoting such energy to dancing in Paris, however, Lois found little time for formal schooling, prompting the ever-resourceful Gladys to hire tutors for her. One of these, a fellow Irishman named Michael Knox, was an intense and eccentric bohemian whom Dorothy Donnell described as being "a trifle mad." Knox had rebelled against his father's wishes that he take up law as a profession and had proclaimed that he would rather starve as a happy artist than grow plump and miserable as an attorney. Gladys retained him to teach Lois Latin and algebra, but Lois told Donnell "he didn't know much about those subjects." Instead, he schooled her in art and in Shakespeare, as well as taking her to museums and to cafés where writers and artists congregated. "I loved the cafés in Montmartre," Lois explained to Donnell, adding that she and Knox "would sit all afternoon talking and arguing.... I learned a good deal from him." She and Knox mingled with a number of artists and literary intellectuals at the cafés. Among the vibrant personalities they met was the lesbian author Radclyffe Hall, whose novel *The Well of Loneliness* had achieved notoriety and whose powerful intellect and curious, masculine appearance made a vivid impression on Lois. Her multifaceted relationship with Knox succeeded. She excelled at dancing and passed her college examinations in Paris when she was fourteen.

It was inevitable that many people would see Lois in Paris. Her celebrity, local though it was, increased. Noticing the attention her daughter was receiving, Gladys began to consider an acting career for her. In a 1931 *Picture Play* interview, she explained her reasons to Mabel Duke: "While I was never theatrically inclined and knew little about the stage, it seemed to me that this profession offered the greatest opportunities and the richest rewards of any occupation for a girl."

The story of the smitten Spanish film director who declared Lois an ideal vestal virgin appears to be the first instance of a filmmaker's taking notice of her. In Paris, however, a French director did so as well, which led to her first two film appearances. Marcel L'Herbier, a pioneer of French cinema, had seen Lois's picture in a photographer's studio and was intrigued by her potential as a film actress. As Lois explained to the *New York American* in 1925, "[L'Herbier] was desperate for a leading lady. You know, over there are no young actresses. Young girls never go on the stage as they do here. So the producers have a hard time."

L'Herbier believed Lois might do well portraying a dancer in his next film, a circus melodrama entitled *La galerie des monstres* that he was preparing with Jaque Catelain, who at seventeen was a popular French matinee idol. She made a test, and L'Herbier awarded her the part of Ralda, a ballerina in a traveling circus. The role was not as dicey as that of a vestal virgin fated to become a lion's lunch, but it was certainly unusual enough. L'Herbier had only one restriction. He required Lois to wear a rather formidable black wig to make her look older.

The wig aged Lois considerably, perhaps too much so, because, with the addition in some parts of the film of a conservative floral dress and a long string of beads, she appeared more a very young student masquerading in a school play than an actress in a film. Regardless of her physical appearance, however, she performed competently in a production that easily could have overwhelmed her. She enjoyed the process of film production, and in 1927 she recalled for Dorothy Donnell the specifics of shooting *La galerie des monstres*.

I had a wonderful time with that company. [L'Herbier] himself called at our hotel for me every morning in his car and we would drive out to some studio in the suburbs.... We got there usually by ten, and sat about talking while the electricians fixed the lights. Then when we finally started to work, the lights would go out! While the electricians tinkered with them, we sat around talking again and by the time the lights were fixed it was lunch time. Lunch always takes two hours in France, no matter how little there is to eat. And of course we finished every afternoon in plenty of time for tea!

La galerie des monstres was filled with curiosities. True to its title, the film followed the theme of circus gothic, presenting scenes rich with sinister clowns (even the boyishly handsome Catelain donned grotesquely exaggerated harlequin make-up); a furious lion that served as a motif throughout the film; a gypsy fortune teller; carnival performers dressed as voodoo priests, military commanders, cowboys, and, of course, monsters. It was a visually engaging movie with a melodramatic plot. Lois danced beautifully and enacted believable outdoor love scenes with Catelain, counterbalancing the melodramatics by providing an anchor of calm and of genuine vulnerability. In contrast to Lois was another performer in the film, the legendary Kiki de Montparnasse (billed here as Kiki), an exotic nightclub singer, autobiographer, actress, painter, and model. The mistress of Man Ray, she was featured in some of his best-known photographs. Lois was dazzled by Kiki, whom she probably had met when Ray photographed Lois earlier.

Lois's performance in the picture pleased L'Herbier enough that he cast her again in his next, more important undertaking, *Feu Mathias Pascal* (also known as *The Living Dead Man*), a project based on a seriocomic novel by Luigi Pirandello. To create the film, the first that Pirandello had allowed to be made of one of his works, L'Herbier joined forces with Alexandre Kamenka's émigré film company in Paris, called Films Albatros, and he cast the Albatros's prime asset, the renowned Russian actor Ivan Mosjoukine, then in his thirties, as the film's lead, Mathias Pascal. Lois played the love interest, Adrienne

Paleari. A visually beautiful production, *Feu Mathias Pascal* was the story of an Italian peasant who, erroneously believed to have been killed in an accident, assumes a new identity in the city. After winning a large sum of money in Monte Carlo, he falls in love with Adrienne, but realizes that while he may have money, without the genuine identity papers he needs in order to marry her he is no more than a "living dead man." All ends well, though, for L'Herbier changed Pirandello's original glum ending and drew the plot to a happy conclusion with the marriage of Pascal and Adrienne.

Lois relished the making of her second film, which was shot largely on location in Italy, and in 1982 she wrote to the film historian Kevin Brownlow about filming at Christmastime in Italy. She went to great lengths, she told Brownlow, to secure a Christmas tree and decorate the production sites festively with ornaments such as popcorn strings. Having developed a schoolgirl's crush on Ivan Mosjoukine, she also hung mistletoe in a doorway, explaining to the object of her affection the American custom of kissing under it. "Alas," she recalled, "all my well-laid plans went awry; Ivan only kissed my hand. I was fourteen, he in his thirties, I expect. . . . First loves are great, aren't they?"

Feu Mathias Pascal did not screen in New York until the spring of 1927. Mordaunt Hall, reviewing the film for the *New York Times*, disliked it, commenting that the story was "interesting in spite of the picture." Otherwise, though, it received generally glowing remarks, both at the time of its original release and in subsequent years. Georges Sadoul, in his often-cited 1972 *Dictionary of Films*, called it "Marcel L'Herbier's best film," notable for its "documentary-like use of exteriors." Noel Burch, in his 1991 *In and Out of Synch: The Awakening of a Cine-Dreamer*, did not agree that it was L'Herbier's best but believed that "the film [was] made with great virtuosity" and explained that it was enhanced by the free-form style of the Albatros Studio.

A teenager with only one previous film credit to her name, Lois was fortunate to have appeared in such an important picture. L'Herbier's casting revealed that he recognized her to be a natural film actress whose abilities were innate, not wholly dependent upon experience. *Feu Mathias Pascal* did not put her over, at least in the United States, but it helped her win her part the following year in the film that would, *Stella Dallas*. In later years, she would recall relatively little about *Feu Mathias Pascal*, although she did reminisce to Michael Ankerich, in his 1993 *Broken Silence*, "I don't remember much about the story, but I do remember Italy. We did a lot of scenes on the Grand Staircase in Rome, across the street from the Coliseum [*sic*], and several scenes in the Coliseum. I remember best the gardens and restaurants. We tried a different one every night." She concluded, "There was a casualness about filmmaking in Europe which my later films in Hollywood never had."

Tryouts in Atlantic City, Samuel Goldwyn, and the "Impressive Vogue" of *Stella Dallas*

2

*A*fter finishing her work for L'Herbier, Lois, with her mother's encouragement, sent photographs of herself to D. W. Griffith and Samuel Goldwyn, who had issued a casting call for an actress to play the lead in a studio production of *Romeo and Juliet* in which he intended to star Ronald Colman. Nothing came of the Griffith attempt. Goldwyn, however, liked what he saw and, forgetting *Romeo and Juliet* entirely, eventually cast her in a film he and the director Henry King had been planning for over a year. It was a vividly produced, strongly constructed picture that would come to be one of the best silent films: *Stella Dallas*, an adaptation of an immensely popular novel by Olive Higgins Prouty.

Lois's timing in sending Goldwyn her photos was fortunate, for *Stella Dallas* was one of the blockbuster books of the 1920s, and filming it was an undertaking of substantial import. Most actresses could only hope for such a film to come along once in their careers, and Lois's involvement in it would bring her considerable attention. In *Stella Dallas*, written as a magazine serial in 1922 and published as a novel in 1923, Prouty had created the most renowned work of her career. A careful and sensitive wordsmith who understood human nature, she also told a good story. And although she perfected and honed each of her novels—which included, in addition to *Stella Dallas*, works such as *The Star in the Window, Home Port*, and, most famously,

Now, Voyager—she was careful to avoid literary artifice, keeping her syntax elegant and free from pretense and obtrusive technique. Her style made her books well received and profitable.

The reading public adored Prouty, and by the time Grosset and Dunlap published *Stella Dallas* as a book, it already had legions of admirers. The story was so popular, in fact, that the producer Edgar Selwyn procured the rights to produce it as a play. That drama, starring the theatrical celebrity Mrs. Patrick Campbell as Stella, garnered poor reviews and never reached Broadway. Nonetheless, it demonstrated that a drama could be made of the book, and even if the play was a failure, a film still had much potential. Prouty believed that the play failed because of Campbell's propensity to overact and to rewrite dialogue and scenes to suit her own melodramatic sensibilities, at the expense of the overall story. To filmgoers, however, such considerations were moot, for few had seen the play but many had read the story, including Lois herself, twice. Innumerable people were caught up in what *Variety* termed the "impressive vogue" of *Stella Dallas* and eager to see it made into a motion picture. Goldwyn, who had an innate sense of what the public wanted, realized that audiences expected him to create a distinguished film.

Accordingly, Goldwyn would oversee the production of *Stella Dallas* with meticulous care and exhaustive attention to detail, the result of which would prove to be, in 1925, a colossal financial and critical success. The film was almost universally acclaimed as one of the great pictures of its day. It was the force that undisputedly propelled Lois's career forward, and while it is popular knowledge that F. Scott Fitzgerald based the *Tender Is the Night* character Rosemary Hoyt, a film actress, on Lois, it is considerably less widely known that the film Rosemary is making in the pages of that novel was a fictional parallel to *Stella Dallas*.

The screen rendering of *Stella Dallas* was an intense study of the sacrifices the title character, a lower-class, gauche, but always good-hearted woman, is forced to make so that her daughter may have an easier life with her wealthy father. After having married the well-meaning but uncouth Stella Martin, Stephen Dallas leaves her because her lack of the social graces impedes his social status and law career. He loves their infant daughter, Laurel, but agrees it is best for her to remain with her mother. Laurel grows up devoted to Stella, but there are problems. She is upset to overhear disparaging remarks from her peers about Stella's garish clothing and coarse mannerisms; and when the headmistress of Laurel's school glimpses Stella and her friend, a gambler named Ed Munn, in what she erroneously perceives to be an immoral situation, she sees to it that none of Laurel's friends, all of whom have been invited, attend her upcoming tenth birthday party. Laurel is left devastated, celebrating her birthday alone with Stella. Several years later, when Laurel has blossomed into a beautiful, poised young woman and engaged to a well-heeled young man, Richard Grosvenor, Stella realizes that she would enjoy a better life with her father, now remarried to the elegant Helen Morrison. Laurel, who loves her father but is strongly attached to Stella, refuses to live with him. Stella then resorts to a painful deception, perhaps the most selfless act of her life. She writes Stephen a letter telling him—falsely—that she and Munn are to be married. Laurel, who is embarrassed by Munn, is mortified, feels betrayed by her mother, and at last moves in with her father and proceeds to make plans for her wedding.

The movie's famous final scene is a haunting one. Laurel, believing her mother to be uninterested in the events of her daughter's life, does not invite Stella to her wedding. It is a lavish affair, but Stella must view it from the rainy street, becoming in essence a stranger, a lonely onlooker standing on the pavement, witnessing her daughter's great moment through a picture window. It is as perverse and sorrowful a situation as has ever been concocted on the screen, but there is also a strange beauty to it, for Stella, reduced as she is to maternal voyeur, realizes that she has done the best for her child. Indeed, the expression on Laurel's face, radiant with happiness and love as she looks to the future, is oddly mirrored in that of her mother, part of her past, whose countenance is teary but glowing. The spell is broken, however, as a street cop coldly tells Stella to move on. With this last, sadistic stroke, the tale ends. Even today one is left battered, if not moist-eyed, by the emotional-roller-coaster plot of *Stella Dallas*; it must have been powerfully unsettling in 1925.

When Goldwyn set out to produce *Stella Dallas,* his first film to be made under an arrangement with United Artists, his primary concern was finding a director. He knew immediately that he wanted Henry King, for he had seen and admired several of King's films, including *Tol'able David* and *Romola*. King initially resisted, as he explained in a series of interviews conducted by David Shepard and Ted Perry and published in the 1995 book *Henry King, Director: From Silents to 'Scope*, because he remembered an unpleasant earlier meeting with Goldwyn. The producer persisted, however, and ultimately King agreed to take on the project. Carol Easton, in her book *The Search for Sam Goldwyn*, quotes King: "As far as Sam was concerned, I could do no wrong. *Stella Dallas* was going to be his first big United Artists release. He believed in the subject. Everything he'd done previously had been show pieces; this was his first 'serious' picture."

Aware of King's taste and sensitivity, Goldwyn worked carefully with him in assembling the cast. The role of Stella was a coveted one. No fewer than seventy-two actresses had been considered before Frances Marion, the film's scenarist, suggested Belle Bennett, a gutsy stage performer who had made appearances in films for over ten years. A comely blonde actress who was more handsome than beautiful, Bennett, in addition, bore a slight resemblance to Olive Higgins Prouty herself. "This woman has just what it takes," Marion told Goldwyn. "She is a mother, she has two children, and she has had everything on earth happen to her...she *is* Stella Dallas." Bennett won the part, and she was indeed an excellent choice—in part because of a personal tragedy, for her sixteen-year-old son died in her arms during the filming of the picture. The death of her child must surely have intensified the mother-child relationship in the film. Watching the loving, wistful looks she directs at Lois in the picture, one can only imagine the anguish she must have been enduring over her own loss. Despite her misfortune, though, she was never anything but professional and collected on the set, and she put her best effort into the film.

For the part of Stephen Dallas, King made a logical selection in the suave Ronald Colman, now free from any commitment to the *Romeo and Juliet* project. For the role of Helen Morrison, King cast Alice Joyce, a gracious actress who at the height of her career was dubbed "the Madonna of the screen." For Ed Munn, King chose Jean Hersholt, who is today remembered for his many humanitarian efforts but was then a highly regarded character actor. And for Grosvenor, King selected the up-and-coming Douglas Fairbanks Jr., who sported a false mustache in parts of this, only his fourth, film so as to appear older.

The role of Laurel was one of the last and in many respects the most difficult to cast. Far from being a typical child role, this part presented demanding challenges. The actress would be required to age some ten years in the course of the film, progressing from a ten-year-old child to a young woman, and she would need also to project the innocent, guileless vulnerability that made Laurel such an appealing character in the novel. At the same time, the actress would have to emanate enough star quality so as to hold her own against an older, experienced actress in a long and grueling film. Laurel may have been, in the jargon of the day, a "juvenile lead," but she was extremely important to the integrity and balance of the picture: if her role were enacted poorly, the production would be compromised.

Goldwyn was in Germany when he received Lois's photograph submission in response to his announced casting of *Romeo and Juliet*. He had received over five hundred responses from Shakespearean aspirants, but Lois's mailing captured his attention. After screening her French films, he met with her while he was in Paris searching for new film talent. Impressed, he thought of casting her not as Juliet but rather as Laurel. Discerning her *Stella Dallas* potential and increasingly enthusiastic about her possibilities, he wired King that he had "found a girl who I think would be wonderful for Laurel" and sent him some tests he had made of her. The tests in question did not entirely satisfy King, however, for they were close-ups that did not show her full body. "Sam had never made a test in his life!" King declared in the Shepard and Perry interviews. "He only shot her face!" King was concerned that because Lois was a dancer her legs may have been too muscular for the girl in the film, especially at the beginning, when Lois, at age fifteen, would have to play a character of ten. He met Lois and her mother at a restaurant in Baltimore and bluntly announced, "Lois, I'm down here to see your legs," whereupon she lifted up her skirt and offered one forth. His fears assuaged, he told Lois, "You're in." His only qualification was that Sophie Wachner, the film's costume designer, put her in ribbed stockings in order to make her appear more childlike in the film's early sequences.

In the spring of 1925, Goldwyn met with Lois and Gladys in New York and offered the actress a long-term contract that would start at approximately $200 a week and increase to $3000 a week by the time she reached twenty-one. Gladys had misgivings about such a sweeping commitment of time for one as young as Lois, but before she could act upon it fate intervened. Later that same day, the two were lunching at the Algonquin Hotel with Beulah Livingston, Goldwyn's publicity agent, when the playwright Marc Connelly noticed them. Connelly, who knew Livingston, approached the table and asked to be introduced. Between cocktails at the hotel's celebrated "round table," he was writing a play entitled *The Wisdom Tooth*. He invited Lois to audition for a part in it.

That afternoon, she did audition for him, winning the role of Lalita, a fairy sprite. Her salary would be $200 a week, precisely the amount that Goldwyn had offered her to play Laurel. Harking back to her days at Seton Hill, when she preferred plays to movies, and desiring stage experience, she accepted Connelly's offer. She reasoned that she could perform in the play during its tryouts in the spring and on Broadway in the fall, and film the Goldwyn vehicle during the summer.

Goldwyn, however, was enraged by her decision, roaring at her that stage actors were inferior to film performers and presenting her with an ultimatum: she would do only his picture or he would recast Laurel. She chose the play. Goldwyn was initially angered by her decision, but, putting the demands of the production over his personal biases, he reconsidered his position. He believed that he had really found in Lois the ideal actress to play Laurel. Consequently, when King later journeyed to Baltimore to glimpse a tryout of *The Wisdom Tooth*, he approached Lois and informed her that Goldwyn had consented to her appearing in both the play and the film. Under these more agreeable terms, she agreed to play Laurel, but only after Gladys had shrewdly negotiated for her to sign on for this film only, which would enable her to freelance afterward. With this turn of events, Lois told *Screenland* in 1925, "I can try both the spoken and silent drama before I finally decide on a permanent career."

Though not among Connelly's best plays, *The Wisdom Tooth*, an imaginative cross between *A Christmas Carol* and *Peter Pan*, afforded Lois an enjoyable, colorful opportunity to hone her acting skills before starting work on *Stella Dallas*. More specifically, it gave her the chance to work with a renowned playwright, one who had already achieved recognition with such works as *Merton of the Movies* and *Beggar on Horseback*, and with a cast of seasoned actors headed by Thomas Mitchell, for whom Connelly had written the play. Appearing in its brief tryouts in Baltimore and Atlantic City in April 1925, Lois played a small role. The experience was nevertheless important for her in that it bolstered her poise and her confidence.

In his 1968 memoir *Voices Offstage*, Connelly described *The Wisdom Tooth* as "a story of a naïve youth's struggle to retain his self-respecting individuality against the stereotyping pressures of New York's business world," a theme that resonates to the present day. The story's central figure, played by Mitchell, is a clerk named Charley Bemis, an average, unimaginative study in mediocrity. One day, however, he goes to a dentist for an aching wisdom tooth. While in the waiting room, he picks up a magazine and begins to read a story about fairy sprites, becoming so engrossed that reality begins to fade away. Soon, three fairies, one of them played by Lois, appear to him in human form, promising that if he believes in them they will transport him to their special world, where he can be different from what he is and can dream and imagine. The fairies and Bemis revisit happy days from his childhood, and he emerges from his reverie refreshed and happy. Curiously, Connelly ended the play darkly, with Bemis encountering his boss, losing his newfound optimism entirely, and admitting that he will never be fit for anything but clerking. Perhaps such a conclusion was Connelly's way of questioning the worldly practicality of the "wisdom" Bemis has acquired, but at the same time it invalidated much of what the play had attempted to accomplish and left the work more a hollow, flawed experiment than an important piece of theater. Connelly recognized the problem and was depressed by it.

In spite of the unevenness of the play, Lois's appearance in it was not a career error. The theatrical experience she gained was invaluable, and an Atlantic City newspaper reviewer praised her performance as Lalita, characterizing it as "charming" and "played with grace," while a Baltimore paper described her part as "important." Such notices were enough to justify the fifteen-year-old girl's insistence on doing the play, and the filming of *Stella Dallas* would proceed with acrimony from neither Goldwyn nor Lois and Gladys. Connelly postponed staging the play on Broadway until the following year, when it had a brief run with a different cast, and this first mounting of the production with Lois remains a bittersweet footnote in the careers of Connelly himself and of the actors who appeared in it.

Upon completing her appearances in *The Wisdom Tooth*, Lois, with Gladys, journeyed for the first time to Hollywood to report to Goldwyn. Now sixteen, she arrived on May 26, 1925. No fanfare greeted her, however. There were no crowds of adoring fans, no streamers, no confetti, none of the familiar Tinseltown fireworks exploding from the glittering silver of camera flashbulbs. Moreover, she wore distinctly unglamorous clothes and no makeup. Though her arrival was dismal, it was Lois herself who had planned for it to unfold in this way, as a Los Angeles newspaper recounted the next day:

> Lois Moran . . . arrived in Hollywood yesterday, entirely unannounced and unheralded. Even the officials of the Samuel Goldwyn organization were unaware of her presence in the city until she walked into their offices to report for duty. . . . Miss Moran's pretty face was entirely innocent of rouge or lipstick, and she was clad most becomingly in a dainty, girlish gown of no flapperist mode.

Once the actual filming of *Stella Dallas* began, the director found, as he explained in the Shepard and Perry interviews, that Goldwyn was a "most charming, wonderful man [who was] always looking upward, forward." Moreover, the ensemble cast meshed well, each actor liking his part and respecting the story he or she was enacting. Accordingly, production progressed relatively smoothly. Of course, there was the death of Bennett's son, and the cameraman was replaced mid-picture; but, under King's coherent direction, the performers sparked the melodrama with conviction and dignity. During production, Lois even developed a schoolgirl crush on Colman, not unlike the one she had had on Ivan Mosjoukine when she filmed *Feu Mathias Pascal* the previous year.

The portrayal of Laurel was enormously important to Lois, not just because she was aware of the career ramifications the role held for her, but also because the character resonated with her as neither Ralda in *La galerie des monstres* nor Adrienne in *Feu Mathias Pascal* had done. Required to convey Laurel's familial conflict from childhood through late adolescence, she was faced with the complex task of portraying a young person struggling to establish her own identity within the confines of a broken home while maintaining strongly felt loyalties to each of her parents.

Lois's work was particularly challenging because while Prouty had had at her disposal the English language with which to convey

Laurel's angst, Lois, working in the medium of silent film, had to do so using only facial expressions and body language. In such a context, it was imperative that she be attuned to the acting nuances and styles of each member of the film's cast, and it was crucial that she swiftly and decisively establish an onscreen chemistry with Bennett. Working diligently under King's thoughtful direction and striving always to learn from his suggestions, even when wounded by them to the point of tears, Lois succeeded masterfully in conveying every aspect of Laurel's troubled young personality and created a screen rendering of power and beauty. Her primary task was to capture the consequences for Laurel of her difficult family circumstances, for parental separation and the impact it had on children was not a common theme of films at the time. She was virtually pioneering this type of characterization.

Lois was a child actress, but in her best moments she was able to temper youthful optimism with adult weariness. Her finest moment in the film was the birthday party scene. Her character goes in the course of minutes from euphoria to enraged despair as she realizes her friends will not be coming. The emotionally wrenching result was a memorable example of silent-era acting at its most electric. It would be inaccurate to say that because of scenes such as this she stole the film from Bennett, but she came close.

Goldwyn, anxious to showcase the result of his efforts, premiered the film at the Apollo Theater in New York City on Monday, November 10, 1925. In response to the crushing demand for tickets to the event, he arranged for two screenings, one in the afternoon and one in the evening. He opened the seating of the earlier screening mainly to critics, to allow them more time to prepare their reviews, and to Broadway and theatrical celebrities, whose attendance, desirable though it was, he deemed more appropriate for earlier in the day. The splashier evening performance was for the film celebrities, whom, as he had told Lois, he considered more important and visible. The matinee proved a success, but it paled compared to evening.

The evening screening, more lavish and better publicized, attracted, as Goldwyn had intended, a variety of film luminaries. Naturally, members of the cast of the film itself were present. Lois and Belle Bennett were seated, along with Gladys and the actress Vera Gordon (best known for Goldwyn's *Potash and Perlmutter* films and a great friend to Bennett), in their own box, from which they could look down at the proceedings. An impressive array of other film personalities attended as well. An hour before this evening viewing, the streets outside the Apollo were jammed by crowds who braved intense gales of wind in order to glimpse the celebrities as they arrived. Owing to police presence, all progressed in an orderly fashion, but the stars nevertheless generated considerable excitement as they entered the theater. They included Gloria Swanson, Leatrice Joy, Anita Loos, James Kirkwood, Mae Murray, Lewis Stone, Will Hays, Hope Hampton, Flo Ziegfeld (with his wife, Billie Burke), Edgar Selwyn, Richard Barthelmess, Adolph Zukor, Jesse Lasky, Dorothy Mackaill, Condé Nast, Rex Beach, Lois Wilson, Thomas Meighan, and an expansive list of other important Hollywood names.

The evening brought frequent bursts of applause and admiration from the audience. New to the lavish excesses of a film premiere such as this, Lois could hardly contain her elation. The festivities and the intense attention being paid to her were indeed a far cry from her almost totally uneventful arrival by train in Hollywood only months earlier. Faced with this stunning, even overwhelming onslaught of glitz and publicity, however, she deported herself with aplomb and humility. She reasoned that the reviews were yet to appear and that they, more than the night's Goldwyn-generated ostentation, would be surer indicators of what the film and her performance in it had done for her career.

She need not have concerned herself with the notices, however, for after the opening, the write-ups in the New York papers concerning both the film itself and her performance as Laurel were complimentary. Critics considered the film to be a well-crafted drama, and many found it profoundly moving. The *Daily News* observed that "this poignant, superb drama is one of the finest achievements of the screen. There is dignity in its simplicity, high drama in its splendid acting." According to the *Telegraph*, "Emotionally, *Stella Dallas* is the big picture of the year. It may be, too, the most perfectly directed, perfectly acted and perfectly photographed picture ever made. One doesn't think of those things while watching it; it goes so flawlessly on its way." Rose Pelswick of the *Journal* wrote, "It is the most tender, the most emotionally artistic film offering of its kind that I have ever seen."

Of Lois's performance, the *Telegraph* remarked, "This lovely child brings to the portrayal of Stella Dallas's daughter emotional power worthy of an experienced trouper." Robert Sherwood, then writing as a film and stage critic and not yet a playwright, noted in the *Buffalo Times*, in advance of later reviews of the film he authored for *Vanity Fair* and *McCall's*, that as Laurel she had been able to "approximate perfection." Dorothy Herzog of the *Mirror* said, "Too much cannot be said in praise of Lois Moran. . . . Miss Moran, a youngster in her teens . . . ascends to the limelight by merit of her excellent characterization." Mordaunt Hall of the *New York Times* agreed with these summations, observing, "Laurel is impersonated by Lois Moran so capably that she won the admiration of the audience. . . . Her portrayal of the daughter [was] nothing short of amazing." And the November 1925 issue of *Photoplay* magazine, which appeared upon newsstands not long after the premiere at the Apollo, featured a particularly glowing assessment of her Laurel that read in part, "Another Cinderella has triumphed. Little Lois Moran is certain of a great success in *Stella Dallas*. We have seen the picture and are ready and willing to concur with Samuel Goldwyn in the belief that he has a great find in this little girl."

Film critics continued to praise Lois for months to come as the picture proceeded to play throughout the rest of the country and, later, the world. Indeed, while the overall film as well as the rest of its cast, Bennett in particular, also received enthusiastic critical accolades, and at a time when several other of the biggest films of the silent era (such as King Vidor's *The Big Parade*, Erich von Stroheim's *The Merry Widow*, and Lon Chaney's *The Phantom of the Opera*), were competing against *Stella Dallas* at the nation's box offices, Lois, by virtue of her portrayal of Laurel, became a critics' pet. Press coverage focused largely upon what the columnists saw as her refreshing and original approach to screen acting. Even Olive Higgins Prouty, who saw the film when it premiered in her hometown of Boston, found Lois captivating both as a person and as an actress. In a widely publicized letter, the author told the actress, "I shall always think of you as Laurel. I think you have all her loveliness and subtle charm, and I imagine her love of beauty." Similarly, Grace Frye, writing in the September 1925 issue of *Screenland* magazine, memorably elucidated Lois's appeal to film audiences of the time:

> Eyes have appetites. And just now the optical appetite of picture fans is demanding a more sensible diet.... The spicy sensational picture, with its exaggerated, painted flappers, is being rapidly placed on the studio shelf. And a normal, rational picture is being served. Featuring a normal, sensible girl that is being termed the "unsophisticated type" [of which] Lois Moran is an outstanding example.

Because of the solid, inspired performance she gave in *Stella Dallas*, Lois had earned the right to blow kisses to the audience from her box at the New York opening, and the glowing reviews the critics accorded her were deserved. Limited though it was, her previous professional experience—dancing in Paris, appearing in *La galerie des monstres* and *Feu Mathias Pascal*, and acting on the stage in *The Wisdom Tooth*—mixed with King's direction and her natural aptitude for the part she was playing to result in an American film debut of uncommon strength and effectiveness. Privately, Lois would be haunted for many months to come by fears that her success in the film had been a fluke, but audiences did not question her talent. As one of her new fans wrote to *Photoplay* in 1926, "The charming and radiant personality of Lois Moran has won the hearts of all who have beheld her."

"*IT* à la Mode," Unsophisticated Sophistication, and a Film *Gatsby* That Nearly Was

3

"*W*ell, hurrah, for the 'New Year'!"

Writing in her journal on January 1, 1926, Lois Moran had good reason to be ebullient. Only a year before, few in Hollywood had known her name, but now, thanks to *Stella Dallas*, she gave new meaning to the adage "overnight success."

> Last night...I went to the Club Lido to celebrate the passing of 1925 and had a very good time. Mabel Normand was there and, though we have never been introduced, she spoke to me [while I was] dancing and said lovely things about my performance in *Stella Dallas*. She declared that I would steal every picture I took part in as I did in *Stella Dallas* which of course is not true but still it was nice of her to say it and for me to hear it.

It was typical of Lois to be self-effacing, for rarely in person or in her journals did she express satisfaction with her work. Nevertheless, Mabel Normand's compliments only echoed those being paid her throughout the film colony.

Samuel Goldwyn's aptitude in devising film publicity helped also to draw attention to Lois. He cunningly placed in her *Stella Dallas* contract an unusual morality clause that he knew would fascinate the press. Such stipulations were not rare in those days following the Fatty Arbuckle sex scandal that had so shaken the picture community, but Goldwyn's particular slant on Lois's contract was unique, for he required her to remain "unmodern and unsophisticated." With his celebrated flair for publicity, he had engineered many ingenious press campaigns for other actresses he had discovered, but Lois presented him with special obstacles: she was at an awkward age, neither a child nor an adult; she possessed little glamour; she had not been in Hollywood long enough to be convincingly linked to any dashing leading men; and, with her early Pittsburgh upbringing, she could not be said to be European.

Another, less resourceful producer might have found such a challenge daunting, but Goldwyn calmly took inventory of what Lois did have. She was indeed young, but with that youth came innocence and naiveté, rare qualities in the fast-living film community. And she did lack glamour, but in its absence she had a homespun, peaches-and-cream appearance. Moreover, in the capable hands of the Goldwyn publicity department, her dearth of romantic filmland attachments and lack of a true European background could be discreetly glossed over. The combined effect of these factors, he reasoned, could be put to compelling use in her favor by exploiting them to their fullest. According to his morality clause, she could not bob her hair, use lipstick or rouge, go barelegged or roll her stockings, smoke cigarettes, or drink alcohol. As *Motion Picture* reported in August 1925, "Bobbed hair, rolled stockings, lipstick, cigarettes or high-balls—and presto! the contract vanishes into thin air and Lois is out of a job."

By today's standards, such provisions seem trivial, and even then Goldwyn probably initiated them more as a means of generating publicity than as a protection against any impending moral threat to his prized ingénue. However, at the time such prohibitory clauses, as a rule, were not taken lightly. Studios expected other actors to abide by comparable rules, most notably in terms of maintaining a specified body weight or not indulging in displays of public drunkenness. Thus, Lois's contractual trick, with its veneer of satire and merriment, nevertheless did contain enough fundamental weight to be assiduously reported on by the press. In conjunction with the contract, Goldwyn created suitable appellations for her, including "The Child Wonder," "The Wistful, Unmodernized Girl," "The Most Innocent Face in the Movies," and, most popularly, "The Fragile Cameo."

The emphasis placed on her level of sophistication approached the absurd, but it was a subject that was evidently enjoyed by all and that did accomplish Goldwyn's aim of promoting his new Hollywood star. In an interview she gave to Katherine Lipke for the *Los Angeles Times* in July 1925, Lois expressed bewilderment about her contract's odd terms. "No child ever raised in France could ever be [unsophisticated]," she protested. "I know about things, and I'm certainly not a little, wide-eyed girl from the country." She added, "I wish there was a word that meant unsophisticated sophistication."

Writers of the day made note of Lois's atypical but pleasing physical appearance. Lipke, for example, observed in the *Los Angeles Times* in July 1925, "She is exactly like a normal sixteen-year old girl of twelve years or so ago, before [World War I] shook growing girls into flappers, and before lipstick was in flower." No one, however, described her as beautiful or as glamorous. These accolades would come later, culminating in F. Scott Fitzgerald's exquisite description of her fictional counterpart in *Tender Is the Night* in 1934, but for the time being, the columnist Grace Frye's description would be the best for which the Fragile Cameo could hope. "Not that Lois...is beautiful," Frye observed. "She certainly is not, according to screen classics. But she is a refreshing, unusual and almost prehistoric type."

After the release of *Stella Dallas*, Lois undertook various social and publicity-oriented outings. Hollywood past met Hollywood present, for example, when, aged sixteen and described by fan magazines as the youngest actress working in the movies, she attended a January 1926 revival presentation in New York City of D. W. Griffith's *Birth of a Nation*. The film had premiered a decade earlier, in 1915, and had featured one of the cinema's founding performers, Lillian Gish, as one of its principal characters, Elsie Stoneman. Although Lois's submission of photographs to Griffith had been unsuccessful a year earlier, she respected his work still and welcomed the opportunity to view this, perhaps his best-known picture. In her journal, she wrote of the film that it was "wonderful, considering that it was 10 years ago" but found, "War scenes not so good."

It was appropriate that Lois should have seen this particular film, for her career thus far bore remarkable similarities to that of Gish. Despite a decade's age difference between the two actresses, certain commonalties between them are worth noting. For example, both women had commenced film acting at an early age and had done so under the watchful eyes of their much-admired mothers. Both adored their sisters (in the near future Lois would have a sister by adoption). Both had achieved initial success under the auspices of larger-than-life film virtuosos. Both were intellectually curious. In conjunction with their mothers, both had an innate shrewdness about matters pertaining to their careers. Both respected the stage and would later achieve success on it. And, perhaps most important, both were beautiful but not glamorous and were known for gentleness and virtue, both in life and in the parts they enacted upon the screen. It would not have been difficult to imagine, in 1926, a younger Gish enacting the part of Laurel, nor to envision Lois portraying Elsie.

Lois attended other film screenings as well, especially premieres of new pictures; participated in various industry-related banquets, usually held in hotel dining rooms; and made numerous public appearances to promote *Stella Dallas*. Now part of the film establishment, she realized that she needed to maintain high visibility to ensure that she would not be forgotten once the brouhaha generated by her Laurel performance began to wane. These forums afforded her ample opportunities to interact with her peers, the public, and the press.

A noteworthy example of her attendance at film screenings was the December 1925 New York premiere of Metro-Goldwyn-Mayer's *Ben-Hur*, the pivotal silent-era epic that starred Ramon Novarro and Francis X. Bushman. Attending the overblown affair in the more glamorous company of actresses such as Aileen Pringle and Alma

Rubens, Lois appeared comparatively plain. Nonetheless, she radiated charm and magnetism, captivating those around her and attracting much attention, and she stood out for her total lack of affectation. While Novarro himself could not attend owing to a cold he caught coming in on the train from Hollywood, the evening was a sparkling success for Lois.

The industry banquets she attended were more subdued affairs that, while lacking the frenetic unpredictability of a film premiere, did give her opportunities to make public appearances and be recognized. One such function to include Lois on its guest list was a "Welcome Home" dinner for Dorothy Gish held in December 1925 at the St. Regis Hotel. Dorothy had just returned from filming *Nell Gwynne* in England, one of her finest pictures, and those present that evening to pay tribute to her included Lois and Gladys, Richard Barthelmess, and various film producers and business executives. Afterward, Gish made an appearance at a lavish ball. The evening provided Lois with welcome publicity in addition to marking one of her early public appearances with Barthelmess, who was soon to play a major role in the development of her career.

Lois remained in the public eye by making what one New York paper described as "startlingly numerous" public appearances at movie theaters throughout the country to promote *Stella Dallas*. On April 2, 1926, for example, she appeared at the film's glittering Los Angeles premiere at the Forum Theater, a glamorous event that was heavily attended by celebrities, even more than had attended the New York opening of the picture, and that drew much notice from the public and the press. When Lois was introduced onstage after the screening, the audience accorded her a thunderous ovation.

In light of such popular success, however, Lois and Gladys remained pragmatic. They knew that the success of *Stella Dallas* would carry Lois only so far and that it was of utmost importance for her to choose—and choose wisely—that all-important second American film. As a freelance performer, Lois was not obligated to appear in material chosen for her by a studio, a situation that had potential both for good and for bad. Had she been bound by a studio contract, she might have benefited from working for experienced production heads, who could have propelled and nurtured her career in a better, more knowing manner than she herself could have done. On the other hand, studio brass was not infallible and certainly had erred before in casting. Lois was free to carefully and at her leisure choose the role and the vehicle she thought would be best for her. Fortunately, the selection turned out to be surprisingly uncomplicated, for just at the right moment Richard Barthelmess, one of the most popular leading men of the day, offered her a leading part in his next picture.

A friend of Marc Connelly, Barthelmess had seen Lois in the *Wisdom Tooth* tryouts in Baltimore and had discerned her promise as a screen actress. He was so impressed, in fact, that he determined she would be ideal for the part of Linda Lee Stafford in a stage property he was preparing for the screen, *Just Suppose*. Lois, recognizing Barthelmess's importance and realizing that a fine opportunity had come her way, readily accepted his invitation. Any picture she did following *Stella Dallas* was almost certain to be to some degree a critical and/or financial disappointment, but in consultation with Gladys she decided that appearing with such a popular and renowned actor would virtually guarantee that the picture would be taken seriously and that, if it was a failure, would at least be a noble one. The project was to be directed in New York by Kenneth Webb for Inspiration Pictures and released through First National.

A. E. Thomas's 1924 play *Just Suppose* had been a topical fantasy that had enjoyed moderate success. In it, the Prince of Wales visits America (which the real prince had done recently) and falls in love with an American girl from the South, only to face heartbreak when he realizes that his royal station prevents him from marrying a commoner. When Mrs. V. E. Powell adapted the stage drama for the cinema, however, she effected major changes. The Prince of Wales became the fictional creation Prince Rupert, and his kingdom was no longer

England but rather "Koronia," a made-up land supposedly situated somewhere near Austria. These alterations achieved two purposes. First, they modified the plot so as to avoid offending British audiences, who may have objected to a Hollywood film containing such a cavalier (for the English) portrayal of a character based on a member of the royal family. Second, they created a storyline that allowed for a happy ending, for, had the plot retained the real Prince of Wales, a resolution in which he marries the Southern girl, which in a Hollywood movie he must inevitably do, would not have been possible.

Barthelmess was suitably urbane and appealing as Prince Rupert, but perhaps the finest element of *Just Suppose* was Lois's thoughtful performance as Linda Lee, the American girl the prince marries. A far less complex part for Lois than that of Laurel, this role made few dramatic demands upon her, but she performed believably and unselfconsciously. Skillfully photographed by Stuart Kelson in floral settings, strolling through gardens or pining upon vine-strewn balconies, she looked lovely but carried few histrionic responsibilities. She was not merely decorative in the film, however. Linda Lee may have appeared to be uncomplicated and unassuming, but Lois, responding both to her own instincts and to Webb's careful direction, imbued the character with a kind of country wisdom and subtly wove her into the context of the plot so that she became an ingratiating and integral part of it. As a counterpart to Barthelmess, in fact, Lois magnetized and considerably elevated the quality of the film, for it was her relationship with him that gave the story its center.

While both Lois and Barthelmess gave fine performances of which each could be proud, it is to Lois's credit that, as she had done in *Stella Dallas*, she held her own against an older, more experienced actor. In fact, the pair displayed a convincing chemistry that was surprising in light of an anecdote she related to Kevin Brownlow in 1989 about the filming of a particular scene in which she was required to kiss Barthelmess. This portion of the film, she wrote, took place "at a swank Long Island estate, with all the matrons watching, including my Mother." She went on, "After a long kiss, I said, innocently to Richard, 'Do all grown-ups kiss with their mouths open?' He could have killed me gladly, but instead mumbled something about camera angles."

Just Suppose premiered in January 1926. Most critics lambasted the film's story line, which they found weak and implausible, but they were almost universally complimentary to the actors, particularly Lois. As she had done in *Stella Dallas*, she garnered favorable reviews for her performance. A film writer for the *Pittsburgh Post* believed that she possessed "an inborn genius for pantomime that will place her among the really great before she is very much older," and Harriette Underhill exclaimed in the *New York Tribune*, "What a fine little actress she is!" *Just Suppose*, then, proved a meritorious vehicle for Lois's follow-up film to *Stella Dallas*. The part of Linda Lee was but a shadow of that of Laurel Dallas, yet it was nonetheless a worthy undertaking, and it kept the wind in the sails of Lois's career.

As she had done for *Stella Dallas*, Lois made a variety of public appearances to promote *Just Suppose*. Now, however, she took such engagements a step further and appeared for charitable causes as well. In New York, during the Thanksgiving holiday of 1925, even before the picture had been released, she and Barthelmess visited the Newsboys Home orphanage to distribute baskets of food. The following January, the two actors followed up this orphanage visit by appearing at a lavish hospital benefit, a special pre-release screening of *Just Suppose* that First National sponsored at the Plaza Hotel ballroom in New York City. Tickets for the function sold for $5.00, the proceeds going to the Babies' Ward of the Tonsil Hospital in New York. Lois believed in the Tonsil Hospital cause: the facility badly needed wards and surgical facilities, and she and Barthelmess had in fact visited the hospital weeks before the benefit.

Of further interest at this time is that one of the earliest published, albeit tangential, linkings of Lois and F. Scott Fitzgerald appeared in an unidentified 1926 newspaper clipping that survives in one of her scrapbooks. Nestled almost imperceptibly amidst longer and more prominent items in the album, this brief account reports that Paramount had considered Lois for a lead role in its film production of Fitzgerald's novel *The Great Gatsby*, a picture the studio released that same year. (Today it is a lost but nonetheless legendary title, the most noteworthy contemporary filming of a Fitzgerald work and a veritable Holy Grail to modern film preservationists, who seek to locate a print of it.) Most likely because of scheduling conflicts, she did not go on to appear in the movie, although in the near future she would make other films for Paramount. It is intriguing, nonetheless, to imagine the appearance of Lois Moran, an actress who became renowned for her association with Fitzgerald, in a silent-era film of his most famous novel. It is also fascinating to consider that even though she may not at this time have known Fitzgerald personally, she did at least, as evinced by this clipping, know of his writing.

Paramount's consideration of Lois for a production as complex and important as *The Great Gatsby* reflected her rapidly increasing distinction in the film world. *Stella Dallas* was still a major cinema event and was just now beginning to play in many cities across the country. *Just Suppose*, although viewed as weakly plotted, had proven a financial success for which she had accrued excellent personal notices. Robert Sherwood perhaps best represented Lois's elevated status in the film world in his May 1926 *McCall's* magazine review of *Stella Dallas*. "[Lois's] triumph is deserved," he wrote. "She is not only beautiful, charming and extremely young; she has a genuine sense of dramatic values and a subconscious safety valve which tells her when to stop." Lois would later appear onstage in two of his dramas, *This Is New York* and *The Petrified Forest*.

Because Lois approached acting with discipline and worked to improve her abilities, and because she had already begun to resent being labeled a "child star," she believed that she needed to prove that her swift acting success had been attributable to more than just good luck. She began devoting time and energy to bettering herself, for she believed that the more fit she was both mentally and physically, the better her acting and onscreen presence must inevitably be. She was determined to be well read, intellectual, and athletic.

In spite of the demands made on the time of a film performer, Lois habitually fit books into her schedule, as she considered reading to be one of the most important aspects of her life. Studio publicists considered this a novelty and distributed still photos of the bookworm starlet curled up with some tome, but her quest for knowledge was very real and had nothing to do with publicity. She pursued reading zealously, favoring the classics but perusing most anything she could find, for she felt that books were the surest means for her to understand human nature and would help her to become a better actress. Noting her love for the written word, her friends happily gave her books as gifts, and she began 1926 by immersing herself in an edition of Herman Melville's *Moby-Dick* that she had received as a Christmas present.

In addition to reading, Lois attended the theater and visited art museums. Living in New York, she had ample opportunity to pursue her cultural interests. In early 1926 alone, for example, she saw such stage productions as *The Student Prince, Easy Come, Easy Go* (starring Victor Moore, with whom she would work during her Gershwin years in the 1930s and whom she described in her journal as "darling"), *Young Woodley, The Man of Destiny*, and a review featuring Phil Baker, whom she described in her journal as "a very attractive man." Her museum visits were frequent and included an outing to the Metropolitan Museum of Art one afternoon after she had partaken of tea with Barthelmess. Possessed of energy and intellectual curiosity, she fit as much as possible into each day.

Her typical day also included some form of physical exercise, for she believed that her body as well as her mind required discipline. To this end, she continued to dance, and whenever possible she also swam, played tennis, fenced, rode horses, jogged, or golfed. Such pursuits, coupled with her fitness-oriented diet, ensured that she remained the same small, well-built creature she had been in *Stella Dallas*. She pursued another physical discipline at this time: singing. Although she had made her peace with films and had opted to stay with them, the thought of a stage career was seldom far from her mind, and she particularly fancied in time becoming a musical or opera performer. She studied voice and took singing lessons, applying herself with the same determination she directed toward films, so that she was soon able to perform pieces by Victor Herbert and Franz Schubert, including several of his lieder in German.

No exercise or self-improvement regimen could have been more rigorous, however, than the exacting process by which she set about selecting her next film project. She told one columnist at the time that she badly wanted to play Peter Pan or Cinderella, roles that indeed would have been ideal for her but did not come her way. With Gladys's help, however, and as she had done in choosing *Just Suppose*, she considered a variety of other stories before deciding that her next picture would be *The Reckless Lady*, to be made, as had been *Just Suppose*, for First National in New York.

This new picture had much to offer her. Based on a popular novel by Sir Philip Gibbs, a respected writer best known for his blistering World War I exposé *Now It Can Be Told*, it was the unusual story of a gambling-addicted mother who nearly destroys the lives of all around her, especially that of her young daughter, Sylvia Fleming, the part Lois would play. Lois appreciated the social relevance of *The Reckless Lady*, but she was particularly intrigued that Belle Bennett would be playing the part of the mother. Eager to work again with Bennett, whom she admired, and realizing that appearing in another mother-daughter picture with her would most likely be a popular choice at a time when *Stella Dallas* was still compelling to audiences, she signed on for the film. Appearing with her and Bennett in the film were Ben Lyon, James Kirkwood, Lowell Sherman, and Charles Murray.

Produced by Robert T. Kane and directed by Howard Higgin, the film received tepid reviews, and the reunion of Lois and Bennett in another mother-daughter picture did not impress critics. In fact, the casting backfired. The *New York Post* noted, "Something tells us that Broadway is in for a lot of little 'Stella Dallae' if it doesn't watch out," and Dorothy Herzog wrote, "If you can imagine... *Stella Dallas*'s weak sister trying to out-attract Stella, you savvy what *The Reckless Lady* is all about." Many critics were respectful of Lois's own work in the film, however. One wrote, "Although the mechanical devices of the scenario often show like ribs on an ill-fed horse, Lois and an excellent cast hold the story together," and another remarked, "The personality of Lois Moran, that elusive sweetness that brought her fame over night on the silver sheet, dominates the picture."

After completing *The Reckless Lady*, Lois enjoyed a brief period of leisure and recreation. Savoring some rare free time, she went to see *Stella Dallas* with some girlfriends, lunched with the *Silver Screen* editor Ruth Waterbury (who, she noted in her journal, was "very amusing"), and visited art galleries, including one exhibiting portraits by Walter Goldbeck, a gifted artist who had sketched Lois not long before. She also indulged herself and purchased a powder-blue evening dress designed especially for her by Charles LeMaire, best known for his costuming work on stage for the *Ziegfeld Follies* and *George White's Scandals*. LeMaire created several outfits for her, and she noted in her journal that he was "one of the few men that can get away with wearing bright colors—for instance a vivid blue suit, red carnation and red tie."

During this interlude, Lois also went to see a Princeton Triangle play, a musical that she enjoyed and that, as will be seen, is of some significance today in consideration of her later relationship with F. Scott Fitzgerald. Additionally, she frequented the Park Lane nightclub, which, she noted in her journal, was "a nice place to dance away." One columnist spotted her there: "Lois Moran, the exquisite young thing, was about the other night, looking pleased with the world and its treatment of her." She also attended a variety of afternoon teas. At one, she was impressed by a handsome young man she met and for whom she offered to arrange a screen test. Nothing came either of her offer or of the young man, but this would not be the first time she would offer to arrange a screen test for a dashing gentleman.

She had originally intended, after completing work on *The Reckless Lady*, to appear in another picture with Richard Barthelmess. The proposed vehicle, to be made, as had been *Just Suppose*, for Inspiration in New York and released through First National, was to be an adaptation of Katherine Newlin Burt's novel *Q*, retitled *The Kid from Montana*, directed by Sidney Olcott. The plot concerned a wild and wooly cowboy who falls in love with an East Coast heiress. Though hardly original—it seemed suspiciously like a reworking of *Just Suppose*—the vehicle appealed to both Lois and Barthelmess, and it went into the early stages of production. Lois recorded in her journal in early 1926, "Had some tests made for *The Kid from Montana* in which I will commence work opposite Dick in a few weeks. Dick looks wonderful in his cowboy outfit. Sidney Olcott seems to be an excellent director. Doesn't let a thing pass. Makes me play to the camera and reminds me continually to stop wiggling my mouth."

Just as these tests were being made, however, Jesse Lasky and Walter Wanger of Paramount approached her and asked her to appear in a film to be produced in Hollywood entitled *Padlocked*. Lois knew of the project, for it had been a highly popular *Cosmopolitan* magazine serial authored by Rex Beach that had been read by an estimated five million people and was currently due to appear in book form from Harper and Brothers. Although she had verbally committed to the Barthelmess film, this new offer was extremely tempting.

Beach, best known for concocting outdoor action adventures set in the American north, had changed his approach and written a topical, urban tale. The story concerned a puritanical modern-day reformer, probably based on the notorious real-life crusader Anthony Comstock (1844–1915), whose beliefs cause anguish to his family, particularly alienating his free-spirited but virtuous daughter, who runs away from home to find love and a career as a cabaret dancer in New York. Beach had utilized a religious framework in his story to mirror the real-life chasm, which F. Scott Fitzgerald had first brought to light in 1920 with his novel *This Side of Paradise* and had become pronounced by the middle of the decade, between the staid, more conservative older generation and the more liberal younger one. By abandoning his trademark wilds of the frontier, which he had immortalized in works such as *The Spoilers*, and opting instead to explore the wilds of moral hypocrisy, Beach had created a story that was both popular literature and sociological exposé, a tale that had been widely read, influential, and much discussed, germane to the times and spellbinding.

Upon its appearance in print, *Padlocked* caused considerable furor. Now, a staunch army of readers who had followed the serial awaited its appearance in book form, and many more had not actually read it but had heard of it. As a result of such popularity, many filmgoers anxiously awaited a Hollywood film interpretation of the narrative, a fact lost upon neither Lois nor Gladys, both of whom were quick to identify the story's potential to be an artistic as well as a commercial tour de force. The producers selected a first-rate and prolific director, Allan Dwan, best known for a series of pictures he had made with Gloria Swanson. They took equal care in choosing a cast, which would include some of the most gifted acting talent of the era: Noah Beery, Louise Dresser, Helen Jerome Eddy, and Douglas Fairbanks Jr., Lois's *Stella Dallas* costar. As the leading man, the producers made a novel yet shrewd choice: Allan Simpson, an amiable and handsome young actor with too little acting experience to be considered a matinee idol who was renowned as the model for the famous Arrow Collar advertisements seen everywhere on billboards and in magazines. The producers also chose an exemplary cameraman, James Wong Howe, best known for films such as *Peter Pan* and *Sea Horses*. Additionally, they made sure to point out to Lois, they had hired a respected, flamboyantly talented film choreographer, Ernest Belcher, to handle two dance sequences that were being created especially for the character of the daughter.

Lois found *Padlocked* fascinating. She sensed that appearing in this film would indeed be a prudent career choice for her, but she was rethinking the wisdom of starring again with Barthelmess. *The Kid from Montana* would, no doubt, turn out to be a fine picture, and it almost certainly would achieve lucrative box office returns with the Barthelmess name on the marquee, but by playing in a film so similar to *Just Suppose*, and with the same costar, she had to concede that she would be exposing herself to dangerous typecasting. She realized that her film parts since *Stella Dallas* had been somewhat weak and sketchily written, and, ever uneasy that she would become viewed as a one-picture wonder by critics and by a public grown weary of waiting on her potential, she began to fear the professional consequences of acting in another picture with Barthelmess, much as she enjoyed working with him. Barthelmess agreed that *Padlocked* would be an important career move for her and released her from her obligation to *The Kid from Montana*. He subsequently lost interest in the project.

The sixteen-year-old movie star bid farewell to New York in early 1926 and boarded a train for Hollywood. She cheerfully welcomed the cross-country journey, for she enjoyed traveling by rail. Her second arrival in the film city differed considerably from her first. Then, she had been obscure and unknown; now, she was celebrated and ascendant. Still, the prospect of publicity and attention made her uneasy, and she characteristically attempted to keep her travel plans as hushed as possible. Her efforts were unsuccessful, however, and a group of journalists and photographers greeted her at the station. In truth, she must have anticipated the reception, because she dressed for the occasion, sporting a chic "leopard's paw" coat, the current fashion rage, and looking poised and assured as she smiled with Gladys from the locomotive platform.

Lois and Dwan got along smashingly and remained friends long after shooting of the picture had concluded. "He is young, short and more round than stocky with a brusque, shy manner," she observed of him in her journal in September 1926. "He is sentimental but ridicules sentiment—Talks little but excellently when he does and, above all, knows his business." Professionally, she respected his assured manner in handling a picture as well as his attention to detail: "He sketches the scene roughly—then lets the actor give his interpretation of it—then corrects, changes, or leaves intact the result according to how satisfactory it is—He will accept nothing but the very best from both the actors and his assistants—and they all either adore him or fear him—I do the former." He in turn was impressed by her determination, talent, and physical attractiveness, telling an Indianapolis newspaper when the film came out, "Lois Moran possesses every quality that goes into the making of film successes. She has perfect photographic features."

Dwan was a strict taskmaster, however, and demanded competence as well as speed. Pressing her to bring depth to the part of Edith Gilbert, he expected her to think about each scene and to try to actually become the character. The end result was well worth the trouble. Unlike Linda Lee Stafford and Sylvia Fleming, Lois's characters in *Just Suppose* and *The Reckless Lady*, young Edith is not in the least passive, and the character thus marked an important and vivid step forward in Lois's gallery of screen creations.

Padlocked was a landmark film for Lois for another reason as well: it gave her an exceptional opportunity to display her abilities as a dancer. The choreographer Ernest Belcher, popularly known as "the Dance Master of the Movies," had built a reputation on the flair of his vivid and imaginative routines. He is remembered today for being the first choreographer to have his work presented on the stage of the Hollywood Bowl, as well as for being the father of the dancer Marge Champion and the stepfather of the silent-film actress Lina Basquette. His task in *Padlocked* was to prepare two original dances that Lois could perform in the cabaret scenes; aware of the modern proclivities of the story and its heroine, he created two variations of that most cutting-edge of youthful fancies, the charleston.

For the "Charleston à la Tamale," Belcher adapted the new dance fashion from America to an ancient one from Spain, creating a number that was a modified charleston from the hips down and a graceful traditional Spanish dance from the hips up. Lois wore a flamenco-influenced outfit that included a flowered fringed shawl and bolero hat. For the "Charleston à la King," Belcher turned to France for inspiration and devised an intriguing routine in which the movement of the feet was typically charleston but the sway of the body and the movement of the arms and head were taken from classical ballet, which originated in the French court. Lois performed this number in one of the most memorable outfits she ever wore in the movies, a white ostrich-feather gown and hat that today reminds one of the famous ostrich-feather gown Ginger Rogers wore a decade later when she danced with Fred Astaire in *Top Hat.*

Padlocked was filmed on a Paramount set adjoining the one for *Old Ironsides,* an Esther Ralston picture that was one of the studio's biggest and most ambitious productions that year. According to an anecdote that appeared in a newspaper column, Dwan was an admirer of the charleston, but James Cruze, the producer of *Old Ironsides,* purportedly frowned upon the dance, whereupon a rivalry between the two sets ensued. While charleston-themed dance and music became a hallmark of the *Padlocked* set, the *Old Ironsides* set was comparatively austere and silent, as Cruze had forbidden his principals, extras, and crew from dancing or playing music on any set where he was working. Though popular on its release, *Old Ironsides* turned out to be overlong and dreary, and one can only wonder what would have happened had it had just a bit of dancing and music.

Critics greeted the release of *Padlocked* with mixed opinions. They were divided in their evaluation of the film as a whole, some reviling it and some declaring it a masterpiece, but they were once again for the most part united in their support of Lois's work. As in the past, the personal reviews she garnered were largely complimentary. Reviewers noted that Lois's portrayal of Edith marked a step forward for her.

Many admired the charm and winsomeness of her characterization, which never seemed saccharine or forced, and several made note of the strengths she brought to the part. The consensus of critical opinion was perhaps best stated in an uncredited write-up that Lois pasted into her scrapbook: "The girl is done by Lois Moran, who shows immense advance in her portrayal of an innocent youngster filled with curiosity as to her emotions. Besides getting the psychology of the part, Miss Moran is delightfully pretty and with a personality that is always charming." According to another unidentified writer, "Li'l Lois Moran. Going great guns. Why not? Looks. Ability. Wistfulness. Personality. *IT*, à la mode." This writer's belief that Lois possessed "It," the term coined by Eleanor Glyn to describe an indefinable mixture of sex appeal, intelligence, and personality, was particularly fascinating because it implied that Lois was sexy, an attribute that until now had not been obvious in her. Moreover, the sobriquet "The *IT* Girl" belonged to Clara Bow, who some critics believed should have played the part of Edith.

But Lois also received a few negative reviews for her work in *Padlocked*. These write-ups originated from critics who saw her as having tried too hard, as having been miscast, and as having enacted her role with a lack of believability, especially in her romantic scenes with Allan Simpson. One critic wrote that she "plays this role as if determined to show she can." Dorothy Herzog wrote that Lois "lacks fire and spontaneity and sincerity." Lois read her reviews, even the poor ones, and tried to learn from them.

Padlocked proved to be far more important to her career than *The Reckless Lady*. Dudley Burrows of the *San Francisco Call* had noted that by the conclusion of *Padlocked*, Lois's character had been "exalt[ed] to the skies," and the same could now be said for Lois's career upon the picture's release. Her next project would be an even bigger, more important undertaking, a darkly themed Lon Chaney melodrama to be shot at Metro-Goldwyn-Mayer in Hollywood in which she would

Lon Chaney, Tod Browning, and *The Road to Mandalay*

4

*U*pon the June 1926 release of her next picture, MGM's *The Road to Mandalay*, Lois realized one of her most striking Hollywood successes. Although the film suffered from a contrived plot and garnered uneven reviews, it featured intense characterizations and benefited from the considerable talents of its director and co-writer, Tod Browning, and star, Lon Chaney. Bold, innovative collaborators of undisputed brilliance, Browning and Chaney had previously created such films together as *Outside the Law*, *The Blackbird*, and *The Unholy Three*, all unusual and powerful outings that had enjoyed critical and commercial favor. *The Road to Mandalay*, which Lois described in her journal in 1926 as "pure gruesome melodrama well-done," was also an atypical picture, a grim study of a twisted father-daughter relationship set in the exotic locales of Mandalay and Singapore and featuring Chaney, the astonishing master of theatrical disguise, in some of his most original and unsettling makeup.

Predictably from the pairing of Browning and Chaney, the new film generated enormous attention from the public and the press. The resulting ballyhoo placed Lois, billed second behind Chaney, in a position of extraordinary visibility and elevated her to a height of popularity that rivaled even what she had enjoyed during the *Stella Dallas* furor the previous year. Indeed, at the time of *The Road to Mandalay*'s initial release, Lois's photograph and accompanying articles about her could be glimpsed in any number of newspapers and magazines. Her personal notices for the picture were excellent, and some cinema managers that summer granted her spectacular star billing by designing for their theaters majestic marquees, topped by imposing cardboard cutouts of the Buddha in honor of the film's settings, that featured her name in towering letters. One filmgoing couple even wrote in a letter to a film magazine that they wanted their daughter to grow up to be just like her. Clearly, in the course of only a year, Lois had achieved another milestone in her brief career. Yet, as successful as the film was, it was only one of several projects she and Gladys had considered as a follow-up to *Padlocked*, and one about which the two women had shared initial reservations.

Two proposed films had intrigued Lois before she agreed to appear in *The Road to Mandalay*. One was an adaptation Universal was planning of Victor Hugo's novel *The Man Who Laughs*. The tale concerned Gwynplaine, a sad, sensitive man afflicted by an ironic permanent grin, his blind sweetheart Dea, and the intrigue that ensues when he learns that he is heir to a title. It was rumored that a high-voltage film icon such as John Barrymore, the European actor Conrad Veidt, or even Chaney himself would play the lead (it eventually went to Veidt), while the part of Dea called for a diminutive young actress who could be unsophisticated and sacrificing. Lois, impressed by a project to be based upon a classic story and realizing that Dea would be highly suitable for her, found the film attractive. However, Universal awarded the role to Mary Philbin, a lovely young actress who shortly before had appeared for that studio as Christine in Chaney's classic *The Phantom of the Opera*. The other film Lois considered was a project she liked less but that would feature her friend Douglas Fairbanks Jr. in a small part. It promised to be a popular commercial production, a glittery Paramount spectacle planned as a kind of Ziegfeld Follies set on the boardwalk, a tale of Atlantic City beauty pageants entitled *The American Venus*.

The film world for a time took a good deal of interest in *The American Venus*, a slick, glossy undertaking, especially in terms of its casting. Because of her dancing abilities, and because she had just appeared in *Padlocked*, another important Paramount film, Lois seemed a logical choice for its lead. The studio considered other actresses for the picture, as well, however, among them Esther Ralston, a more established actress newly emerged from starring in *Old Ironsides*, and Louise Brooks, a beautiful newcomer who like Lois had come to films as an experienced dancer. Gladys was aware that Lois was being considered for the film amid this formidable competition and even took the girl to New York to discuss the project with Paramount executives there. Ultimately, however, she flatly rejected the picture: it would call for costumes that would reveal too much of her daughter's body, a prospect she thought vulgar. She remembered with disdain a skimpy dance garment Lois had worn in *La galerie des monstres* and feared that outfits for this new picture would also be scanty and inappropriate for a teenager. Gladys drew a bright line between film art and film pornography, and a requirement that her daughter again attire herself in revealing apparel seemed to her to fall into the latter category. Lois, herself not wild for the project, respected her mother's wishes, and the matter was dropped, but not before note of it had reached the press. One columnist compared her to Elsie Janis, another young actress of the day, and remarked that "Miss Moran, who, like [Janis], has a mother, suddenly withdrew with great swishing of skirts, said to indicate extreme distaste for the matter at hand."

Ralston, who resembled Lillian Lorraine, a renowned Ziegfeld Follies star, won the lead role in *The American Venus*, and the finished product became one of her biggest hits, its title providing her a sobriquet for years to come. Brooks also appeared in the film in a smaller part and made a remarkable impression. Lois was not daunted when she learned of the film's success, however, for she admired both actresses, and she herself would go on to make a splashy vehicle like it a few years later at Fox when she appeared in one of that studio's

Movietone Follies episodes and starred in a lavish, Ziegfeld-inspired production number. Her work on that picture was in the future, though. Now, she was back at square one in what was becoming the challenging process of selecting her next movie.

Gladys believed that the ideal film part for Lois at this time, one that could move her daughter's career forward without jeopardizing it, would be one that incorporated the sweetness of the Dea role in *The Man Who Laughs* while retaining some of the lacquer and free modernism of the characters in *The American Venus* and still remaining what she as a mother considered appropriate and in good taste. Such requirements were not easy to fulfill, and she began to worry that a suitable role would not soon materialize. She began to suffer from agonizing headaches, which her doctor attributed to the strain of managing Lois's burgeoning career. Relief came in March, however, when Browning offered Lois the role of Chaney's daughter in *The Road to Mandalay*. Having seen *Stella Dallas* and *Just Suppose*, he believed that Lois was the ideal choice to play the supporting lead in his film, and Gladys, although she disliked the project, approved it.

In retrospect, it is interesting to consider that Gladys rejected a film such as *The American Venus* because she felt it teetered on the pornographic but endorsed *The Road to Mandalay*, a considerably darker picture that did not require Lois's character to wear sexy clothing but did call for her to butcher her father with a knife. It would seem that Gladys's acceptance of this film was typical of the age-old battle in American films of violence being more acceptable than sexuality, but in fact there were other considerations. For one, in an era in which actors routinely made several films a year, she wanted to keep Lois's name perpetually before the filmgoing public. After losing *The Man Who Laughs* and refusing *The American Venus*, she did not want to wait much longer before again placing her daughter before the cameras.

Moreover, Gladys was impressed with the credentials of the *Mandalay* film, a project that would afford Lois the opportunity of working with two of the brightest and most respected talents in

Hollywood at MGM, then a young studio but one that was already distinguished by a reputation—thanks to its head of production, Irving Thalberg—for consistently turning out films of substance and quality. In truth, Gladys did abhor the violent aspects of the plot, especially because Lois had in real life lost both her father and stepfather and certainly did not need to go about slashing at father figures in the movies, but she believed it to be an outstanding opportunity in other ways. Lois also appreciated the potential benefit that the picture presented to her career, and although she, too, found its plot gritty and readily grasped the irony of a twice-orphaned actress being required in a photoplay to literally stab her father in the back, she contracted with MGM to appear in it.

Lois was familiar with the films Chaney had made with Browning, and she appreciated the gripping characterizations and visual effects the actor had achieved in them. In *Outside the Law* (1920), he had played, she knew, a dual role of a gangster and a Chinese man. In *The Unholy Three* (1925), he had portrayed a crooked ventriloquist who masquerades as an old woman. In *The Blackbird*, released earlier in 1926, he had played a Limehouse criminal who disguises himself as a crippled bishop. And in the film he was about to make with her, he would play a menacing one-eyed saloonkeeper and criminal whose one virtue is his love for his daughter. Lois was at first uneasy about playing a part in the newest entry in this gallery of peculiar films, but she relaxed when she realized that *The Road to Mandalay* would be no less strange, really, than *La galerie des monstres* had been two years earlier. She also realized that she was about to appear in what was in essence another parent-child drama, and she knew without doubt that she was fast becoming one of the best actresses of all in this particular arena.

The story of *The Road to Mandalay*, originally entitled *Singapore*, had nothing to do with Kipling's famous poem of the same name. Browning wrote it with Herman J. Mankiewicz, a drama critic brought from the *New Yorker* to work on his first screenplay (he would later become renowned for his writing on pictures such as *Dinner at Eight* in the 1930s and *Citizen Kane* in 1940s), and their tale was, on the surface, stark, brutal, and as prosaic as it could be, a dark swirl of sordid family politics, crime, and murder. However, the two writers infused their narrative with its own unique lyricism. They structured the turbulent relationship between the story's two major characters, the father and daughter, so as to contrast bristling tension with moments of affection, counterbalancing conflict with tenderness, and in so doing they blended the two extremes and blurred boundaries so that nothing at the core of the film was really as it seemed.

In Chaney's Singapore Joe, the writers created a figure who is outwardly repellent, violent, and amoral but inwardly thoughtful, compassionate, and capable of great love for his daughter, even though the nature of that love, as will be seen, is open to interpretation. Conversely, they wrote Lois's Rosemary as an outwardly soft, loving, sheltered young girl who appears meek and unassuming but who is actually possessed of fire and capable of passion and even murder. The paradoxical pairing of these personalities, of a father and daughter who seem polar opposites but who in fact share the same intertwining of emotional extremes, endowed the film with depth and complexity, and without the crisscrossing, intricate emotional framework that supports the interactions of these two characters *The Road to Mandalay* would be of little interest and an almost certain artistic failure. This becomes clear upon a consideration of its otherwise overblown story line, which must be set forth in detail, as the film is one of Chaney's most overlooked efforts.

The plot of the film as retold here is taken from a print that can be found on underground home video. There is presently no known complete print of the film. The existing version, which is that found on video, is missing the first twenty-five minutes, which concerned Joe's youth and background, and is marred by poor picture quality. Film preservationists located some of the missing footage in the 1980s, but acrimonious negotiations with MGM prevented the assembly of a more complete print. The available version opens with an unpleasant confrontation in the ramshackle saloon that Joe owns (MGM's art director, Cedric Gibbons, achieved the stark look of the film). He is angered because the police, in an episode that is presumably in the missing footage, have just raided his establishment and confronted him with his criminal activities, which include dealings in drugs and weapons, and he is certain that they have done so based on information leaked by his supposed friend and cohort, English Charlie Wing (played by Kamiyama Sojin), a vicious Chinese ne'er-do-well who is as enmeshed as Joe in local crime and resents his power. Joe, who goes through most of the film wearing a skimpy vest open over his bare chest, denounces Charlie to the customers in the bar. A tense confrontation between the two ensues, but although Charlie draws a knife, Joe uses his one good eye to stare his rival down, and the episode is forgotten. This sordid episode establishes the intense personalities of two of its pivotal characters, especially Charlie, who is not seen in much of the remaining film but who will be a major player in its dramatic ending.

The tone changes considerably in the next scene, in which a pretty and demure girl, Rosemary (Lois), is introduced as she tends a lace counter at a bazaar in a Singapore convent. Surrounded by fine doilies and collars, she wears a fluffy white dress and is shown in close-up holding her wares delicately to her face. The bazaar itself is densely decorated with religious statuary, and several nuns can be seen milling about in the background. Watching over Rosemary at the shop is a strict-looking priest (Henry B. Walthall) who scrutinizes her every move. Among the customers who visit her counter is, surprisingly, Joe, who has traveled there from Mandalay for as yet unknown reasons. In a coy early scene, the priest looks on with an expression suggestive of possessiveness and jealousy as Joe speaks to her while throwing her longing, smitten looks, and the audience is given the distinct impression that neither of these men has honorable intentions toward her. Rosemary knows the priest and addresses him by his name,

Father James, but she is disgusted by Joe's raunchy appearance and refers to him only as "that horrible man." She is impressed, however, that he speaks lovingly of his daughter, for she believes that her own father has abandoned her. "Even he doesn't forget his daughter," she tells Father James about Joe, "as low and vile as they say he is."

In a subsequent scene, it is revealed that Father James and Joe are actually brothers. We also learn that Rosemary, whose mother died in childbirth, is Joe's daughter. In a vivid interchange in which Joe, fresh from visiting the girl, gushes to his brother, "I've seen her again, Jim! Ain't she wonderful?," it is further brought out that Joe adores his daughter and wants her to have an upbringing free of the knowledge that her father is a repulsive-looking crime lord. He has consequently never revealed his identity to her and has instead left her in the hands of his brother and of the church. He contributes money to her upbringing and to the bazaar but refuses to present himself to her as her father until he has saved enough cash to one day retire from his profession and have surgery to repair his appearance, a process he anticipates will take two years. Father James believes that the time has come to be honest with Rosemary, indicating to Joe that she is extremely anxious to know her father, but the priest respects his brother's wishes and reveals nothing to the girl, who has in the meantime built up great rage toward the father she knows exists somewhere but who she believes abandoned her. Joe's anonymous devotion to her is glimpsed in a brief but haunting scene in which he peers lovingly at her through a window at the bazaar, an episode strikingly reminiscent of the ending of *Stella Dallas*.

The odd triangular relationship between the brothers and the girl is given a new dimension when one of Joe's friends and cohorts (Owen Moore) comes to the bazaar. Known as the Admiral because he at one time served as an officer in the Royal Navy, he is a degenerate whose notorious past is rife with crime and debauchery, and even Joe is wary of him. At the time of the film, however, the Admiral is a reformed and seemingly mellower man, wearing a variety of linen suits (which, inexplicably, range from filthy to spotless) and looking more haunted and sad than villainous and calculating. Still a young man when he sees Rosemary in the bazaar, he is quickly smitten with this innocent girl who so differs from the more worldly women he has known. She in turn adores him and sees in him gentleness and beauty that she believes is obscured by his reputation and often shabby appearance. Inspired by Father James's advice that "love is the most beautiful thing in all the world," they soon decide to marry.

When Joe learns of his daughter's intentions, he is enraged. He views the Admiral as "slimy, dirty scum" and is totally opposed to his associate in crime's becoming engaged to his pure daughter. He pleads with Father James not to perform the marriage, and although James tells Joe that "God has brought them together and I shall marry them," he remains adamant in his belief that the Admiral is "filth" beyond redemption. Accordingly, in Singapore, on the day of the wedding, Joe dramatically kidnaps the Admiral from the church before the ceremony can take place and transports him back to Mandalay. A servant tells a distraught Rosemary what has happened.

Clad in a form-fitting, angular, modern white dress, in stark contrast to the more maidenly frock she wore at the film's beginning, Rosemary leaves the shelter of the Singapore convent and journeys to the wilds of Mandalay to retrieve her lost groom. She locates Joe's saloon and there asks English Charlie Wing, who is as seedy and conniving as he was earlier in the film, where she can find the Admiral. With the intent of molesting her, Charlie shows Rosemary to an upstairs room. Joe comes in before Charlie can assault Rosemary, however, and Charlie retreats downstairs, where, malevolently, he instructs a patron in the bar to fetch the Admiral, knowing Joe will want to kill him. In the meantime, Joe tells Rosemary that by abducting her fiancé he was only acting on her father's wishes, whereupon she becomes infuriated and sneers, "I hate my father for what he's done. I hate him! I've despised him for neglecting me! Now he has taken away the man I love...and I loathe him!"

Joe is visibly shocked and wounded by the girl's words, but before he can reply the Admiral enters. The two men struggle violently, but Joe overpowers the Admiral and attempts to strangle him. Rosemary, seeing what is happening, runs to them with a knife and stabs Joe in the back before he can kill her lover. After this unknowing act of patricide, she faints, and Joe, dying but suddenly realizing the depth of the girl's love for the Admiral, says to him, "She must have loved you...to do this." Now understanding what is truly best for his daughter, and apprehensive of English Charlie, he instructs the Admiral to leave immediately with the girl. The Admiral picks Rosemary up from the floor and carries her out of the bar, pushing Charlie Wing aside as he does so. Joe then stumbles out of the upstairs room and falls from the upper landing to the floor of the bar below. Father James rushes to his side, and Joe utters these dying words about his daughter, which echo those he spoke earlier in the film: "I've seen her again, Jim! Ain't she wonderful?"

In essence a bizarre reworking of the parent-child drama that was *Stella Dallas*, this story did not make for a film that was particularly heartwarming or uplifting in spirit. However, Browning, filming from a scenario Elliott Clawson had prepared from the original story, did stress colorful characterizations and created a fascinating psychological character study of its three major characters—Joe, Rosemary, and the Admiral—which is important to consider when trying to determine the picture's overall quality and its resulting importance to Lois's career. The curious interaction between Joe and Rosemary is indeed the central and most stimulating aspect of characterization in *The Road to Mandalay*, but the viewer is left also to ponder another important relationship, that between Joe and the Admiral, for their conflict, in addition to propelling the story to its impassioned conclusion, adds a possible new dimension to Joe's adoration for Rosemary. Why is it that Joe so dislikes the Admiral, his former friend? On one level, it seems obvious that he considers the sailor a hardened criminal who is unworthy of his daughter's affections; but Joe himself is no better, if not worse, and of all people would seem likely to believe in the concept that it is what is in a person's heart that is most important. Moreover, Rosemary clearly does love the Admiral, a man who may have had a despicable past but who now has changed and reciprocates her affections. And even allowing for a father's prerogative of being overprotective and cautious, Joe's abduction of the groom on the day of the wedding is extreme.

The inevitable conclusion, then, is one suggested in the earlier scene at the bazaar: Joe himself has repressed romantic feelings for the girl. The incestuous subtext, subtle but evident, better explains his behavior, which is more like that of a scorned lover than of a concerned parent, and also helps account for his insistence upon becoming more cosmetically pleasing before revealing his identity to her, when he knows how desperately she wants to know her father and how little his physical appearance would ultimately matter in such a context. In their illuminating 1995 biography of Browning, *Dark Carnival: The Secret World of Tod Browning, Hollywood's Master of the Macabre*, David Skal and Elias Savada agree with this approach and observe that Browning and Mankiewicz may have made use of Freudian theory in their story: according to Freud, whose work was well known by 1926, the subconscious mind equates a single eye with the phallus. Applying this line of thought to the film may at first seem absurd, but there is more to it than meets the eye, so to speak, for it is plausible, given the intelligence and sophistication of its writers and given Chaney's predilection of using makeup as a means to mirror a character's personality. Seen from this point of view, the film takes on chilling new thematic weight, and certain scenes become particularly disturbing, in particular those in which Joe remarks of Rosemary, "I've seen her again. Ain't she wonderful?" as well as the sequence that depicts him, scruffy and single-eyed, peering at her through a window.

For Lois, appearing in *The Road to Mandalay* marked an unusual progression in her Hollywood career. One might expect that this star of comparatively wholesome pictures such as *Stella Dallas* and *Just*

Suppose would have found the project unpleasant and distasteful, no matter how carefully it was crafted. In truth, though she went into the production wary of the narrative's violence, she respected Browning, considered acting with Chaney a privilege, and came to regard the curious plot as a disguised blessing, because it was unusual enough that she thought it might safeguard her against future typecasting. As the production went on, she concluded that the picture's somber tone might keep it from being the guaranteed hit she and Gladys had believed it would be, but she had faith in Browning and Chaney and trusted that their expertise as filmmakers would transcend the weaknesses of the story. She was almost certainly unaware the existence of any potential incest theme—had she been, Gladys would have intervened and more than likely would have sought to withdraw her daughter's services—but it is probable that she was aware of the finer points of the characterizations. More important, she undoubtedly clicked with Browning. A notorious alcoholic who drank on the set, under different circumstances the director might easily have been dismissed by both Lois and Gladys as little more than a drunk; however, his drinking did not concern Lois. She admired his creative, searching mind and natty Brooks Brothers manner of dress (in much the same way as she admired F. Scott Fitzgerald a short time later), and she diligently followed his direction, striving to convey the vivid mixture of demureness and fire that made the part of Rosemary so opalescent.

She found it easy to enact the early scenes at the lace counter as well as the romantic sequences with Owen Moore, a warm, natural actor and the former husband of Mary Pickford, but the later confrontations with Chaney called for the exploration of what was for her a new dimension in film acting: the believable expression of intense, undiluted rage. Not the kind of hurt, vulnerable anger she had portrayed in the birthday party scene in *Stella Dallas*, but rather a fury so intense and so powerful that it drives her to commit murder. She knew that if she did not adequately meet this challenge she would diminish the characterization, one of the central elements of the entire film, and she was determined that this not happen. Browning himself was acutely aware of the importance of properly setting forth Rosemary's ire and worked carefully with Lois. He believed, however, that mere coaching would not produce the white-hot results he wanted, so when the time came to film the anguished stabbing scene, he stood behind the camera and screamed furiously at her so as to intensify the murderous rage she needed to convey. A writer for the *Cleveland News* reported upon this aspect of the filming: "Browning, being a bit of a psychologist, lashed himself into a fit of anger and began to scold the innocent little Lois, making certain, however, to throw an occasional wink to Lon Chaney."

Although shaken by these tactics, Lois respected Browning's abilities as a director and believed that his harsh methods were for the good of the picture. Indeed, when she saw the rushes she was surprised by the intensity of her performance and grateful to him for eliciting such high-level work from her, even if he had resorted to bullying to do so. Later, when she made *Behind That Curtain* for Fox in 1929, she drew on and refined the lessons Browning had taught her about the expression of on-camera rage, and these techniques, learned during the production of one of her earliest films, helped her to give one of the finest performances of her entire career.

By the time filming of *The Road to Mandalay* began in March 1926, Lois was accustomed to appearing in films with large casts of older, more experienced actors. Still, she had never worked with an actor as renowned or as intense as Chaney, and she worried that she would not be able to meet the demands of costarring with him. She was especially apprehensive when she noticed the meticulous care he was taking to create Singapore Joe's unusual physical appearance. The character's facial scarring was easy enough for Chaney to achieve with makeup, but in order to effect the blind left eye he wore painful glass shields that covered the entire visible sclera and made it appear an opaque white. These devices, which predated the established use of contact lenses, had been designed for him by Hugo Keifer, a local optician, but while they gave Chaney the eerie look he wanted and for which the picture became known, they were also extremely painful and necessitated that he film for only brief periods of time while wearing them. Lois was astonished that he would endure the agony caused by the shields, two of which have survived and can be found in his makeup case at the Natural History Museum in Los Angeles, and she realized that he was a remarkable performer who was willing to make extraordinary sacrifices for the sake of a film.

Awestruck and nervous, she nevertheless applied herself to her own work in the picture, concentrating on Browning's direction, and quickly came into her own as Rosemary. The disdain she feels for Chaney's character in the film seems so real, the viewer could easily conclude that she felt the same way about the actor in real life. This was not the case, however, and in later years, when she discussed her career, she frequently said that she considered costarring with him a high point of her years in Hollywood. She had good reason to think so. Her scenes with Walthall and Moore were for the most part standard screen fare, even though they all tried their best in them, but there was clearly a unique, bubbling, volatile chemistry between her and Chaney that did indeed make *The Road to Mandalay* one of her finer, more compelling films. Regretfully, they never appeared together again: Chaney died four years later, and Lois retired from Hollywood in 1931. As it was, Lois went on to appear in film with only one other legendary horror star: Boris Karloff, who would have an uncredited role in *Sharp Shooters* in 1928 and who would play a servant in *Behind That Curtain*. Additionally, in 1928 Chaney publicly praised Lois and the photographer William Mortensen for the use of cosmetics and effect in a December 1927 *Vanity Fair* spread entitled "The Seven Ages of Lois Moran," in which Mortensen recreated Shakespeare's seven ages of man in appropriate makeup and costume for each period. Chaney was particularly impressed by the old-age makeup, which was applied so well as to make Lois virtually unrecognizable.

When *The Road to Mandalay* opened in June 1926, managers of movie theaters exhibiting it played up its Oriental theme. They also featured, in addition to the film itself, live entertainment: exotic Chinese-themed dance shows and, time and time again, the performance of a song that bore no relevance to the picture, a 1907 setting by Oley Speaks of Kipling's poem. The studio itself, however, marketed the picture differently, choosing to promote it primarily as a weighty thriller, and publicists aimed it at fans of the horror and crime genres. Poster and advertisement art featured images of Chaney looking predatory and grotesque, his blind eye much in evidence, and Lois as a terrorized victim in white. To emphasize the film's status as an intense mood piece in the tradition of Chaney's earlier pictures, some newspaper ads additionally incorporated drawings of him in costume from other roles, including those he played in *The Unholy Three*, *The Blackbird*, and *He Who Gets Slapped*, an MGM film made independently of Browning in 1924 in which he had portrayed a circus clown. Bloody daggers, Venetian blinds, and bold Oriental-style lettering were other motifs utilized by publicists to add atmosphere and punch to their promotional efforts. A movie-edition pulp novel of the story even appeared featuring a cover photo of a bare-chested Chaney clutching a dagger and furiously threatening Lois and Owen Moore.

The studio, obviously, believed that the best way to market its new film was to promote it as Grand Guignol, although its marketing campaign made passing reference to the film's romantic subplot. The publicity made no mention of the film's more pervasive theme of parent-child conflict, and anyone who saw this original publicity today would be hard pressed to deduce that Chaney and Lois were actually father and daughter in the picture. Such a promotional scheme did prove to be shrewd, because the film opened to excellent box office and went on to gross more than had any of Chaney's other MGM pictures to date, with the exception of *He Who Gets Slapped*. However, as years passed and it became much easier for film enthusiasts to gain access to the promotional memorabilia than to see the film itself, this approach proved damaging to the picture's long-term reputation, as it resulted in its undeservedly being stigmatized as nothing more than a melodramatic, over-the-top curiosity, a situation that only now is changing with the film's availability, if only in fragmented form, on home video.

Contemporary reviewers of *The Road to Mandalay* afford it a better-informed if mixed reception. Those who liked it were excited by a new Chaney offering and were generous with praise for what they considered a worthwhile and original effort. The *Detroit Evening News* described it as a "movie of flesh, blood and bone," while the *Motion Picture News Review* said it was "a man sized picture with a deadly wallop." The *New Haven Times Leader* thought it a "masterpiece" and "one of the most beautiful love stories ever told on the screen." The *Chicago American* agreed, calling it "a remarkably good melodrama with a fine cast, and undoubtedly one of Chaney's greatest pictures," while the *Paterson (N.J.) News* offered, "It's a picture everybody will remember—and love." A writer for the *Philadelphia Inquirer* enthused, "*The Road to Mandalay* is more than red-blooded film fare. It's crimson! There is nothing effete about this rip-roaring melodrama, with the accent emphatically on the 'rip.'" The *Brooklyn Eagle*'s critic opined, "It's easily, I believe, the best movie of the sinister East that has come out of the studios this season." And the *Motion Picture World* observed, "Here is a story which deals with the very dregs of humanity in contrast with purity and innocence. It is exceedingly melodramatic at times but we do not recall a picture in which there is better sustained suspense and more hair-trigger nerve-tingling tension." Some write-ups made special mention of Browning's work on the picture. The *New York City World* noted, "He has excitement. He has suspense. He builds to beauty," while the *Boston Herald* remarked, "The picture is Tod Browning's who knows more about the lighting and staging of a screen melodrama than any one now in Hollywood. He knows, too, the value of under emphasis and of gestures that are well timed."

The critics who disliked the film believed that it suffered from a flawed plot, one that turned the film into a sour and unappealing product distinguished only as one of Chaney's noble failures. Lois's admirer Palmer Smith, of the *New York Evening World*, perhaps best expressed the views of these critics when he observed simply, "It left me cold and with a rather bad taste in the mouth." A critic at the *New York Daily News* concurred, describing the film as "a raw and unpretty drama." And *Variety* termed it "a slumming party abroad": "It appeals to the modern taste for what is called 'morbid,' but which nowadays is called 'sensational.' The Grand Guignol, maybe, was ahead of the times."

But if the critics were divided in their opinions of the film as a whole, they were almost unanimously complimentary to Chaney and to Lois. For his portrayal of Singapore Joe, Chaney received a variety of accolades: "Chaney Outchaneys Chaney" (*Motion Picture*); "Chaney has seldom, if ever, been better" (*Dallas Herald*); "Chaney is splendid" (*Variety*); and "*The Road to Mandalay* is one of the most stirringly dramatic and virile [films] that Chaney has ever had and adds another laurel to his masterful characterizations" (*Motion Picture World*). *Photoplay* even chose his performance as one of its picks of the week. Reviewers also praised his use of makeup; according to the *Brooklyn Times*, "He is a master of brutish makeup, to be sure, and leaves nothing undone to make himself as hateful and nasty in appearance as possible." As could be expected, film writers made particular note of his unsettling blind eye: *Variety* marveled, "It is remarkable how this particular detail contributes a sort of mood and tempo to the whole production"; the *New York City Telegram* noted, "The effect is sufficiently revolting to satisfy even Mr. Chaney's fastidious tastes in the matter of makeup"; and *Motion Picture World* said, "In an intensely dramatic story Lon Chaney...again demonstrates that he is without peer as a genius of makeup." In view of these kinds of notices, it is not surprising that Chaney went on to make several more pictures with Browning, including such well-known titles as

The Unknown, London after Midnight, and *West of Zanzibar,* which, interestingly, began as *Mandalay* had ended, with Chaney falling from an upper-story landing.

Lois's own reviews for *The Road to Mandalay* were generally positive, although most critics overlooked the expansion of range she accomplished in it and instead focused upon the softer, gentler qualities—which they termed "innocence"—evinced by her Rosemary at the picture's beginning. To this end, *Variety* observed that she "put over youth and innocence as no other screen actress who comes to mind"; the *Paterson (N.J.) News* remarked that "she's just too charming for words"; and the *Detroit Times* observed that "she portrays [the part] in her best manner. She is innocence personified." Some reviewers did note the dramatic advances she made in the movie. The *San Francisco Chronicle* believed that she "shows surprising power in the scene in which she upbraids Joe for stopping her marriage to the man she loved." *New York Telegraph* agreed: "The little star has never appeared to better advantage and her big dramatic moments were played to an exacting tempo." The relatively few critics with opposing views included a columnist for the *New York City Telegram* who felt that she was too inexperienced for her role and that future directors "must content themselves with teaching her how to walk before they try to enter her in races for which she is so obviously untrained," as well as a film writer for the *Indianapolis News* who remarked, " She still seems much more like a school girl than an actress."

In considering Lois's work in *The Road to Mandalay* in relation to her career as a whole, it is clear that she was successful overall in her quick progression from dancing ballet in Paris to emoting for Tod Browning on a Hollywood sound stage. Chaney's presence in the film may have been its central force, but Lois contributed substantially to the picture's overall effect. She never again appeared in as bleak or uncompromisingly violent an undertaking, and for that matter would not do another MGM production until she made her last film in 1931, but if the film could be said to mark her lone foray, literally and figuratively, into a world of leather and lace, she carried it through with style and a vibrant screen presence. Most who watch it today do so to see Chaney; but, the viewer who looks beyond Singapore Joe will discover Lois's in many ways equally complex Rosemary. Browning elicited intense, powerful performances from both of his stars, and, all elements considered, Lois was justified in later years for looking back at *The Road to Mandalay* as a highlight of her career. It had been filmed in a brief twenty-eight days at a cost of $209,000, and it had made a profit of $267,000, prompting Lois to write in her journal at the time that it "broke records all over country." In the 1950s, designers for the Pirates of the Caribbean ride at Disneyland in California based one of the pirate characters on Chaney's one-eyed Singapore Joe; and it may or may not have been coincidence that in 1934 F. Scott Fitzgerald chose the name Rosemary for the character he based on Lois in *Tender Is the Night*.

George Gershwin, Lya de Putti, and Reaching for the Moon

*T*he Road to Mandalay heralded a new period in Lois's career. With its success she began to relax, dwelling less on her anxiety that her peers and the public would not regard her an actress of lasting merit. She now approached her life and film career with strengthened confidence, enthusiasm, and resolve. Although she continued to nurture the thought of again acting upon the stage, she had with experience come to respect the medium of movie making, and, after appearing in her quartet of pictures that followed *Stella Dallas—Just Suppose, The Reckless Lady, Padlocked*, and *The Road to Mandalay*—she realized it was increasingly important to become the most capable of cinema actresses. As she wrote in her journal, "It seems to me that one must reach for the moon if one wishes to get anywhere near it."

To achieve her ambitions, Lois continued to accept work in atypical, demanding films and surrounded herself with gifted people. In the summer and fall of 1926, these strategies resulted in a career and personal renaissance for her, one that sparkled with accomplishment and was populated by some of the most brilliant personalities of the day. In films, she made two singular pictures, *The Prince of Tempters* and *God Gave Me Twenty Cents*. She was also F. W. Murnau's first choice for the role Janet Gaynor played in one of the most famous of all silents, *Sunrise*. Her personal life glittered with legends from film, theater, music, and literature, and her social calendar included

George Gershwin, George White, Gloria Swanson, Malcolm St. Clair, George Jean Nathan, Condé Nast, and James Quirk. During the final half of 1926, she enjoyed, at the age of seventeen, one of the most rewarding periods of her career.

Before the events of that summer and fall could unfold, however, Lois had again to face the task of selecting her next film. After completing *The Road to Mandalay*, she found herself in a problematic position that resulted from her continued desire to freelance rather than sign a long-term contract with one studio. This most recent film was highly successful and brought her greater renown. For practical purposes, however, she emerged from it beset by the same stress that had long plagued her and Gladys: locating that next suitable screen property. Mother and daughter once believed that as Lois became more accomplished and well known she would find it easier to choose her projects because more material would inevitably become available to her. This was true to some extent, for she received a greater number of film offers after each movie she made, but it did not allow for one important qualification: with Lois's fame came expectations—from her peers, the public, and herself—that each successive picture would be better than the last and would offer her new and more challenging acting opportunities. The pressure of living up to such standards took an increasing toll on the two women, to the extent that gradually they were inching toward what up to then had been unthinkable, the possibility that it would be prudent for Lois to sign a prolonged studio contract.

But even as Lois was having personal doubts about the wisdom of continuing to freelance, one columnist strongly encouraged her to resist a studio contract. Aileen St. John-Brenon, writing for the *New York Telegraph*, published an impassioned open letter to her on July 4, 1926, in which she went into considerable detail about the damage she felt such a contract would do to Lois's career. St. John-Brenon was of the opinion that it would be a colossal misstep for an actress of Lois's disposition and sensitivity to commit to one studio and submit herself to the machinations of a huge organization in which her individuality and direction could be lost. She warned, "There will be times when, because you are on salary, because perhaps no one has been detailed to pick out stories that are suitable for you, you will be shoved into inappropriate and ineffectual parts." Lois was haunted by this grim view. Indeed, St. John-Brenon had put into words the fears Lois herself had harbored since she started in films. She determined to continue freelancing for as long as possible.

Theoretically, the films she most wanted to make at this time were productions of *Alice in Wonderland*, *Cinderella*, and *Peter Pan*, stories many people, including she herself, believed she was born to enact. However, no such projects materialized for her. She did receive a variety of offers for films she considered unsuitable, and two projects she did like—screen adaptations of popular stories of the day, *The Garden of Eden* and *Sorrel and Son*—were not yet even through the planning stages.

Realistically, the most promising offer Lois received was once again from First National in New York, for whom she had made *Just Suppose* and *The Reckless Lady* and which held no grudges over her having backed out of *The Kid from Montana* earlier that year. The studio was preparing a film version of E. Phillips Oppenheim's popular novel *The Ex-Duke*, a melodramatic but involving tale of a monk who leaves the monastery to enter the secular world when he discovers that he is heir to a fortune. The film's producer, Robert T. Kane, who had worked with Lois on *The Reckless Lady*, considered her an excellent choice to play the part of one of the women the monk encounters outside the confines of his cloistered life. Lois's first reaction to the project was tepid, however, because the plot lines of both *Padlocked* and *The Road to Mandalay* had featured religion, and she feared becoming typecast as a heroine of religious-themed dramas. The more she learned of the proposed picture, though, the more she liked it.

She was especially pleased when she learned that Kane had retained a German director from the esteemed UFA studio, Lothar Mendes, to direct it. Mendes had made only a handful of films, most of which were virtually unknown in America, but Lois found the prospect of working with him appealing: she knew other German film makers such as G. W. Pabst and F. W. Murnau were held in high regard for their ability to create stylized films, often distinguished by innovative photography. A further enticement was the cast Kane had assembled for the picture, which included Ben Lyon, her young costar from *The Reckless Lady*, as the story's monk hero; Ian Keith and Lya de Putti as a pair of schemers who plot to bilk him of his fortune; and Mary Brian, borrowed from Famous Players for a brief moment of comic relief as a server of hors d'oeuvres.

Lois was intrigued by Kane's casting of Lya de Putti. Worldly, vampish, often characterized by an austere black bob, and seven years Lois's senior, this Hungarian siren was a fascinating film hybrid, a cross between Theda Bara and Louise Brooks, although she borrowed too much of the former's gloss and lacked the puzzling iciness of the latter. Having starred in successful films abroad, most notably E. A. Dupont's *Variety*, she was in the process of importing her European glamour to America. Lois admired de Putti as a gifted screen performer whose exoticism masked genuine talent.

Perhaps because of the serious tone of the stark *Mandalay*, she enjoyed making *The Prince of Tempters*, which was solemn but not as grim. Because the picture was to be produced in New York, the bicoastal actress once again changed addresses, temporarily leaving the Elm Street residence in Beverly Hills that she and Gladys had purchased and moving for the rest of the summer to a luxurious New York City apartment across the hall from the residence of Abby Rockefeller, in a building called the Old Colony House. When Lois and Gladys arrived, their first concern was not the actress's career, however. Rather, they sought to ensure that their personal life was in order before proceeding with filmmaking.

Family and home life continued to be of great importance to the twice-widowed Gladys, in particular, and it was with these values

in mind that she now legally adopted a five-year-old orphaned relation, Betty Evans, who had for the last couple of years languished in
boarding schools. Upon her arrival at Old Colony House, this dark-
eyed child added considerably to the Morans' domesticity and quickly
earned the adoration of her new adoptive mother and sister. Although
the press unfairly compared her to Lois, and Gladys with the best of
intentions groomed her from the start to follow in her famous sister's
film footsteps, an upbringing no child could have found pleasant,
young Betty possessed strength of character and developed a distinct
personality.

Now reestablished in New York and possessed of a newly accentuated family, Lois flourished. Her relationship with Gladys continued
to be primary in her life, and she lived professionally and personally
according to the dictates of her parent. With her stiff posture and
a stern scowl, Gladys appeared outwardly to be the quintessential
domineering stage mother. But Gladys had never nurtured stage aspirations of her own, maintained her own life with her own friends, and
did not live vicariously through her daughter. What is important is
that she was indeed instrumental in guiding Lois's career and did so
shrewdly and successfully.

Lois's existence when she first returned to New York was relatively self-contained and limited to Gladys and to Betty, but, as she
became more settled at Old Colony House and better acclimated to
the closed-in bustle of the city, after having become accustomed to
the more leisurely pace of the wide-open spaces of Los Angeles in
its youth, she concentrated less on her home life and more intently
on her career. This resulted in a gradual progression of her personal
life over the next several months from one concentrated primarily on
her family to one that was fortified by the host of friendships that she
cultivated in the course of her film work and that helped to shape
her creativity and professional ambitions. But before this blossoming,
Lois needed to enmesh herself once again in New York film produc-

tion, and in June she reported to Mendes to begin production on *The Prince of Tempters*.

She began work on the picture in enthusiastic spirits, for she was confident in Mendes's talent and optimistic that he would create a superlative film that would benefit her career. He was consumed with the creation of his picture, plunging headlong into its production and filming from a scenario that had been prepared from Oppenheim's novel by Paul Bern. He clearly loved the tale he was directing. Lois herself read both the novel and the scenario, and she, too, in spite of her initial reservations, came to like the plot, at least at the beginning of filming. Neither she nor Mendes realized then that it was a story that played much better on paper than it would on film, as a brief retelling of its plot may demonstrate.

Francis (Ben Lyon) has grown up in a monastery and as a young man, in contrast to his friend Mario (Ian Keith), intends to become a monk. News comes to him, however, that he is an English duke who has recently inherited a fortune. He ventures into the world and finds its luxuries appealing. Mario and his girlfriend Dolores (de Putti) conspire to bilk Francis of gifts and cash, but he meets a sincere girl, Monica (Lois), with whom he has a pleasant afternoon at a lake and who helps to balance the excesses of his new life. Dolores, threatened by Monica, devises a scene in which Monica is set up to walk into a room while Dolores has literally thrown herself at his feet. Upon seeing this, Monica flees. Francis, having found nonreligious life "Bitter! Bitter!," returns to the monastery. Meanwhile, Dolores, who has come to genuinely love Francis, realizes that he would be happy with Monica, and in a selfless gesture she tells Monica of her deception before committing suicide. Monica returns to Francis, who, it is presumed at the film's conclusion, will once again leave the monastery and marry her.

Mendes approached the production of *The Prince of Tempters* with vigor and flair, his motivation high: he was passionate about the plot and had much to prove in directing his first American film. His overall achievement was a visually striking production that was unlike anything in which Lois had before appeared. The young director did stumble in his handling of the actors in that he unwisely allowed the villainy of the characters played by Keith and de Putti to border on crude caricature and to dominate a film whose focus should have been the spiritual conflict of Lyon's monk character, but he compensated for this flaw by obsessing over his film's look, which he achieved with intricately detailed sets, vivid costumes, and painstakingly engineered camera angles executed with his cameraman, Ernest Haller.

Between the extremes of the sublime visuals and the melodramatic plot could be found the acting, which ranged from reflective, careful, and restrained to brash, outrageous, and over the top. Though Lyon, who strove to create a believable, three-dimensional interpretation of Francis, and Keith, who enacted the Baron with free-flowing, confident excess, embodied two completely different approaches to acting, the memorable pairing of Lois and de Putti created a dichotomy that really made the screen bristle. Lois outwardly played Monica as a seemingly weak, submissive character, who in consistently putting the interests of Francis before her own, appeared deceptively soft and fragile. Clad in simple, girlish clothes, and being most daring only in the innocent swimming scene, she at first appeared a pale contender for the affections of Francis. De Putti's Dolores, on the other hand, was an outwardly much more flamboyant, and, it would seem, stronger personality. Outfitted in a garish wardrobe that included an exotic clinging black satin dress with a high collar and expansive train, she volleyed for Francis using sex as her weapon, for the sole benefit of herself. Yet, as the film progressed, it was the seemingly disadvantaged Lois who won the day, because hers was the character who was honest, went deeper in spiritual strength, and best understood that Francis could be happy only when incorporating his religiosity into the worldly climate into which he had been thrust. Her basic goodness overrode de Putti's outlandish glamour and sexuality.

Such contrast casting worked remarkably well to showcase the talents of each actress and resulted onscreen in a jigsaw-puzzle-piece relationship between the two, for what de Putti lacked in sincerity and warmth, the earnest and sincere Lois made up for, and what Lois lacked in glamour and overt sensuality, the elaborately gowned and sultry de Putti provided. The result of this intriguing combination of talents was a charismatic chemistry that proved beneficial to the careers of both actresses. In 1986, Albert Guérard of Stanford University authored an unpublished study of Lois and de Putti that he entitled, appropriately, *Snow White and Rose Red*.

The Prince of Tempters opened in New York at the Mark Strand Theater at Broadway and Forty-seventh Street in July 1926. Lois did not like the finished picture: she felt that it had turned out to be uneven and decidedly uninspirational. Critics agreed with her. They loved Mendes's visuals and original filmmaking, but they derided the plot, which they considered anemic and meandering. The female leads, however, were a different matter.

Film reviewers noticed de Putti's "vigorous and serpentine" (*Exhibitors Herald*) portrayal of Dolores, agreeing that she was fascinating to watch: the *Cincinnati Times Standard* noted that "Lya de Putti of the scorching orbs demonstrated the 1927 model superheated European vamp, should you happen to care for vamping," and the *New York Daily Mirror* remarked, "Her last scene with Ben and her death is beautifully done." However, other critics agreed that she overacted and that her performance was at times a silly mirroring of Theda Bara's vamp days from the previous decade.

Lois, in contrast, had seldom come off better than in when enacting her role of the guileless Monica against the maelstrom of de Putti at full voltage. As a result, she earned some of the best notices of her career. The *Los Angeles Express* believed that she "walks away with all honors"; the *Cincinnati Times Standard* remarked that "her work continues to show growing artistic intelligence and emotional breadth"; the Detroit *Times* opined that "she is positively a revela-

Lois, age 14 months, 1910.

Lois, 1911.

Lois, 1912, at the time she was known in Pittsburgh as "Billy."

Lois's mother, Gladys, and Lois, Pittsburgh, 1912.

Lois and friend in France, 1924.

Lois, an unknown friend, and Marc Connelly in Atlantic City during the brief run of *The Wisdom Tooth* in 1925.

Jaque Catelain, Marcel L'Herbier, and Lois vacationing in France during the production of *La galerie des monstres* in 1924.

Catelain, Lois, and L'Herbier frolicking at the shore, 1924.

is Moran at the time of *Feu Mathias* *scal*, 1924.

As Ralda in *La galerie des monstres*, complete with black wig and string of beads designed by L'Herbier to make her appear older.

is, gowned for the famous wedding ene in *Stella Dallas*.

The major players of *Stella Dallas*, 1925. *Standing, left to right*: Samuel Goldwyn, Ronald Colman, Alice Joyce, Douglas Fairbanks Jr., and Jean Hersholt. *Seated, left to right*: Belle Bennett, Henry King, and Lois.

Richard Barthelmess and Lois in *Just Suppose*, 1926.

In flamenco costume for the "Charleston à Tamale" in *Padlocked*.

With Allan Simpson, better known as the model for the Arrow Shirt Collar advertisements than as an actor, in *Padlocked*, 1926.

In ostrich feathers for the "Charleston à la King" in *Padlocked*.

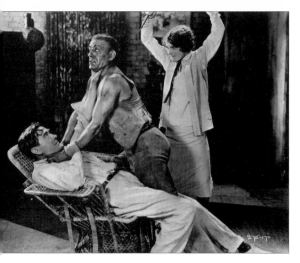

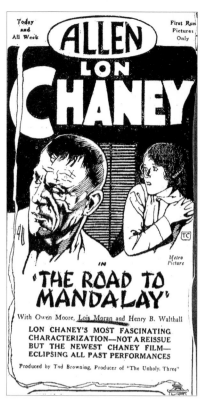

ove: The climactic moment of *The Road to Mandalay*,
26, with Lon Chaney and Owen Moore.

;ht: Newspaper advertisement for *The Road to
mdalay*, 1926.

nneth Alexander, who proclaimed himself
a photographer of actresses exclusively,
nposed this portrait of Lois shortly after
completed *Stella Dallas*.

William Mortensen created this portrait of
Lois in conjunction with his celebrated "The
Seven Ages of Lois Moran" that appeared in
Vanity Fair in 1927.

In festive spirits, as photographed by
William Mortensen ca. 1927.

Lois as the devoted Mary in *God Gave Me
Twenty Cents*, 1926, her favorite of her
films.

Poised and assured, in a ca. 1926 photograph
by Irving Chidnoff, New York.

Lya de Putti oozing bobbed glamour, as
depicted on a German postcard in 1926.

Lois's emotional breakdown in *God Gave Me Twenty Cents*, when she believes her husband has left her, afforded her some of her finest acting opportunities.

envisioned by theatrical photographer
ᵣrence Vandamm in New York in 1925.

ᵈio coming attraction herald for *The
ᵢnce of Tempters*, 1926, which depicts
is in her well-known swimming scene
ᵈ de Putti in the clinging black dress that
ᵣe to be one of the most renowned film
ᵗumes of the 1920s.

Cast photo taken on the set of *The Prince of Tempters*. Among those depicted are, *from left to right in the front row*, Mary Brian, de Putti, Ben Lyon, and Lois.

Lois inscribed this photograph of herself by Witzel to costar Jean Hersholt on the set of *Stella Dallas* in 1925.

Another study of Lois by Witzel, ca. 1925

Sloe-eyed and ascendant, Lois poses for photographer Eugene Robert Richee at Paramount in 1926.

Lois breaks from filming to take tea with Thomas Lipton, ca. 1927.

tion"; and Regina Cannon of the *Evening Graphic* wrote, "Lois Moran is utterly delightful as the sweet young thing." To these warm reviews was added a particularly negative write-up, however, by the *New York Daily Mirror*'s Dorothy Herzog, who attacked Lois's believability in enacting love scenes: "[Lois] is a curious contradiction. She runs the emotional gamut with technical perfection. Yet no sincerity warms her technique. Her love scenes made us shiver. She shrinks when she should yield to Mr. Lyon."

As always, Lois read all of her notices, even the unflattering ones, and tried to benefit from them. She was particularly mindful of Herzog's remarks. A short time after Herzog's review, she specifically addressed her criticisms in a studio press release, saying, "Romantic love scenes aren't difficult. All young girls have secret visions and dreams. I suppose that's the real secret of the whole thing—to be able to conjure up visions of people, emotions and situations—that are real and truthful. Experience is just a measuring stick."

Love-scene controversy notwithstanding, *The Prince of Tempters* marked for Lois a successful and creative return to New York film production, and although in her journal she expressed disappointment in the finished picture, she knew, when production wrapped in July, that her appearance in it would boost her popularity as an actress. She emerged from her obligation to Mendes in an ebullient mood and enjoyed a brief respite from the cameras in which she again devoted time to her personal life. Now, though, she went beyond the domesticity at Old Colony House with Gladys and Betty and cultivated a rich social life, founding and strengthening a variety of friendships that enriched her as a person and that in some instances also proved helpful to her career. She observed in her journal, "Mixing people, like drinks, is very good for one, I think. It's interesting to see a brilliant, scintillating person one day—and become mentally stimulated—and then see a soothing, quietly intelligent person the next."

As publications such as *Vanity Fair* frequently pointed out, film was not considered an intellectual medium, but it was one that nevertheless allowed Lois to meet the intelligentsia head-on, a feat she managed through her clout as a well-known film actress, which allowed her to pass in and out of the social gatherings often attended by 1920s New York's intellectual elite. In Paris, her friend Michael Knox had taken her to cafés that were meeting places for such people. Now, her name alone was all that was required to bring her in contact with them. Because she was ingratiating, intelligent, and curious, she was usually warmly welcomed by an array of accomplished and articulate personalities.

One such person who particularly impressed her was George Gershwin, whom she and Gladys visited with Henrietta Malkiel at a tea at his Riverside Drive apartment on August 25. Malkiel, a friend of Gershwin's brother, Ira, and Ira's wife, Leonore, had met Lois at a party, believed she and George would get along famously, and arranged for the two to meet. Lois, who continued to take singing lessons and dreamed still of one day appearing in a Broadway musical, revered Gershwin and viewed his compositions as the apotheosis of what it was possible to accomplish in modern music. Her tea with the composer was a fabulous experience for her, and she was awed by his personal charm, as well as by an impromptu piano performance. In turn, he recognized that although she was young, she was unique and sufficiently talented to be a potential star in one of his future stage musicals.

Lois recorded the details of the meeting with Gershwin in her journal.

> Went to George Gershwin's for tea.... He is darling. (I've been racking my brain for some less absurd sounding adjective—they don't seem to have any nice ones for men)—He's not a bit spoiled, plays the piano marvelously, and is one of the few people who "fit" (by that I mean people that are especially congenial to Mother and me).... He thinks I have fine possibilities for musical comedy.... And maybe he'll even write [a show] for me when I'm ready!! Thrilling??!

From a personal perspective, this encounter was one of the most cherished of Lois's life, but it also had profound career implications for her. The popularly accepted account is that she first met Gershwin in New York in 1931 while on vacation from Hollywood and looking for stage work. But Lois's journal entry places her relationship with him a full five years earlier and helps to better explain why she eventually won the coveted part in *Of Thee I Sing* over competition that today may be politely termed as fierce.

On several other occasions, she encountered George Jean Nathan, one of the era's toughest literary critics, who respected and befriended her during the next several years. A perceptive and erudite critic, Nathan was fond of Lois and later, in an October, 1958 article for *Esquire* magazine about his life in the 1920s, remembered her as "a lovely kid of such tender years that it was rumored she still wore the kind of flannel nightie that was bound around her ankles with ribbons." For her part, Lois appreciated his intellect and personality, writing in her journal later in the year, "I love him—He is very dark—of medium height with beautiful brown eyes with a fascinating sparkle in them and a lovely, soothing speaking voice—Sometimes, when talking, a little hesitancy comes into his voice and eyes—It is very charming—And he will say the most amusing things in his gentle way." A couple of years later she would revise her opinion of him, writing in her journal that he was a pompous social climber who lacked genuine talent, but for the time being she held him in highest regard.

Lois also met the writer and amateur photographer Carl Van Vechten, whose witty and eccentric novels about New York Society, such as *Firecrackers* and *The Blind Bow-Boy*, delighted her. She adored the urbane and charming Van Vechten and would speak fondly of him all her life; and he later said, as quoted by Edward Lueders in his 1965 biography *Carl Van Vechten*, "I knew most of the film stars, including Garbo, but my more intimate friends were Aileen Pringle, Carmel Myers, Lois Moran." Van Vechten would later take a series of memorable photographs of Lois when she was appearing in Gershwin musicals.

Other cerebral luminaries she met during this period in New York included *Vanity Fair*'s publisher, Condé Nast, whose sophisticated manner she found magnetic and whom she described in her journal as "darling... apparently one of the happiest people I have ever met"; the writer Michael Arlen, about whom she wrote in her 1970s autobiography notes, "Seemed an awfully nice man, but, aside from *The Green Hat* [his best-known work], not much appreciated as a writer"; and the film-magazine editors James Quirk (*Photoplay*) and Ruth Waterbury (*Silver Screen*), with whom she enjoyed festive luncheons at which gossip was the prime entrée. She also encountered two esteemed playwrights, her friend Marc Connelly, in whose play *The Wisdom Tooth* she had appeared the previous year, and Robert Sherwood, who had positively reviewed *Stella Dallas* and who would go on to author two works in which she would star on stage, *This Is New York* and *The Petrified Forest*.

Lois considered her education an ongoing, lifelong process that had only begun when she had passed her college boards in Paris, a belief shared by Gladys, and consequently she valued the friendships she made with New York intellectuals not only because she enjoyed their company and was flattered by their attentions but also because she learned from them and found their accomplishments a source of inspiration. Through their influence, she became even more intent upon reading, absorbing knowledge, and strengthening her mind. Her journal from that summer forward, in fact, became increasingly sprinkled with phrases such as "learned a lot," "beautiful mind," and "philosophy of life," and it was not uncommon for her to write entries in it in French about books she had read. She linked her academic pursuits to her acting skills that summer when she explained to the columnist Roscoe McGowen that the ability to think was of great importance to a young actress because it "substitutes for a lack of experience," and because "a crisp imagination... enables her to place herself in another person's shoes. . . . One must be able to feel the sadness or joy in other people's lives and be quick to weep or laugh with them."

In that era, which preceded the flowering of feminism some years later, Lois was inevitably criticized by some for placing too much emphasis on her intellectual attainments. One film magazine even published a photo caption that read, "Lois Moran is too intellectual. She hasn't yet learned the cleverness that conceals cleverness." She, however, did not consider herself a snob and devoted considerable time to activities that did not involve her books, including socializing with her friends from the film community, attending picture screenings and other industry functions, often even becoming a star-struck fan who wrote in her diary about movies she saw or actors she met. A chief way in which she kept up with her film connections while not actually on the set was through her friendship with Allan Dwan, the director of *Padlocked*, who long after the film wrapped welcomed Lois into his home, which some of the biggest movie names of the day frequented. It was at the Dwan residence, for example, that she met Gloria Swanson, who had collaborated with him on several films and of whom Lois remarked in her journal, "Find her lovely looking in a very unusual way off the screen. Has such an intriguing, thin face—she's ever so nice, methinks." Also through Dwan that summer she met the prolific Irish actor Matt Moore, the handsome brother of her *Road to Mandalay* costar Owen Moore, as well as the film directors Malcom St. Clair and Herbert Brenon.

When not socializing with movie performers, Lois enjoyed watching them on the screen. She was particularly impressed with two film actresses whom she appears never to have met but who nonetheless appealed to her, Greta Garbo and Louise Brooks. Although at that time Garbo had filmed few American photoplays, Lois had seen some of the Swedish actress's European work, discerned her disarming and soulful talent, and admired her ability to use her compelling personality as a means of transcending her physical appearance so that no audience would ever leave a theater with the impression that she was just another pretty face. Lois saw in Garbo intelligence and integrity. She claimed to have seen each of her films three times.

Today, the fact that Lois also admired Louise Brooks does not seem surprising, given the legendary status she now holds, but in fact Lois's admiration just demonstrates her perceptiveness. Brooks in the 1920s was not considered unusual; it was only years later, in the 1950s, that she became a cult icon. Lois viewed her onscreen that summer in *The Show Off* and was struck by the actress's highly individual screen presence, observing in her journal, "Louise Brooks perfectly exquisite, no, gorgeous, looking but *blank—blank—blank*—Has a divine head and neck—exactly like the Modernistic drawings" (Lois's emphases). She saw that behind Brooks's calculated blankness of expression, which in later years would be much discussed by her admirers, there was at work trenchant drive and intelligence. This, combined with her severely bobbed hair and intense physical beauty, made her a very appealing performer to Lois.

Lois was pleased with the course her nonprofessional life had taken. Nevertheless, her powerful work ethic did inevitably resurface, and soon after commencing her brief holiday away from the cameras she grew eager to begin production on another picture. In spite of many offers, she braced for what she feared would be another anxiety-ridden film selection process, especially since she was feeling discouraged. She had been disappointed with *The Prince of Tempters*, and the jolt of professional confidence she experienced after *The Road to Mandalay* had waned. She pined for something special, but based on her previous experience, she anticipated that locating such a project would be an arduous, frustrating process.

To her amazement, the decision proved to be effortless, for Paramount approached her with a picture that was well suited to her talents, an adaptation of a popular *Cosmopolitan* magazine short story entitled *God Gave Me Twenty Cents*. Authored by Dixie Willson, a prolific young magazine writer, this odd tale seemed ideally crafted as a source for a film. Its plot was both sensational and lyrical, on one level a torrid melodrama about a triangular relationship between a sailor, a young waitress he marries, and a worldly siren who seeks to separate them, on another level a haunting character study of a girl, the waitress, who is so defined by the love she feels for her husband that when she believes he has sailed away with another woman she contemplates suicide, believing that in death she will be transformed into a seagull and can fly behind his ship in perpetual expression of her love.

In preparing such a story for the screen, Paramount had recognized that it was a project which, if handled tastefully, could yield a film of superior quality and public popularity. In consequence, the studio assigned it a top-notch director, Herbert Brenon, at the height of his powers and fresh from recent films such as *The Great Gatsby* and *Beau Geste*, and carefully considered the casting of the actors. Jack Mulhall won the part of the sailor; William "Buster" Collier Jr. was cast as a young fugitive; and Lya de Putti, like Lois newly emerged from *The Prince of Tempters*, was retained to enact the role of the plotting femme fatale. For the part of the waitress, the pivotal role of the film, Brenon was convinced that Lois, whom he had remembered from *Stella Dallas* and whose onscreen voltage with de Putti had impressed him more recently, would be the ideal selection. Lois, pleased to be offered such a poetic role, welcomed the opportunity of working for the first time with Brenon and again with de Putti.

At the time, Lois considered appearing in *God Gave Me Twenty Cents* a coup for her career—and, indeed, the finished film would feature some of her most accomplished work—but, in retrospect, the casting can be viewed as an inadvertently adverse progression, because by contracting for it she was unavailable a short time later for another, more important film for which she was considered. In June 1926, the respected German director F. W. Murnau, a contemporary of Lothar Mendes at the UFA studio who was renowned for powerful films such as *Nosferatu the Vampire* and *The Last Laugh*, arrived in America with considerable fanfare to begin filming a project for Fox entitled *A Trip to Tilsit*, a simple but moving story of the reconciliation between a farmer and his wife after he has been unfaithful to her with a more sophisticated woman from the city. Murnau had seen Lois's films, had visited the set of *The Prince of Tempters*, and believed that she possessed the innate warmth and gentleness that would be perfect for the part of the wife, and his choice of casting was duly reported on August 14 by Louella Parsons in her syndicated column. Parsons concluded, "If I am any judge of human nature Murnau will get what he wants," but sadly for Lois he did not. Because she had signed for the Brenon picture, she was unavailable to film at Fox, and as a result, and to her great disappointment, she lost the role to Janet Gaynor. The finished picture, released as *Sunrise*, went on to become one of the most beautiful of all films and was one of three pictures that year for which Gaynor received the first Best Actress Academy Award, in the days when those trophies were given for multiple performances. Lois was understandably upset about missing out on the film but not bitter.

Once the sting of the *Sunrise* loss lessened, she threw herself into *God Gave Me Twenty Cents*. She began by carefully reading the screen treatment of Wilson's story, which had been prepared at Paramount by John Russell and Elizabeth Meehan. The two had worked to create a screen narrative that featured romance, action, and plot twists but that would, at the same time, focus upon the fragile, soulful beauty of Lois's character.

In New Orleans during Mardi Gras, a handsome sailor, Steve Doran (Mulhall), meets Mary (Lois), a young, unaffected waitress. Smitten with the girl's naiveté, he places a rose in her hair and makes her queen of the Mardi Gras parade. They soon wed, and Mary adores her new husband. One of Steve's old girlfriends, Cassie (de Putti) then reemerges. When he declines to take her with him on his next voyage, she challenges him to a coin toss with two fake dimes that are marked with heads on both sides. Cassie, of course, wins her bet and carelessly tosses the dimes onto the ground. Mary's landlord tells the heartbroken wife that Steve has sailed off with Cassie. Desiring to become a seagull that can fly behind Steve's ship in devotion to him, she walks toward the wharf with the intent of drowning herself. On her way, she passes a florist shop and espies roses in the window, for sale for twenty cents. She has no money but wishes to wear a rose in her hair as a remembrance of the one Steve gave to her in the Mardi Gras parade. As she makes her way to the water, she prays for the required twenty cents and is overjoyed to find two dimes on the ground. Picking them up, she rushes back to the florist to buy a rose. Soon the florist, realizing that the dimes are fake, chases her and involves the police. An ugly shooting match ensues, and one of those shot happens to be Cassie, who has not sailed with Steve after all. On her deathbed at the hospital, she tells Mary of her deceptive coins. Mary and Steve reunite.

Lois very much liked this plot and the part she was to enact in it. Finding the role of Mary moving, complex, and the most challenging to come her way since that of *Stella Dallas*'s Laurel, she began work on the picture in high spirits, relieved and happy to have the chance to again prove her merits as an actress in challenging and worthwhile material. She realized the part needed to be approached carefully: it ran the risk of becoming maudlin and overly sentimental, and as a result Lois applied herself even more determinedly than usual, thoroughly absorbing herself in the complexities of the character and doing her best to portray her in a lifelike, believable way.

As filming of *God Gave Me Twenty Cents* got under way, Lois became increasingly fond of Brenon, who shared her enthusiasm for the project. Actress and director, in fact, quickly evolved into friends, and Lois was so taken with him that she wrote a detailed entry in her journal about him: "Mr. Brenon is a charming English gentleman with a whisky face, soft, straggly, thin white hair and an harassed look in his eyes—He has a very definite, domineering personality, though not an aggressive one, combined with a great sympathy for and understanding of people and an Irish sense of humor." She continued, also, to be fascinated by de Putti, noting in her journal that "I do enjoy being with her" and taking time to creatively analyze what it was about this actress that so intrigued her. "She gives such a lot of enthusiasm to everything she does.... I think she has one of the most beautifully shaped faces I have ever seen.—It is so like a flower or a cameo—and rather incongruous for a person of her type.—Her hair is dark and sleek like a savage's—her fingernails are rather repulsive in as much as they are slightly curved like animal claws—but her smile is fascinatingly human and attractive.—Her philosophy of life is simple and frank—without scruple or moral."

Working on such a film with such a cast, Lois happily recorded in her journal, "Work is going beautifully." This is not to say that filming proceeded without problem. Rudolph Valentino died during its production, and Lois was greatly upset that her work at the studio prevented her from attending his funeral. She complained in her journal on August 30, "Reported for work at the studio but my call was a false alarm. Was so sorry that we missed Valentino's funeral as a consequence—such a shame that he died, so young, only 32, and with a lovely career ahead of him, perhaps." She publicly expressed her grief by telling the *Film Daily*, "To me it was Valentino's youth which makes his death so sad."

In spite of this mishap, Lois emerged refreshed and optimistic from production of *God Gave Me Twenty Cents*. As late as 1963 she remarked in the *San Francisco Examiner*, "My favorite early [film] was *God Gave Me Twenty Cents*...it gave me a lot of satisfaction." Paramount's Adolph Zukor and Jesse Lasky shared her enthusiasm. After reviewing rushes of the film, they selected it for a rare honor: when it premiered that November in New York, it would be the feature film at the gala opening of their Paramount Theater, one of the most grandiose, imposing movie palaces ever erected, and as the featured attraction it would enjoy a lavishly engineered debut. The advent of the Paramount was a milestone in the history both of New York and of the cinema, and its unveiling was a spectacular event. Erected at a cost of $13.5 million, then a staggering sum, this theater was a monument both to the Art Deco stylization of the day and to antiquity, an awesome, thirty-five-story structure that towered over Broadway, occupied almost a full square block, seated nearly 4000 patrons, and featured an imaginative decor that included exquisite ornamentation and a myriad of antiques. A bold and important new structure, the Paramount on the night of its public opening was a spectacle, bathed in colored lights and swathed in blue smoke from camera flashbulbs, a glittering, incandescent structure that reached toward the sky and could be seen for blocks. The excitement resulted in the theater's nearly being overrun by the press, still and newsreel photographers, and hordes of curious onlookers. Police had to intervene to control the crowds and the traffic.

Adding to the excitement that autumn evening were the celebrity attendees, who arrived to the theater in taxis and limousines and battled their way into the foyer amidst the gleam of the flash photography and shrieks and gasps from the crowd. Naturally, the cast and crew of *God Gave Me Twenty Cents* were present. Lya de Putti sat a few rows behind William Collier Jr. and across the aisle from Lois, who came with Gladys and who, Roscoe McGowen reported in the *New York News* the next day, "sat well forward where she could watch herself with a (possibly) critical eye." Robert T. Kane, Dixie Willson, and Jack Mulhall were other *Twenty Cents* alumni in attendance.

Most of the film celebrities present had not been involved with the film, however, and included, among many others, Gloria Swanson, Richard Dix, Lois Wilson, Betty Bronson, Neil Hamilton, Mack Sennett, Sid Grauman, Lothar Mendes, Louise Brooks, and Alice Joyce. Others present included Sinclair Lewis, Fannie Hurst, David Belasco, Rex Beach, and Charles Dana Gibson. The highly sought after tickets for the event were being scalped for as much as $100 a pair. One nightclub proprietress even made it known that she would pay $200 for a pair anywhere in the house.

The program itself featured a speech by Mayor Jimmy Walker, who, though suffering from a cold, charmed the crowed and paid tribute to Adolph Zukor, thanking him for opening such a theater during his administration. Will Hays, then the president of the Motion Picture Distributors of America, Inc., also spoke in tribute to Thomas Edison, the inventor who helped to found the cinema and who sat straight backed and stony faced in the audience. Additionally featured in the program was a film history retrospective, *Pageant of Progress*, compiled by John Murray Anderson.

Initially, Lois was elated that *God Gave Me Twenty Cents* would play a part in such a historic event; but, as the evening itself wore on, she became fatigued and irritated because on such a crowded bill her film did not screen until well past eleven. Many of those present, including several critics, left the theater, exhausted, before watching it. In her journal a few days later, Lois discussed the evening: "After two hours of an excruciatingly boring program the picture came on and of course went over badly—It ended at 12:45 and how I wept when we arrived home—That certainly was a miserable night, even if everyone did say that I gave a beautiful performance."

Although dwarfed at its New York opening by the festivities for the film palace at which it played, *God Gave Me Twenty Cents* was actually better received than Lois thought. Critics throughout the country were not universally impressed, but they were generally respectful toward the film as a whole and appreciative of its finer points, in particular, as had been true of *The Prince of Tempters*, the performances given by de Putti and Lois. In discussing de Putti's performance, they were more enthusiastic than they had been when reviewing her work in *The Prince of Tempters* and in fact generally praised her. Harriette Underhill of the *New York Herald Tribune* trumpeted, "Lya de Putti does far better work than she has done in America. She is sincere and intensely interesting," and a columnist at *Variety* noted, "In this one she is almost as good as in *Variety* [her earlier German film]. And she looks like a million dollars in some of the shots here." Other critics disliked her performance and believed that she overacted, a view typified by the unhappy writer at the *New York American*, who complained, "Lya de Putti is the only player who attracts attention. She does so by reason of her continual overacting. In other words, she is so bad one is unable to forget her." Reviews such as this notwithstanding, de Putti proved in this picture that was a capable actress, and it is unfortunate that she never became a major star in American films. In November 1931, after a brief troubled life and before her potential had ever been fully realized, Lya de Putti died of pneumonia at the age of thirty-two in a New York hospital after having undergone surgery to remove a chicken bone that had lodged in her throat.

As for Lois, her careful depiction of Mary did not go unnoticed, and the intensity and soul with which she played her key scenes in the film—the moment when Mulhall crowns her queen of the Mardi Gras parade, her anguished suicide walk toward the sea, her hearing de Putti's confession at the hospital—prompted critics to lavish her with praise and to award her the best reviews she had received since *Stella Dallas*. The *San Francisco News* observed that "Lois Moran, appealingly pretty and naïve, gives a surpassingly delightful performance, easily her best effort"; Regina Cannon of the *New York Evening Graphic* wrote, "Lois Moran is superb. . . . This is [her] finest screen performance thus far, exceeding even her excellent characterization in *Stella Dallas*"; Palmer Smith of the *New York Evening World* remarked that "I thought her performance almost perfect"; and *Variety* gushed, "That girl is a wonder. She troupes all over the place. Women are going to love her, suffer with her, and just about want to kill the sailor husband who they believe has walked out on her because of his former love."

Lois read the reviews with elation. She was pleased to have been validated as an actress, of course, but, perhaps even more important, she was at greater peace with herself. She believed that she had at last given a screen performance that would open a new chapter in her career because it would, once and for all, prove her merits as an actress and put to rest any rumors that her performance in *Stella*

Dallas had been a fluke. "Personally," she wrote in her journal shortly after the premiere at the Paramount, "I think it my best performance to date. I think I understand what it's all about better and have more technique, poise and depth—Hope I'm not mistaken because I should hate not to have progressed at all in eight months." As evidenced by her reviews and by the solid commercial success that the film went on to achieve, she was not mistaken. Her future as a film actress was now more promising than ever.

At the time, she enjoyed using a term she had learned from George Jean Nathan: the word "much" used as a term of praise in an unusual context, as in "He is very *much*" (her description in her journal, and her emphases, of *Vanity Fair*'s managing editor, Donald Freeman). It was a phrase that could easily have been applied to her, as well, for as a teenaged film actress she had thus far made nine films, including her two European titles, all of which had been to varying degrees successful. As she steadily honed her natural acting talent, she garnered ever increasing popularity with the public and respect from her film peers. By adding to these professional factors a stimulating private life, Lois became one of the most well rounded actresses of the day. Lois Moran was, indeed, very *much*, and it was with well-justified pride that she noted in her journal in October 1926 that she had recently glimpsed a memo at Paramount written by Jesse Lasky in which he had assessed her on-camera abilities. "[It] said that I had matured beautifully," she excitedly reported, "and that I had acquired 'it'! Hooray! It's about time!"

Book II

"Darling, Dumbbell, Upsetting, Adorable Scott"

Golly, it was a happy time. . . . I was floating on a cloud.

Lois Moran, 1948, describing her early acquaintance
with F. Scott Fitzgerald

Tender Is the Night was only a fairy tale,
though a beautiful one.

Lois Moran, 1988

Pickfair, Strawberries and Caviar, and F. Scott Fitzgerald

6

*W*hat about love, everyone says," Lois Moran pondered in a journal entry dated November 22, 1926. "Never having experienced that upsetting condition, I wouldn't be too sure of myself." By that autumn, the seventeen-year-old actress had experienced romantic relationships in the plot lines of her films but not in her personal life. While she flourished enacting lovestruck heroines upon the screen, she believed that in her personal life the time was not right for her to experience a romance of her own. A variety of engaging individuals enriched her existence and she was not lonely, but she did not place great importance upon men and dating. She remained steadfast in her future goals of marriage and family; however, as 1926 progressed, she determined that with the demands placed upon her time by the movie studios, and given her close attachments to Gladys and Betty, the circumstances of her life were not conducive to her seeking out a romantic relationship.

Lois, like most other young girls, was certainly aware of the opposite sex and seldom lost sight of her ultimate goal of marriage and family. With her inherited Irish pragmatism, however, she reasoned that her previous attractions, which had been directed to her older leading men such as Ivan Mosjoukine, Ronald Colman, and Richard Barthelmess, were merely fleeting infatuations and not of lasting importance. She had yet to experience a substantive, deeply felt romantic attachment and was, she assured herself, happy to keep it that way. She noted in her journal that she was put off by girls her age "exchang[ing] silly platitudes with boys as inexperienced as themselves." For Lois, love was something to be savored in her future. What she did not realize was that she could not so easily dismiss matters of the heart, a lesson she would learn when in early 1927 she attended a party at Pickfair, the palatial home of Mary Pickford and Douglas Fairbanks Sr., and met there a certain writer who was in town to author a movie scenario, a novelist by the name of F. Scott Fitzgerald.

As 1926 drew to a close with the approach of autumn and winter, Lois could not have known that a literary celebrity such as Fitzgerald would soon enter into and play such a vivid part in her life. Her steadily ascendant film career virtually overwhelmed her, and she saw more of her cinema colleagues than she did of her friends in the worlds of arts and letters. Film critics, moreover, accelerated her enthusiasm for movie work when they commenced awarding her year's-end accolades in their columns. In December, for example, *Photoplay* placed her on its Honor Roll for 1926, a prestigious tribute in the days before the Academy Awards. The magazine cited her performances in *Stella Dallas* and *Padlocked* as among the best of the year and ranked her with the likes of John Gilbert, Gloria Swanson, Ramon Novarro, and Clara Bow as one of the actors who had made the most important onscreen contributions during the previous twelve months. The *New York Tribune* columnist Richard Watts Jr. followed the film magazine's example and named Lois as one of the screen actors who had made the greatest progress in 1926, a list that included Greta Garbo, Vilma Banky (Samuel Goldwyn's other film "discovery" of recent months), Harry Langdon, and William Powell. The *Chicago Journal* summed up the critics' prevailing opinion of Lois when it observed succinctly that she was "one of the most brilliant of the younger stars."

Tributes such as these, in combination with the lucrative box-office returns that flowed in from her films, surprised but gratified Lois and bolstered her self-confidence. Later, in 1929, she wrote in her journal a self-observation that characterized her thinking at this time. "The thing," she would write, "which always moves me in a really sincere way is my desire to create, to *be*. It is the only thing in this world. Even though all may be futile, at least one has made as beautiful a creation as is possible." Lois believed that, despite her anxieties over having selected the right films and having left her mark as a serious actress, she had accomplished much in 1926, and that the year had been creatively fertile for her, a time in which she had established a solid foundation for her future in the movies and, in time, on the stage.

In consequence, as 1927 approached, Lois and Gladys found themselves in buoyant, forward-looking spirits. The two had determined that Lois's next film would be an adaptation of a 1900 David Belasco–produced stage play, *The Music Master*, to be made for William Fox and to costar Alec B. Francis and Neil Hamilton. But a host of other happenings occupied her time as well, and in a rare turn of events, the production of her newest film was not of primary importance to her. Rather, this was a period of great color in her life away from the set, a joyous respite. She took part in career-related publicity activities, which she enjoyed and viewed more as recreation than as work, attended parties and various other social functions, and spent many evenings at the theater. These diversions were exhilarating and Lois was happy to be experiencing them, but she did not know that their greatest significance would be that they would culminate in her meeting Fitzgerald in January of 1927.

In late 1926, Lois took pleasure in attending the theater, although she was blunt in her opinions of the plays at hand. In October in New York, she attended the opening of the dramatized version of Theodore Dreiser's 1925 novel *An American Tragedy*. She had not liked the book, noting in her journal that she believed Dreiser to be "all repressed and mixed-up—Poor Man—His style in writing is interesting, though, before it becomes monotonous." The stage production of *An American Tragedy*, however, made a more favorable impression upon her. Also that October in New York, she saw *Rain*, the dramatization of Somerset Maugham's story, starring Jeanne Eagels. Lois enjoyed Eagels's performance as the story's main character, Sadie Thompson, but otherwise was "greatly disappointed in" the play and penned in her journal, "Imagine it was one of the first 'sexy' plays and therefore was successful—all about a 'bad, bad woman' and a 'good, good preacher' who has repressed all sex emotion for so long that he can't help letting go at last after which the woman announces 'all men are pigs'—Quite childish—methinks—people make such a row about nothing and the most natural things these days."

She also saw Helen Hayes in J. M. Barrie's *What Every Woman Knows.* She admired Hayes and described her as "quite an ideal 'Barrie' actress" but added, in an uncommon assertion of ego that had its roots perhaps in her continued desire to play Barrie's *Peter Pan*, "I do hope to someday be better than she in his plays." Lois's mention of Hayes was an intriguing foreshadowing of a memorable weekend she would spend with Hayes and the writer Charles MacArthur, Hayes's husband-to-be, a short time later at a party at F. Scott Fitzgerald's home, Ellerslie.

In keeping with their celebratory dispositions that winter, and given the fact that Lois had worked virtually nonstop for nearly two years, Gladys decided spending the Christmas holidays abroad would be an enjoyable rest. Early in December, she, Lois, and Betty set sail from New York aboard the enormous luxury liner *Leviathan* bound for Cherbourg, from where they planned to travel to Paris and St. Moritz for a month's vacation. Lois, elated by the prospect of vacationing in France and Switzerland, boarded the ship wearing a fur coat, black gloves, and cloche hat and in the winter weather posed on deck for photographers by aiming snowballs at their cameras.

In its early stages, the excursion was a happy experience for Lois. She enjoyed solitary early morning walks on the deck of the *Leviathan*, at that time of day when there was, as she recorded in her journal, "not a soul on deck excepting a few sailors." She was gleeful when the ship arrived in Cherbourg and was soon again enjoying "dusk and Paris." The family would remain in Paris for a short time before moving on to Switzerland. As pleased as Lois was to be back in the City of Light, she grew uncharacteristically melancholy when it conjured memories of her earlier life there that she had spent with her Irish tutor, Michael Knox. Those days with Knox, spent chatting with artists and writers in cafés, seemed far off and halcyon to her now. The fame and success that had come to her since then had brought her weighty responsibilities and extinguished her childhood, because it had exposed her too soon to the realities of the world. She dined and danced in the city and wrote fondly in her journal of "that Paris feeling...hazy...quiet...dreams preparing," but at the same time made ominous references to experiencing "unrest" and an "odd feeling." After spending less than four days in the city she announced to her mother that she was homesick and wished to return to the States. Gladys, aware that the months of grueling work at the studios had fatigued her daughter and suspecting that nostalgia was causing her to feel ill at ease, decided to truncate the trip and sail immediately back to America.

The Morans made their return voyage on the *Leviathan*, and although Lois had been depressed and homesick in Paris, she was now peppy and bright and found the journey home the most exciting part of the trip. On board the luxury liner with her were a variety of well-known travelers headed for New York for Christmas: the governor of Massachusetts, Alvan T. Fuller, and his wife; Alanson B. Houghton, the United States ambassador to Great Britain, and his two daughters; and the stage actresses Peggy O'Neil and Vesta Victoria. Lois also met the renowned French playwright Sacha Guitry and his wife, the actress Yvonne Printemps. In addition to celebrating the holidays, they were coming to New York to present Guitry's newest play, *Mozart,* with Printemps in the role of the composer as a very young man. Lois also met a group of college boys from Cambridge as well as a jazz pianist with whom she discussed modern music.

Lois was particularly fond of chatting with Guitry, an older man whose intellect fascinated her and whose insights into Mozart inspired her resolve to one day appear in a Mozart opera. Guitry's extroverted and glamorous wife also intrigued Lois. Oozing heavy European glamour, Printemps sashayed about the deck wearing a stylish fur coat, leather boots, and orchid corsage while clutching a small bewildered puppy under her arm. Playing shamelessly to press photographers, Printemps was every inch the star, giving full meaning to Carl Van Vechten's often-quoted Hollywood adjective "orchidaceous," and she made sure the world was well aware of her impending arrival in America. She made a strong impression on Lois, who was struck by the French actress's bravura style and personality.

Possibly the greatest hullabaloo of the voyage came for Lois, however, when a bomb scare threatened the *Leviathan*'s docking in New York. As one of the city's papers put it at the time, "anonymous [bomb] threats had been made by a fanatic," and when the ship reached port a bomb squad and four detectives descended upon it. They located no explosives, however, and the threats, aimed apparently at Ambassador Houghton, proved in all ways groundless. Once this potential terrorism had been settled, the ship's famous occupants emerged from their staterooms to meet anxious family, friends, and a frenzied army of reporters and photographers who were eager to report on both the bomb threat and the celebrity holiday arrivals. So it was, amidst Christmas adornment, the pop of camera flashbulbs, and an almost palpable sense of relief that disaster had been averted, that the ship's inhabitants made their way back onto land. Lois, pleased to be home and not to have been blown to bits, emerged looking poised and increasingly the movie star, attired in an Art Deco–patterned coat accentuated with hat and pearl-trimmed handbag. She had no regrets over having aborted her overseas holiday and was ready to return to life as usual in America.

For Lois, life as usual, as Christmas and New Year's melted away into 1927, was festive and mirthful. Free for the moment from any studio obligations and, intent upon having the fun she had anticipated would have come her way in Europe, she led a glossy social existence in New York before returning to Hollywood. She attended several parties in New York at which she renewed acquaintances with several friends, including George Jean Nathan, Condé Nast, and the editor of *Vanity Fair*, Donald Freeman. She also met the tennis star Bill Tilden, whose 1920 book *The Art of Lawn Tennis* she had admired and for whom she would help to procure a film role in *The Music Master*; the actress Rosamunde Prichot, whom she named in her journal as one of the most intriguing people she had encountered that year; and the book and theatrical illustrator Ralph Barton, who is today best remembered for the droll drawings he created for Anita Loos's 1925 novel *Gentlemen Prefer Blondes* and its 1928 sequel, *But Gentlemen Marry Brunettes*. Barton, in particular, played a significant role in Lois's life at this time. She described him in her journal as "a charming man with a marriage complex—He has been married four times already and is considering going through the process again in spite of having known the girl for a few days." In keeping with his obvious interest in the relationships between men and women, he would a few months later make an astonishing contemporary visual comment on Lois's relationship with Fitzgerald in an illustration for *Vanity Fair*. Unfortunately, Barton's interest in multiple marriages and male-female relations would also prove his undoing, for he committed suicide in 1931, after his most recent wife, the actress Carlotta Monterey, had divorced him to marry Eugene O'Neill.

In addition to attending parties, Lois took part in some scattered film-related activities, both as spectator and participant. Although she believed that attending film screenings at this time was rather like embarking upon a busman's holiday, she in the former capacity went out to see the 1921 celluloid version of a novel her *Prince of Tempters* costar Ian Keith had given her that Christmas, George du Maurier's 1891 *Peter Ibbetson*. The film, retitled *Forever*, featured the late Wallace Reid and Elsie Ferguson, and although Lois liked it, she rather petulantly remarked of it in her journal, "could be worse."

She also appeared, as a lark, in a brief scene for a mock four-reel silent short subject of *Camille* that Ralph Barton was filming as a home movie with an astonishing cast that included Anita Loos, who in 1927 would write the scenario for Lois's film *Publicity Madness*, in the title role, and Charles Green Shaw, a writer and acquaintance of F. Scott Fitzgerald's, as Armand, as well as, among others, Charles Chaplin, Paul Robeson, Theodore Dreiser, John Emerson, Roland Young, W. Somerset Maugham, George Jean Nathan, H. L. Mencken, Sinclair Lewis, Joseph Hergesheimer, Alfred A. Knopf, Ethel Barrymore, Rex Ingram, Aileen Pringle, Dorothy Gish, Carmel Myers, and Richard Barthelmess. The "real picture people," Lois wrote in her journal, were playing extra parts, and she did a small drunken scene for it, playing the part of Kitty. "In my devotion to my art, [I] spilt a glass of whisky all down my frock." Nothing of lasting significance came of any of this burst of recreational merriment—nothing, that is, until, in Hollywood in early 1927, she attended that fateful party at Pickfair.

Lois's association with Fitzgerald had its genesis in December 1926, when he, his wife, Zelda, and their daughter, Scottie, returned to America after having resided for the past three years in Europe, primarily on the French Riviera. Fitzgerald's life in Europe had been wild and unstructured, and as his drinking and partying had escalated, his writing had diminished to the point where he had not authored a story in nearly sixteen months. It had been what he would later characterize as a period of "one thousand parties and no work." A return to the United States, he hoped, would help him discipline himself, rejuvenate his literary creativity, and settle into a more productive, patterned existence. In the early days of his return, he and Zelda visited their families in Washington, D.C., and Montgomery, Alabama, and he remained focused on returning to the basics and creating a sense of order and work in his heretofore chaotic life.

Shortly after Christmas, however, fate altered Fitzgerald's hopes for a new modulated routine. An opportunity arose for him to travel to Hollywood to write for the movies. John Considine Jr., a Yale graduate and Fitzgerald admirer, sent him a telegram on December 30 inviting him to come out to the West Coast to write a screen scenario. Considine was in charge of a production company, Feature Productions, and was searching for a story he could produce for United Artists that would star Constance Talmadge, one of the most popular comedic screen actresses of the day. Considine liked the contemporary flavor of Fitzgerald's work and believed that Fitzgerald could create a "fine modern college story" for Talmadge.

Considine's offer tantalized Fitzgerald. Movies had been produced of several of his works: the short stories "Head and Shoulders," filmed as *The Chorus Girl's Romance* in 1920, "Myra Meets His Family," filmed as *The Husband Hunter* in 1920, "The Off-Shore Pirate" (1921), and "Grit" (1924), as well as the novels *The Beautiful and Damned* (1922) and *The Great Gatsby* (1926). Moreover, he had previously written for films, albeit with little success, in the early 1920s when he prepared scenarios and titles for the likes of the producer Lewis J. Selznick, the director Allan Dwan, and actresses such as Elaine Hammerstein. He had never actually been to Hollywood, however, and he was intrigued by Considine's proposal and confident that he could excel at preparing a story for Talmadge. He was also in need of additional income and had been alert to reports from fellow writers such as Carl Van Vechten, Marc Connelly, and Charles MacArthur of the vast amounts of money to be made in the film industry.

After negotiating, he agreed to go to Hollywood for what was then a small fortune, $3500 down and $8500 payable upon the completion and acceptance of the story. In early January 1927, he boarded the Twentieth Century Limited for Los Angeles, taking Zelda along with him and depositing Scottie with his parents in Washington, D.C., and although he wanted his arrival in Hollywood kept low profile, the press was quick to report on it. The columnist Allene Talmey wrote, for example, in an article Zelda pasted into her and Fitzgerald's scrapbook, "As blondes, ash, yellow or brass, have been the heroines of Mr. Fitzgerald's tales ever since he came up on the crest of the younger generation in *This Side of Paradise*, he will be set immediately to fashion one of his blonde, reckless, willful and irresponsible girls for Constance Talmadge to use as background for her sparkle." The Fitzgeralds' tenure in Hollywood was brief, lasting only eight weeks from January to mid-March of 1927, but Lois played a substantial role in it.

Upon their arrival in Hollywood, Scott and Zelda stayed in a four-apartment bungalow at the Ambassador Hotel on Wilshire Boulevard. Their neighbors in the bungalow made up an illustrious group: the actors John Barrymore and Carmel Myers and the novelist Carl Van Vechten. In "Show Mr. and Mrs. F. to Number —," a 1934 *Esquire* magazine article authored by them (more by Zelda than by Scott, though), the Fitzgeralds briefly discussed their Hollywood trip. The article explained that they had arrived in Los Angeles in time to experience an earthquake, and, as they described their surroundings at the hotel, outside their window "white roses swung luminous in the mist from a trellis" and nearby "a bright exaggerated parrot droned incomprehensible shouts in an aquamarine pool—of course everybody interpreted them to be obscenities." The Fitzgeralds' lodgings at the lively bungalow were, as Zelda wrote to Scottie, "just between the leading vamps of the cinema: Pola Negri on one side and John Barrymore on the other." Zelda perhaps believed that telling her daughter that Negri was living next door would be of more interest to the girl than telling her the truth, that the less notorious Myers occupied the suite. The Fitzgeralds also socialized with Lillian Gish, about whom Lois had earlier written in her journal when she had seen a revival of *The Birth of a Nation*, and Lois's friend and costar Richard Barthelmess. Moreover, Douglas Fairbanks and Mary Pickford gave a lavish luncheon in their honor at Pickfair where, the Fitzgeralds noted in *Esquire*, they marveled at Pickford's "dynamic subjugation of life."

Fitzgerald noted in a ledger he kept at the time that he and Zelda also met such Hollywood denizens as Bessie Love, Patsy Ruth Miller, Marion Davies, and the writer Ben Hecht. Fitzgerald enjoyed the company of these particular friends and basked in their attentions to him, but otherwise he did not like film people. He described Hollywood as "a tragic city of beautiful girls" and was wary of its inhabitants' "almost hysterical egotism and excitability hidden under an extremely thin veil of elaborate good-fellowship." There were exceptions, however. He considered Van Vechten a true and trusted friend, even if he did call him a "pederast" in his notebooks; he found in Barrymore a jovial drinking chum and fellow doting father who was devoted to his daughter, Diana, and had placed numerous pictures of her in his bungalow; he liked and respected Myers, whom he and Zelda had met in Rome in 1924 while she was filming *Ben-Hur*; and, most important, he adored Lois, whom he met early on in his trip.

Fitzgerald had probably already known *of* Lois. It would have been difficult for anyone at the time not to have heard of her success in *Stella Dallas*. He was acquainted with Edgar Selwyn, the producer of the original stage version of *Stella Dallas*. On the French Riviera, he had also known E. Phillips Oppenheim, the author of *The Ex-Duke*, on which Lois's film *The Prince of Tempters* had been based. He was most likely aware of *Padlocked*, in which Lois had played a young girl at odds with the older generation. The character personified the type of strong, willful young heroine Fitzgerald had enjoyed creating in novels such as *The Beautiful and Damned* and in stories such as "Bernice Bobs Her Hair" and "The Off-Shore Pirate."

From 1948 to 1951, Lois corresponded with Arthur Mizener, who was then researching *The Far Side of Paradise*, the first biography of Fitzgerald, and in her letters to him, which are housed today in his papers at Princeton, she was more effusive and forthcoming about Fitzgerald than she would be in later years. At the time Fitzgerald was staying at the Ambassador, she wrote to Mizener, she and Gladys had taken an apartment on Mariposa Street, which ran alongside the hotel: "I don't recall when or where we all met," soon a clique had formed including herself, the Fitzgeralds, Van Vechten, Barrymore, and Barthelmess. Sara Mayfield, a friend of Zelda's, wrote a memoir about the Fitzgeralds in 1971 entitled *Exiles from Paradise* in which she stated that Lois met Fitzgerald at the Pickfair luncheon; and Matthew Bruccoli, in his 1981 biography of Fitzgerald *Some Sort of Epic Grandeur*, said that the introduction most likely occurred through Van Vechten. Once they met, Lois and Fitzgerald quickly became the best of friends. "Golly, it was a happy time," Lois wrote to Mizener. "I was floating on a cloud." The Morans entertained from their Mariposa apartment, which was closer to the studios than was their house on 517 North Elm Drive in Beverly Hills. They ordered meals to be sent over from the hotel, and, as Lois told Mizener, "Scott and I liked strawberries and caviar." Even more precious to her, though, were delicacies of a different sort: conversations she and Fitzgerald had when the parties at the apartment became too crowded and the pair would spill out into the hallway, sit on the stairs, and chat. "Those brief talks are my loveliest memories of Scott," she wrote to Mizener. "I can't remember a thing he said, but everything was right and everything was beautiful."

Fitzgerald found the seventeen-year-old Lois as refreshing as the white roses that clung to the walls of the Ambassador. At thirty, the once boyish, handsome writer who had become famous for novels and stories about youth was now a depressed man who saw himself as spent and middle-aged. Additionally, his popular success had dwindled: his last novel, *The Great Gatsby*, had sold considerably fewer copies than his first, *This Side of Paradise*. Even his renowned marriage to his beloved Zelda had become difficult and strained. In Lois, he saw youth, beauty, and promise, things he believed no longer existed in his own life, and he was captivated by her intelligence and social grace. He was impressed by her passion for reading; by her ability to speak fluent French, something he was never able to do; by her love of music, even though he himself, as both his daughter and the novelist John dos Passos pointed out, possessed what director Billy Wilder would have called "Van Gogh's ear for music"; and by her keeping a journal and a poetic chapbook. He also related to her ambition. "We were [both] awfully keen about our own work," Lois told Mizener.

Moreover, Fitzgerald was almost certainly aware of certain aspects of *Stella Dallas* that bore an uncanny resemblance to his own life. For Fitzgerald's seventh birthday in 1903, his mother had thrown him a party and had sent out invitations, but it rained, and no one came. He and his mother celebrated his birthday alone, and he devoured the cake by himself. This episode, one of the most miserable episodes of his childhood, strikingly recalled the famous scene in *Stella Dallas* in which no one came to Laurel's tenth birthday party, which was perhaps Lois's best-remembered sequence from the film. Also reminiscent of *Stella Dallas* was the fact that Fitzgerald loved his mother but was embarrassed by her dress and behavior, a situation that was similar to how Laurel felt about Stella in the relationship that formed the most important part of the story. It would seem that Fitzgerald, who no doubt had either heard of or seen the film, could not have helped but develop a fondness for the young actress who had enacted situations that bore such remarkable similarities to incidents in his own life.

Fitzgerald may have been uneasy with many of the people he met in Hollywood, but he saw Lois as an unaffected and successful young woman to whom he could open his heart. There were others in his Hollywood circle at the time—Van Vechten, Barthelmess, Barrymore, Myers—but Lois made the strongest impression upon him. In his ledger, in fact, he made a point of noting in February 1927, in his own particular shorthand, "Party at Lois," a detail Lois later confirmed for Mizener: "To sum up the Hollywood (1927) period—we went to many parties, night clubs, etc." Fitzgerald believed that events in his life often occurred in seven-year cycles, and he saw it as a positive sign that almost seven years earlier, long before he knew Lois, he had written a short story entitled "Benediction" with a teenage heroine he called Lois.

Lois was awestruck by Fitzgerald. In a 1928 journal entry, she proclaimed, "What prose that man can create!," and she later wrote to Mizener, "My worship for him was based on admiration of his talent." She had acquired her love of books and respect for writers as a child in her grandparents' library in Pittsburgh, and while her tastes generally ran more to Victorians such as George du Maurier than to contemporary novelists of the Jazz Age, she knew of Fitzgerald and his work. In the winter of 1926, she had attended a Princeton University Triangle play when it came to New York. The Triangle Club was a Princeton theatrical group that had been founded by Booth Tarkington that created and staged a musical comedy every year that toured during the Christmas holidays. Anyone seeing a Triangle play probably would have been aware of Fitzgerald, who while at Princeton had been a highly visible and active participant in the club from approximately 1914 to 1916, wrote and published song lyrics for three of its productions (*Fie! Fie! Fi-Fi!*, 1914; *The Evil Eye*, 1915; and *Safety First*, 1916), and had emerged as one of the club's most celebrated alumni. Also, Lois had read *The Great Gatsby*, and of course, Paramount had even considered her some months earlier for a part in its film of that novel. Furthermore, Lois knew Dorothy Gish socially and would most likely have known that Gish's husband, the actor James Reny, was a close drinking buddy of Fitzgerald's who was then preparing to play the title role in the New York stage production of *The Great Gatsby*, which would premiere a short time later.

When Lois actually met Fitzgerald, she became his instant admirer and was dazzled by his sophistication and intellect. He may have considered himself an aged relic, but she found him strikingly handsome and appealing; she had, after all, often developed crushes on older men. Like Lois, Fitzgerald was self-made, a product of the American Midwest, and, as Charles Green Shaw once described him, "congenitally shy." He had also retained enough of his natural optimism to be quite compatible with her forward-looking personality. His mother had written in his baby book that the first word he had had spoken was "up!", reminiscent of Lois's motto that "Nothing is impossible to a Moran."

Lois anxiously pursued her friendship with Fitzgerald that spring of 1927 in Hollywood. "I thought he was perfect," she recalled in 1971 in a letter to a Fitzgerald enthusiast. "A writer to me was the greatest thing in the world. I lived for books from the time I was three. To know and be with one of the great writers...it was just a beautiful experience as far as I was concerned."

The relationship that developed between Lois and Fitzgerald may have been the one redeeming feature of his 1927 trip to Hollywood, for his time there was otherwise misspent and unsuccessful. He may have been on his best behavior when he was with Lois, but at other times he and Zelda took to crashing parties in vulgar ways and indulging in behavior that offended many. They arrived uninvited, for example, at a party given by Samuel Goldwyn for the Talmadge sisters. Showing up at the door on their hands and knees, they barked like puppies to be let in. Once admitted, Zelda wandered upstairs with Colleen Moore and, much to Moore's astonishment, proceeded to take a bath. Episodes such as this recall the humorist Ring Lardner's 1925 description of the Fitzgeralds: "Mr. Fitzgerald is a novelist and Mrs. Fitzgerald is a novelty." At another party, they arrived wearing only their pajamas. At a tea given by the Morans at the Ambassador for Carmel Myers, they went from guest to guest asking for watches and jewelry on the pretext of performing a magic trick. They then retired to the kitchen where, tipsy and feeling clever, they set about cooking their new acquisitions in a pot of tomato sauce. And at one point Fitzgerald procured $100 in change and threw it at the windows of the Ambassador, chortling, "It's money, it's money, it's money! It's free!"

Carmel Myers enjoyed Fitzgerald's pranks and later commented, "It required the special quality of Scott's personality to infuse such sophomoric behavior with an atmosphere of explosive gaiety." However, they did little to endear Fitzgerald to other members of the film community. Lois wrote to Mizener that the tomato sauce prank particularly outraged Constance Talmadge and Ronald Colman. With hindsight, it now seems apparent that the Fitzgeralds were guilty more of false conceptions about what was appropriate behavior in Hollywood than they were of intentional bad manners, for they did not realize that film people, contrary to popular belief, were actually hard working and had to be quite self-disciplined in order to rise early day after day and put in long hours on the set.

Scott was aware of this work ethic in Lois but otherwise falsely assumed that Hollywood in general was loose and morally lax. Zelda came to realize, as she wrote to Scottie, that "Hollywood is not gay like the magazines say but very quiet. The stars almost never go out in public and every place closes at mid-night." It is not surprising, then, that many there would have perceived the Fitzgeralds as snooty, rude, and condescending. When asked about Fitzgerald late in her life, for example, Joan Crawford, who had encountered him in the heyday of her film-acting career, regularly replied quite icily that he was little more than a sad drunk. Louise Brooks, an admirer of Scott and Zelda, later observed that in Hollywood the Fitzgeralds were "like a comedy team" and that Zelda possessed "the profile of a witch." Lois expressed more favorable views, however, describing Scott and Zelda in 1948 to Mizener as "two beautiful people," "the golden Fitzgeralds": "They simply got tight and pulled a lot of sophomoric pranks. . . . Of course they behaved badly, but they were never mean or cruel or unkind."

Parties notwithstanding, Fitzgerald spent much of his time in Hollywood writing on the film scenario he had journeyed there to prepare. As Matthew Bruccoli told the *New York Times* in 2004, "He took screenwriting very seriously, and it's heartbreaking to see how much effort he put into it." He found time to attend a screening of the film that Paramount had made of *The Great Gatsby* (a production he and Zelda disliked), to visit film sets, and to be photographed with the likes of Barthelmess, Wallace Beery, and the illustrator Harrison Fisher. Otherwise, he worked diligently in his room at the Ambassador, having his food sent there.

The end result of Fitzgerald's efforts, however, was substandard. His story, "Lipstick," was more or less a reworking of an earlier short story, "Head and Shoulders." Set at a college modeled after Princeton, it concerned romance and intrigue: a girl (to be played by Constance Talmadge) who has been falsely imprisoned, is released, comes into possession of a magical lipstick that makes men want to kiss her, and sets her sights on an aloof undergraduate, who, of course, eventually falls in love with her. Perhaps because he was out of practice after not having written stories for so long, however, Fitzgerald was not at his best. The tale was sketchy and improbable, even for the movies, and the characters were one-dimensional.

With its clever fantasy theme, "Lipstick" might have been unique and worthwhile, but it turned out to be a pedestrian enterprise that was not worthy of Fitzgerald's talents. Nevertheless, projects of lesser quality were regularly produced in Hollywood, and he had good reason to believe that Considine would accept his story. To his shock, however, the producer rejected it, telling Fitzgerald in a telegram that he found the story "weak" and refusing to pay him the remaining $8500. One reason the story was declined may have been simply that Talmadge disliked Fitzgerald. She had found his antics at the Goldwyn party distasteful and had subsequently quarreled with him over the scenario. Studio heads, including Considine, must surely have been aware of the powerful star's displeasure. Fitzgerald's agent, Harold Ober, wrote in a memo at the time, "He [Fitzgerald] says he got into a row with Constance Talmadge for whom the story was written and he thinks this is the reason they didn't want to do it."

Whatever went on between Fitzgerald and Talmadge remained a source of bitterness to Fitzgerald for years to come. When he first arrived in Hollywood in 1927, he described Talmadge glowingly to the press as "the epitome of young sophistication . . . she is the flapper *de luxe.*" By the time he wrote "Jacob's Ladder" later that year, however, he included a less flattering reference to her when he not-so-subtly implied that she was pretentious by having a film director refer to her as retaining a personal "water boy," and in the notebooks he kept in the 1930s he wrote, "There is undoubtedly something funny about not being a lady, or rather about being a gold digger. You've got to laugh a lot like Constance Talmadge." Today, when visiting the gravesites of Fitzgerald at St. Mary's Cemetery in Rockville, Maryland, or of Talmadge in the Abbey of the Psalms at Hollywood Forever in Los Angeles, both peaceful and beautiful, one is perplexed by how utterly seriously the two self-absorbed celebrities took themselves during this short-lived debacle.

The "Lipstick" fiasco caused Fitzgerald considerable anguish, for he felt belittled, humiliated, and angry. He was also financially com-promised: the $3500 retainer the studio had initially paid him had barely covered his traveling expenses. Ober tried to place the story elsewhere, such as with B. P. Schulberg of Famous Players as a vehicle for Bebe Daniels, whom Lois knew, but he was not successful. The Fitzgeralds left Hollywood, and as a good-bye gesture they stacked the furniture of their Ambassador suite in the middle of the room and placed their hotel bill atop the pile. Fitzgerald did not again attempt film work during the 1920s and in fact would not return to the movies until November 1931, when Irving Thalberg, whom he met during that 1927 Hollywood venture and upon whom he based the main character in his unfinished novel *The Last Tycoon*, invited him to MGM to write on a Jean Harlow picture, *Red-Headed Woman*, an assignment that would mark the beginning of even more difficult and heartbreaking film writing and failure for him throughout the 1930s. He even edited dialogue, unsuccessfully, for *Gone with the Wind* in 1939.

Their experience with "Lipstick" was certainly unpleasant for the Fitzgeralds. Scott came away from it humbled and embarrassed. He had gone to Hollywood, he later admitted, "confident to the point of conceit" and noted that the sting of the failure was particularly hurtful to him because "I had been generally acknowledged as the top American writer both seriously and, as far as prices went, popularly. . . . I honestly believed that *with no effort on my part* I was a sort of magician with words—an odd delusion when I had worked so desperately hard to develop a hard, colorful prose style" (his emphases). He thought of revising "Lipstick" as a short story for *College Humor* but ultimately abandoned the idea. But he had met Lois, and she was the reason he did not consider his excursion west a total loss.

As for Zelda, she had been bored and unhappy in Hollywood and at the time had written to her Scottie, "If we ever get out of here I will *never go near* another moving picture theatre or actor again." She was also resentful of her husband's attentions to Lois, which he assured Zelda were platonic but were nevertheless increasingly irritating to her. In one particularly bitter argument in their rooms at the Ambassador, after Scott had taken Lois and Gladys to dinner, she complained to Fitzgerald in her hurt and anger that he was neglecting her in favor of Lois. He cuttingly replied, perhaps because he was drunk, that Lois at least was making use of her talents and actively working to make something of her life. Stung, Zelda retaliated by destroying something she herself had created. In the bathtub, she burnt her clothes, which she herself had sewn. This sad, self-destructive act was indicative of her growing fury over Fitzgerald's relationship with Lois. The episode haunted Fitzgerald, who was so pained by it that he referred to it in his notebooks simply as the incident of the "burning clothes." He also wrote in his notebooks, in an observation that he incorporated into his short story "Babylon Revisited" (1931) and that recalls episodes in his marriage such as the bathtub incident, "Family quarrels are bitter things. They don't go according to any rules. They're not like aches or wounds; they're more like splits in the skin that won't heal because there's not enough material."

In spite of Zelda's animosity, Lois helped to recharge Fitzgerald's creative flow, and after he left the film community he commenced writing short stories again and in rapid succession based characters on her in at least three efforts published in the *Saturday Evening Post*: "Jacob's Ladder," "Magnetism," and "The Rough Crossing." More important still, he would also eventually model one of the major characters in

Tender Is the Night on her. Clearly, she was a strong presence in his life and was very important to his writing.

Fitzgerald's interest in Lois was complex. He was drawn to her youth, vivacious personality, and intelligence. He also found her physical appearance appealing, especially her particular mannerism of holding her head so as to appear to be looking upward. Equally attractive to him was Lois's reciprocal adoration of him, for he was at a stage in his life when he craved ego reinforcement. As he noted in a 1930 letter to Zelda, he "woke up in Hollywood no longer my egotistic, certain self," and anyone who could make him believe in himself again was "precious" to him.

Lois was a well of reassurance and comfort to Fitzgerald. She read his books and noted in her journal in 1927 that she was fond of *The Great Gatsby,* his short story collection *All the Sad Young Men,* and *This Side of Paradise*, a copy of which he inscribed, "For Lois Moran from hers devotedly F. Scott Fitzgerald." She also read other books that he recommended to her, including David Garnett's *The Sailor's Return*, Paul Morand's *Open All Night*, Hemingway's *The Sun Also Rises*, and the poems of Rupert Brooke, who had been killed in World War I. Lois respected Fitzgerald and looked up to him as a mentor. "Everything he said to me about literature, people or the world in general was gospel," she wrote to Mizener. "He could think no wrong." Fitzgerald so inspired Lois, in fact, that she even wrote a few short stories of her own in which she based characters on him. Perhaps aware of Lois's admiration for Fitzgerald, Charles Green Shaw in 1928 wrote a profile of Fitzgerald in which he remarked upon Fitzgerald's vision of the perfect woman, and the description does, to a degree, fit Lois at the time. "His preference in women," Shaw wrote, "is a not-too-light blonde, who is intelligent, unopinionated and responsive."

Lois even went so far as to arrange for Fitzgerald to take a screen test so that he could remain in Hollywood to be her leading man in her next film, an event that caused considerable stir in his life. Temporarily forgetting her resentment of Lois, Zelda wrote excitedly to Scottie,

"Daddy was offered a job to be a leading man in a picture with Lois Moran!!," and sources as diverse as Fitzgerald's hometown newspaper, the *St. Paul Dispatch*, and the more widely circulated *Bookman* published references to it. The latter reported in April 1927, "They do say that [Fitzgerald] is taking screen tests and wishes to try out for leading man to Lois Moran." Lois confirmed to Mizener that the test did indeed take place and that "we laughed about it." The studio purportedly told Fitzgerald that he was too old to face the scrutiny of the camera, and in any case the test has never been located. He may have been referring to this episode when he observed in his notebooks in the 1930s that there might be possibilities in creating a story "about a man looking as if he was made up for a role he couldn't play"; and a 1976 television biography starring Jason Miller, *F. Scott Fitzgerald in Hollywood*, opened with Fitzgerald in make-up as he was about to make the test.

Even if her attempts to procure a screen role for Fitzgerald failed, however, Lois appears, a short time later, to have enacted a kind of onscreen acknowledgment of his talent and renown. In a film she made in 1927, *Publicity Madness*, written by her and Fitzgerald's mutual friend Anita Loos, she did a scene with Edmund Lowe in which she played a young girl who goes to a barber, sits in his chair, and proceeds daringly (for the time) to have her hair bobbed. This sequence vividly recalled Fitzgerald's highly popular 1920 *Saturday Evening Post* short story, "Bernice Bobs Her Hair," in which the heroine had also gone to a barber in order to have him shear her locks. In fact, a still photograph was circulated of Lois seated in the barber chair that bore a strong resemblance to the well-remembered dust jacket of Fitzgerald's 1920 short story collection in which "Bernice Bobs Her Hair" had been published, *Flappers and Philosophers*, which had featured an illustration by W. E. Hill of Bernice seated in the barber's chair.

In should be noted, however, that in spite of the Fitzgerald hero-worship Lois seemed to be demonstrating by arranging his screen test and by appearing in the apparently "Bernice"-inspired film scene, she maintained a delicate balance with him and was careful not to be overly reverential, something he probably appreciated. There may have been elements of a father-daughter or teacher-student relationship between them, but Lois, as she always pointed out, never lost sight of the fact that they were, first and foremost, chums. "Mother viewed Scott as a friend," explains Lois's son, Tim Young. "She did not view him as a means of advancing her own career, and she never mentioned that she and Scott had ever discussed his writing a screen story for her. She did not ever draw attention to herself, at the time she knew him or later, by dropping Scott's name." In fact, Lois even went so far as to criticize Fitzgerald in a July 9, 1928, journal entry. "Where are our American authors?" she complained. "The Germans, Norwegian, Swedish, seem so far ahead of us in thought—American literature seems so horribly external—all story, all frivolity, lack of depth and thought—Scott Fitzgerald, *why* don't you do something. You could be so great."

As Fitzgerald's not-always-admiring friend, then, Lois affectionately kidded and joked with him, in one letter even addressing him as "Darling, dumbbell, upsetting, adorable Scott." In a cable to him and Zelda that reached them on the train en route back east after the "Lipstick" unpleasantness, Lois wrote:

> HOLLYWOOD COMPLETELY DISRUPTED SINCE YOU LEFT BOOTLEGGERS GONE OUT OF BUSINESS COTTON CLUB CLOSED ALL FLAGS AT HALF MAST EVEN JOHN BARRYMORE HAS GONE OUT OF TOWN BOTTLES OF LOVE TO YOU BOTH.

She followed this telegram with a chatty letter to Fitzgerald that she mailed to him later that spring. Addressing him as "Darling Scott," she told him that her life since he left Hollywood was boring. "I miss you enormously," she wrote. "Life is exceedingly dull out here now—Have just been bumming around the studios and seeing people I am not the least interested in." She went on to tell him that the kisses she was receiving from her Hollywood leading men, presumably on and off the set, were unsatisfactory and that "maybe I will play with William Haines in his next picture—I rather hope so because I admire him tremendously and he gives very satisfactory kisses," an odd remark considering that Haines was known to be homosexual.

The next time Lois saw Fitzgerald was later that spring at his new home. As a result of his screenwriting failure, he had resolved to return to doing what he did best: writing prose fiction. Recalling his motives for returning to America the previous winter, he once again determined to attain tranquility in his life so that he could focus full force upon his work. He set about searching for living quarters that would afford him the peace and solitude he required. Maxwell Perkins, his editor at Scribner's, suggested that Delaware would be suitable because it would be secluded and quiet, yet within reach of both the *Saturday Evening Post* offices in Philadelphia and the bustle of New York City. With the help of the author and attorney John Biggs, an old and trusted friend from his college days who would later serve as his literary executor, Fitzgerald found Ellerslie, an elegant nineteenth-century Greek Revival mansion at Edgemoor, on the Delaware River.

Ellerslie was enormous, with high ceilings. Surrounded by trees and gardens, it had been constructed with a Greek-columned portico in the back that provided a magnificent view of the river. Lois later described Ellerslie to Mizener: "It was fine. . . . Beauteous old house, lawn, so green, that sloped down to a levee on the river." Zelda, who wrote to Scottie at the time that she was "crazy" to live in a house in America, liked it tremendously. Fitzgerald also found the residence highly appealing, although perhaps for reasons other than aestheticism. Having spent the entire retainer he had received from United Artists as well as the subsidiary publishing income from *The Great Gatsby*, he was attracted to the house's inexpensive rent of $150 per month. In short, the Fitzgeralds found Ellerslie an eminently suitable residence, reasoning that it would be the ideal location for Scott to resume serious writing, and in the late spring of 1927 the family moved in. In May, Fitzgerald, who in 1929 described himself to Biggs as "the Eccentric Earl of Ellerslie," gave a weekend-long housewarming party to which he invited Lois and Gladys.

That springtime party at Ellerslie was one of the most colorful events of Lois's life in the 1920s. In her 1970s working notes, she referred to it as "a big deal with the Fitzgeralds," and Fitzgerald himself mentioned it in his notebooks in the 1930s as a good source for a possible story. It took place on the weekend of May 21, 1927. Charles Lindbergh, whom Lois would come to know personally after her marriage to the aviation pioneer Clarence Young in the 1930s, had just flown across the Atlantic. "We all went mad with enthusiasm," Lois later reminisced to Mizener, and there was a giddy air of festivity and celebration as guests began to arrive. In addition to the Morans, Fitzgerald had invited his parents; Biggs; the writers Van Vechten, Ben Hecht, and Charles MacArthur; the actress Helen Hayes, who was engaged to MacArthur; the critic and essayist Ernest Boyd, whom she later described to Mizener as a "nice brown man"; the dancer Catherine Littlefield; the composer Theodore Chanler; and the wealthy war hero and champion polo competitor Tommy Hitchcock, whom Fitzgerald admired and trusted. Zelda, who appeared to be on her best behavior, seems to have concealed any resentment she felt toward Lois. There was apparently one angry Lois-fueled outburst, but this must have occurred in private, because Lois made no mention of any such episode when she wrote to Zelda's biographer Nancy Milford in 1965 that all she recalled of Zelda that weekend was "the very intent, piercing look in those marvelous eyes." Zelda hosted an elegant cocktail party and picnic under the flowering chestnut trees on the banks of the Delaware River, and the guests listened to an African American jazz band as they sipped champagne while looking skyward in honor of Lindbergh.

Lois chatted with Van Vechten and good-naturedly conversed with Scottie in French. She also comforted MacArthur, who was, as she recalled in her notes, "pale green" with lovesickness over Hayes, whom with great fanfare he would marry a short time later. Lois recalled to Mizener, "Sat on the levee for hours one night with MacArthur while he talked about Helen Hayes. They were not yet married, and he was having a miserable time getting a divorce from his wife. They had been separated for years, but she was being mean about a divorce." Another facet of the party Lois enjoyed was a game devised by Fitzgerald in which the guests enacted an impromptu play called, in deference to Tommy Hitchcock, "Polo Balls." Hitchcock had great fun with the play and wrote to Fitzgerald in May 1928, after Lois had returned to Hollywood, "I understand Lois Moran is coming East the end of July. Could we not have a weekend then . . . with you and Zelda, and write the second act of Polo Balls?" Even more fun ensued when a kind of athletic free-for-all developed in which the guests commenced literally picking each other up. "It was a bright moonlit night," John Biggs later recalled. "Lois Moran, to show how strong she was, picked up her stage mother; Charlie MacArthur then picked up the mothers of both Helen Hayes and Lois Moran, and I, to show how strong I was, picked all of them up, but I couldn't hold them and dropped one of them into the river."

Lindbergh euphoria, riparian picnics, and thespian and athletic creativity were not the only sources of high spirits that weekend. In a letter to the critic H. L. Mencken, Van Vechten referenced the excessive drinking that went on at Ellerslie, noting that the Fitzgeralds kept "a very wet house in Delaware." It was an apt description of the weekend house party. Lois, there with Gladys, partook moderately of champagne, but the party was otherwise punctuated by liberal consumption of cocktails. Unexpected guests from New York and Philadelphia began to appear, many with healthy appetites for libation, and food ran out long before the liquor—many guests had to drive to nearby Wilmington just to procure a sandwich. John Dos Passos arrived shortly after Fitzgerald's parents had departed, and

Sara Mayfield quoted him in *Exiles from Paradise* as reporting that he came upon a "deliriously" wild continual party in progress.

Snapshots taken that weekend survive in the Fitzgeralds' scrapbook, but they reflect a more subdued tone. One of the pictures, which the Fitzgeralds captioned "Guest of Honor," depicts Lois wearing white and looking robust and healthy, smiling directly at the camera, a skill she had honed so often in any number of Hollywood still photography sessions, while her arm is slipped through Fitzgerald's. Another shows her gazing up adoringly at him while Carl Van Vechten looks at them with a sour expression upon his face—whether because he disapproved of their relationship or because he had to squint into the bright sun it is impossible to say. Other photos show the various guests romping about and having fun, seemingly unaware that future generations would have an interest in the goings-on of that weekend. Fitzgerald was fond of these photographs, as evidenced by the impressive layout he gave them in the scrapbook, and Lois wrote to Mizener of having among her mementos two of her own "snaps" from Ellerslie that depicted herself and Scottie. On one, which apparently included Fitzgerald himself, he had written "Two lettuce leaves and a hangover," and on the other, "My two golden girls."

Lois and MacArthur took the same train back to New York after the weekend at Ellerslie. By that time, both were exhausted by the subjects of their respective affections and in need of an emotional refuge from the anxieties produced by the party's romantic undercurrents. When a passenger on the train observed that they looked like a married couple, they seized the opportunity for merriment and pretended to be just that. Posing as man and wife for the duration of the short train journey, they shifted their focus from romance to practical joking. It was a retreat that Fitzgerald himself, ever the prankster, would have appreciated.

Another meeting between Fitzgerald and Lois took place a short time later in New York. Although Fitzgerald did resume writing at Ellerslie and adopted an upper-floor room as his work area, furnishing it only with a kitchen table and a chair, he and Zelda took to making frequent trips to New York, where they partied, drank heavily, and usually stayed at the posh Plaza Hotel, one of Fitzgerald's favorite locales. On one of these excursions, they attended a party for the boxer Gene Tunney, at the time wildly celebrated for having recently defeated Jack Dempsey for the heavyweight crown, and accompanying them were Lois, Gladys, and their friend George Jean Nathan.

To Fitzgerald that evening, Tunney represented the supreme success of the American male, and the writer admired the pugilist for his ability to wield boxing gloves with as much dexterity as he himself did fountain pens and pencils. His fan worship may have stemmed from the fact that Fitzgerald in his youth had dreamed of becoming a football player, or it could simply have been the result of one too many visits to the bar, but whatever the cause, he stayed at Tunney's side most of that evening, and it was difficult for Zelda to convince her husband to leave the party. He finally made his way back to the Plaza in a taxi, stopping to buy all the papers of a newsboy he saw in the rain. This was the thoughtful, if not insecure, Fitzgerald Lois knew in the late 1920s.

Zelda, Confusion and Bedazzlement, and the Fitzgerald Revival

7

By the time of the Tunney party, a boxing match of a different sort had developed, albeit a one-sided one. Zelda had come to actively dislike Lois, and as Scott's fondness for the young actress grew, so did Zelda's animosity toward her. Zelda's feelings form an important aspect of the relationship between Lois and Fitzgerald. Her aversion seems to have had its roots in two factors. She was wounded over the attention Fitzgerald was paying to another woman, and she was jealous of Lois, not so much because she was younger, by nine years, nor even because she was a movie star, but because she was a trained dancer who had performed at the Paris Ballet, a fact that ate away at Zelda because she herself had long dreamed of becoming a professional dancer. Lois wrote to this author in later years that Zelda was "never a bit peculiar" to her, but there is ample evidence that the Alabama-bred Zelda's Southern good manners were little more than a gloss that concealed bitterness and anger. Indeed, the Scott-Zelda-Lois triangle was complicated and multifaceted, and will probably never be fully understood.

Zelda began to resent Fitzgerald's relationship with Lois from their earliest days in Hollywood. She was aware of her husband's propensity for developing crushes on women he idealized. The list of such infatuations went back to before their marriage, when he had pined for the wealthy, unattainable Ginevra King in St. Paul and had continued throughout the 1920s with women such as Sara Murphy, to whom he dedicated *Tender Is the Night*, on the French Riviera, and even the witty author Dorothy Parker in New York. The advent of Lois into her husband's life, however, was particularly threatening to Zelda.

Most of Fitzgerald's attractions to other women had at that time probably not resulted in adultery. Indeed, Ernest Hemingway noted in his posthumous autobiography *A Moveable Feast* that Fitzgerald told him in the late 1920s that Zelda was the only woman with whom he had ever been intimate. His attentions to Lois nonetheless worried Zelda because Lois was pretty and intelligent, and spoke openly of wanting a husband. Zelda remembered that shortly before she married Fitzgerald in 1920 he had, presumably angry over her promiscuity with other men, indulged in a sexual interlude with the actress Rosalinde Fuller, so she believed that he was capable of using other women to retaliate against her. Moreover, the Fitzgeralds' marriage had been compromised in 1924 in the south of France when Zelda had embarked upon a brief sexual affair with Edouard Jozan, an attractive French aviator. Knowing that Fitzgerald was sensitive and had been emotionally wounded by the indiscretion, she feared he might have a similar involvement of his own.

Zelda was irritated by and distrustful of Lois on any number of counts. She worried about what Lois and Fitzgerald were talking about when they slipped away into the hallway at the Mariposa parties. She was initially pleased by the screen test Lois arranged for Scott but soon rethought the subject. Remembering that she herself and Fitzgerald had considered in 1922 the possibility of appearing together in a film adaptation of his second novel, *The Beautiful and Damned*, she felt it was unjust that Scott was now actually making tests for a picture in which he would appear not with her but with Lois. She was furious that Fitzgerald unfavorably compared her to Lois in the argument that precipitated the clothes-burning episode. She was almost equally rankled by the tongue-in-cheek telegram Lois sent to them that they had received on the train back from Hollywood because Lois had signed it LOVE TO YOU BOTH, for she suspected that the love in question was in fact directed only to Scott. The matter worsened when Fitzgerald mimicked the telegram in his story "Jacob's Ladder."

The letter Lois wrote to Fitzgerald following the telegram also probably put off Zelda. She likely saw the missive, in which Lois had spoken of missing him terribly and mentioned that she was not satisfied with the kisses she was forced to endure from Hollywood actors. Zelda could not help but have been outraged that Lois would mention kissing in any form in a letter to her husband. Finally, and perhaps the coups de grâce to all of her resentments of Lois, was the fact that Zelda was uneasy with how well Lois and Scottie had gotten along at the Ellerslie picnic and may even have been aware of and resent the snapshots of Lois and Scottie upon which Fitzgerald had written sentimental captions. Clearly, then, Lois was threatening to Zelda in many ways.

Zelda appears never to have lashed out directly at Lois, however, and most of the time channeled her anger constructively. The most obvious step she took, literally and figuratively, was that she started taking ballet lessons. Intensely aware of Lois's success at the Paris Opéra, she immersed herself in dancing even though she must have known that she was too old to achieve renown. While living at Ellerslie, she went to Philadelphia three times a week, accompanied by Scottie, to study under Catherine Littlefield, who had been a guest at the Ellerslie party and who was the director of the Philadelphia Opera ballet. Zelda also studied modern dancing and attempted to learn the Black Bottom, a syncopated jazz dance then in vogue. In any case, she had to give up dancing a couple of years later. Her mental illness made the pursuit an impossibility, and she wrote to Fitzgerald that for her, "dancing is gone."

Zelda's efforts at dancing were not spurred on solely by jealousy of Lois, for she had wanted to become a professional dancer long before Lois appeared in her life, but it was fueled enough by rivalry with the younger woman that acquaintances of the Fitzgeralds realized that some friction may have existed between the two women. In a 1989 interview with William M. Drew, for example, the actress Eleanor Boardman, whom Scott and Zelda had met in Hollywood, remarked upon Lois's role in Zelda's wanting to become a ballerina: "Zelda had an *idée fixe* about becoming a ballet dancer, because she fancied that Scott was in love with a young girl in Hollywood, Lois Moran, a leading star who had been a ballet dancer. Zelda was as thin as a bean but she would go every morning to ballet lessons."

Another way Zelda coped with her anger over Scott's attentions to Lois was to pursue her own writing. Aware that Lois had begun to author short stories under Fitzgerald's influence, she became intent upon reminding the world that Scott and Lois were not the only ones who could create with words. Zelda was a creative, imaginative wordsmith who was often unjustly overshadowed by her husband. In 1927 alone, she sold articles to *Harper's Bazaar*, *College Humor*, and *Photoplay*. And the resourceful Zelda turned to still other remedies to upsets in her life, some of which seem to have been attempts to refute Fitzgerald's criticism that she was not utilizing her creative abilities. For example, she expanded the range of her creativity by designing oversized furniture for Ellerslie's large rooms and by designing and constructing a beautifully detailed dollhouse for Scottie. She also painted pictures, which were characterized by arresting color and composition, and she created exquisite paper dolls of historical and literary characters, even one of Fitzgerald that was accentuated with angel's wings.

Zelda did not always deal with her anger so productively, however, and there were episodes in which she openly expressed heated rage on the subject of Scott and Lois. The clothes burning at the Ambassador appears to have been the first of such outbursts. Another took place a short time later, when she and Scott were on the train back east from Hollywood. When Lois's telegram arrived, offending Zelda with its declaration of love to them both, and Scott spoke of the prospect of Lois visiting them, the Fitzgeralds once again quarreled. Zelda again retaliated in a self-destructive manner, but in this new action was high art, and it has earned a permanent place in Fitzgerald lore.

Intent upon expressing protest against Lois, who she knew had a fondness for wearing wristwatches, and anxious to strike out at Scott, she quite magnificently achieved both aims simultaneously by throwing from the window of the moving train the diamond and platinum wristwatch Scott had given her when they were engaged in 1920. She could have tossed a ring, a bracelet, a necklace, a brooch, or even an article of clothing, so her selection of a wristwatch most likely was calculated to inflict maximum emotional hurt upon her husband. Perhaps she succeeded in her goal, because Fitzgerald used the episode later in his short story "The Rough Crossing," changing the flung object from a watch to a string of pearls.

Zelda followed this glittering act of dismay, apparently, with an intoxicated outburst at the Ellerslie house party, because she wrote a short time thereafter to Van Vechten, "From the depths of my polluted soul, I am sorry the week-end was such a mess. Do forgive my iniquities and my putrid drunkenness. This *was* such a nice place, and it should have been a good party if I had not explored my abyss in public." The details of what Zelda said at the party about Lois can now only be imagined, because no one appears to have written any of it down—perhaps Van Vechten had been the only witness—but Zelda otherwise made her opinions on the subject of Lois abundantly clear in several ways.

In the fall of 1927, for example, Zelda overtly flirted at a New York party with Richard Knight, an attorney. At the time, Scott had come to New York to see Lois, and the timing of Zelda's attentions to another man seems again to have been a calculated act of revenge. Her strategy worked, for Scott was so upset by her actions that he forbade Zelda ever to see Knight again. Nevertheless, as Zelda observed, Fitzgerald remained "thoroughly entangled sentimentally" with Lois. Later, in 1930, Zelda again took aim at the Scott-Lois relationship in a short story she wrote for the *Saturday Evening Post* entitled "A Millionaire's Girl," in which an ambitious young actress seeks to marry an older man. Zelda seemed to allude to the relationship between Scott and Lois in an acrid line spoken by the story's narrator: "I am a cynical person and, perhaps, no competent judge of idyllic young love affairs."

More directly, Zelda wrote a vituperative description of Lois that Nancy Milford brought to light in her 1970 biography of Zelda. Lois, Zelda observed, was "a young actress like a breakfast food that many men identified with whatever they missed from life since she had no definite characteristics of her own save a slight ebullient hysteria about romance. She walked in the moon by the river. Her hair was tight about her head and she was lush and like a milkmaid." In 1932, Zelda, in her only published novel, *Save Me the Waltz*, also wrote what she considered an autobiographical storyline concerning a man who in retaliation against his wife for her infidelity has an affair with a younger woman.

Interestingly, considering Zelda's belief that Fitzgerald had an adulterous affair with Lois, two of the last writings he composed pertaining to her concerned the subject of marriage. In a November 29, 1940, letter to Scottie, less than a month before his death, he gave the sixteen-year-old advice about her prospects for finding a boyfriend. A doting and caring father, he told her not be discouraged, that soon many romantic opportunities would be coming her way, and to illustrate his point he mentioned Lois, who by then was married and settled. "I remember," he wrote, "that Lois Moran used to worry because all the attractive men she knew were married. She finally inverted it into the credo that if a man *wasn't* married and inaccessible, he wasn't a first-rate man. She gave herself a very bad time." He related this story to his daughter as a way of encouraging her to keep her hopes high and not despair of finding her match: after all, even Lois Moran, who had been on the brink of losing hope, had found her ideal husband.

Matrimony was also the catalyst of what may have been his last letter to Lois, written to her on March 8, 1935, shortly after her marriage. Lois had telephoned Scott on the day of her wedding (*"after* the ceremony," she emphasized to Mizener in 1948), and Louis Azrael, a Baltimore journalist, shortly thereafter had filled him in on the details of the event, as well as providing him with a mailing address for her. Fitzgerald had been touched by Lois's calling him on such an important day, especially because their recent meetings and phone conversations had been strained because of his drinking. In response to her call he wrote her a congratulatory letter, a typed three-page document with holograph additions in which he expressed happiness for her marriage (even though he referred to the groom only in passing); informed her that he had stopped drinking, which was possible, as he did alternate heavy binges with spells of sobriety; and ruminated a bit on their relationship and Lois's personality. It is an erudite and intelligent missive, by turns melancholy and joyful, filled with nostalgia for the past he had shared with Lois and hope for her future. While it also contains a tone of inherent closure, an implied finality indicating that their relationship had come to its inevitable conclusion, it also reflects the unique and in some ways timeless bond that had formed between them.

Fitzgerald could not have given Lois a more treasured wedding gift, for it was something that she kept and prized. Not even Mizener could convince her to donate it to Fitzgerald's archives at Princeton. Indeed, the letter is an important document in any consideration of her relationship with him. In it, he admits that he feels somewhat strange to be writing a congratulatory wedding letter to "a lady who once played such an important role in my life," but he is friendly and supportive. He does refer to an old episode in which Lois apparently had wounded his pride by telling him that she had him "on the spot," but he does not elaborate further on exactly what had happened, although it would seem to have been in regard to his possibly having behaved in a crapulous manner toward her after a bout of heavy drinking, and he signs the letter "Your chattel," which may or may not be a term of endearment. Otherwise, the letter is sweet and devoid of bitterness, positively brimming over with fondness for her, and its contents provide a fascinating overview of the impact she had upon his life. Following is a transcription of that correspondence, taken from the original document. Fitzgerald's notoriously poor spelling has been left intact.

Note the date! Had no address till Lew Azrael gave me one a few minutes ago

1307 Park Avenue
Baltimore, Maryland
March 15, 1935.

Dear Lois,

I was touched that you all called me up on your wedding day, and it more than made up for the somewhat chilled receptions I had come to expect from your telephone. Could I have been there I'd have loved it—the marriage of Columbine, (and Lou Azrael told me it wasn't far from that, with all sorts of amusing circumstances,).

I believe you are going to be just as happy as it is possible for anybody to be with a dash of the Celt in them. For many reasons I want to see you again before many more years drift by and hear about the singing and hear about you and how all your funny old idealisms have worked out. (You will probably like me better because I don't drink any more.)

I have a book of short stories called "Taps at Reveille" coming out in a few weeks and I thought of including that old piece "Jacob's Ladder" but I found that I had so thoroughly disemboweled it of its best descriptions for "Tender is the Night" that it would be offering an empty shell.

This seems an odd congratulatory letter to write to a lady who once played such an important role in my life, but it doesn't seem from this distance that your marriage has changed anything about you—I think one of the strongest impressions I ever got of the absolute seperateness of people, of old friends, of differing destinies and directions was that day in the Belvedere three years ago when you unwound a little of your life for me—gave me glimpses into all the years that I knew nothing of. Somehow we always expect old friends to be static until we see them again, and after thirty this is to some extent realized—but in case of one who started so early and so galvanically as you did, the changes are rung so quickly that no one could be anything but rather confused and dazzled.

I have never quite forgiven you, by the way, for the remark that you made in the dressing room at Ford's that you "had me on the spot" that day. My mind was never working faster than then; all that was true was that I was tired and abstracted. You probably don't even remember the episode, but keep it in mind, young lady, to quote old Sage Fitzgerald, you can stab a man anywhere but in his pride; never touch that unless you mean murder. Anyhow, I love you tremendously always and wish all happiness to you and yours.

Your Chattel
Scott Fitzg

While the news of Lois's marriage saddened Fitzgerald, it did not alienate her from him. He clipped reports of the wedding from newspapers, and, as he indicated at the close of his letter, his feelings for her had changed little over the years. However, by 1935 he was increasingly depressed and alcoholic. *Tender Is the Night* had appeared the previous year to mixed reviews and disappointing sales; Zelda was increasingly ill and indefinitely hospitalized; Scottie was away at school; and sickness, mental instability, and death had recently befallen several of his friends. The result of all this, combined with Lois's retirement from public life into her marriage and burgeoning family, was that his relationship with her came not to an end but to a gentle halt. Although he mentioned her in letters he wrote to Zelda's psychiatrist in 1937 and to Scottie in 1940, it appears that after 1935 he and Lois had no further in-person encounters.

Because of the intensity of Fitzgerald's relationship with Lois, and given Zelda's dislike for her, generations of Fitzgerald readers have wondered whether the relationship between Scott and Lois was sexual. It is, in fact, widely assumed that it was, but Lois was adamant, to her dying day, that she and Fitzgerald had shared a special friendship and nothing more. Nevertheless, speculation persists that she and Scott were lovers, and even Tim Young points out, "Time and time again, everyone wants to know if they slept together." Because of its relevance to the biographies of both Lois and Fitzgerald, and because she in particular is so often identified with him, the subject goes beyond the realm of gossip. To begin any such discussion, it is necessary first to trace the events that have led to the public's linking of Lois and Fitzgerald sexually.

For years after Fitzgerald's death in December 1940, at the winter solstice, no one gave much thought at all to her having known him because at the time of his passing he had fallen out of favor with critics and with the public, both of whom thought of him only as a dated, irrelevant antiquity of a bygone era. Throughout the 1940s, his works did continue to be published—among them his unfinished novel *The Last Tycoon* in 1941, a widely distributed Armed Forces edition of *The Great Gatsby* during World War II, and the Viking Portable Library of his works compiled by his friend and one-time lover Dorothy Parker in 1945—but the hypnotic lyricism of his writing, which is today admired, had not yet been rediscovered by new generations, and there was comparatively little interest in him. All that began to change, however, when in 1949 Paramount remade *The Great Gatsby* as an Alan Ladd vehicle. In 1950 Budd Schulberg came out with *The Disenchanted*, a best-selling novel based on portions of Fitzgerald's life, and in 1951 Mizener came out both with his book *The Far Side of Paradise* and a widely read *Life* magazine article about Fitzgerald.

These events helped set into motion what came to be known as the Fitzgerald revival, a reawakening of interest in his works and life that grew with time and eventually resulted in his becoming in death an acknowledged literary giant and a far more popular cultural icon than he had ever been while alive. In 1951, Lois wrote to Mizener of the revival, "It makes for tears . . . to see Scott selling like mad again. All his books reprinted, he acclaimed a great writer, etc., at this late date. Too late for him to be proud and happy." The revival affected Lois immediately. Zelda had died tragically in a 1948 fire at a sanitarium in which she was housed, and as a result Lois was seen as one of the few vital remaining links to a man whom many had now come to view as one of the most brilliant writers in modern literature.

The Fitzgerald legend took on increasingly gigantic proportions, and books by and about him began to regularly fill bookstore shelves. In contrast to his literary creation Jay Gatsby, who, Fitzgerald had written, had been enveloped in "foul dust," Fitzgerald posthumously took on a magical quality to many people. Anything or anyone even remotely associated with him was, for his admirers, doused in stardust. As a result, researchers and fans began regularly to contact Lois about him, especially with regard to whether the two had been physically intimate. She always replied that they had been friends only, but many believed that they had had an affair. Most of the people who contacted Lois in later years, as she pointed out to a friend in a 1971 letter, were respectful to her and far younger than she.

Yet others were not always deferential and contradicted her, readily expressing their beliefs that she and Fitzgerald had to have been a romantic couple. Her post office box in Sedona, Arizona, her home later in life, often contained letters from people who said as much to her, and some even located her phone number, which was listed, and telephoned her about it. These people were convinced that because Fitzgerald had had sexual relationships with other women in the latter half of the 1930s, particularly with the divorced gossip columnist Sheilah Graham, who documented their relationship in a series of articles and memoirs, it logically followed that the same must have been true of him and Lois in the late 1920s. Not inclined to accept Lois's version of the particulars of the time she spent with Fitzgerald, nor her pointing out to them that a great deal had happened in Fitzgerald's life by the time he knew Graham, namely Zelda's long-term institutionalization in a mental hospital, these people placed Lois in a difficult position. By consistently maintaining her innocence in the matter, she was seen by many as a prevaricator attempting to prevent her "fragile cameo" reputation from becoming sullied; and if she had confirmed that the rumors were true, she would have been crucified as a harlot who had selfishly threatened the Fitzgerald marriage, one of the most beloved popular romantic relationships of the century. Fitzgerald's portrayal of her as Rosemary in *Tender Is the Night* was of little help on the issue, because the character was by turns both innocent naïf and self-absorbed seductress.

With the passing of time, it is possible to more calmly assess the particulars of the debate. There are convincing arguments to be made both for Lois and Fitzgerald's having been lovers and for their having been friends, and it is a case that would puzzle any jury. When the smoke is cleared away, however, the conclusion that they were indeed sexually involved is virtually inescapable. Fitzgerald's biographer Jeffrey Meyers has so stated in his illuminating 1994 *Scott Fitzgerald*, and Tim Young agrees.

> When you asked Mother about Fitzgerald, you always sensed there was something she was hiding. She of course would not have wanted to admit having had an affair with a married man in the twenties, especially when she built a career on being the perpetual vestal virgin, but the facts are there. By today's standards, it isn't a disgrace. She had premarital sex with a man she loved. Big deal. It doesn't matter that she was the pure heroine in *Stella Dallas*. Mother liked men, and she enjoyed sex. To her, Scott Fitzgerald was an irresistible man. It would be naive to believe they were only friends. Fitzgerald knew many women, but Zelda did not dislike all of them as she did Mother. There had to have been a reason. If you read between the lines of Mother's journal, it's all there. With Gladys lurking around, she couldn't have written explicit entries on the subject, but it's there in the tone, in what isn't said. I believe that Mother at the time was ready to defy Gladys, and I believe that Fitzgerald took her virginity. Just imagine how many other women would have given anything to be in Mother's place! In my opinion, Mother's involvement with Fitzgerald was definitely sexual. It was the end of her innocence. For all we know, Fitzgerald and my mother could even have had a drunken sexual involvement that she did not remember, since at the

time she wasn't drinking heavily and would have been susceptible to alcohol. He, of course, remembered everything but probably would have refrained from going into the specifics because it would have embarrassed Mother, not to mention the damage it would have done to his already shaky marriage to Zelda. As for Hemingway saying that Fitzgerald told him he had only ever had sex with Zelda, that is bunk. Fitzgerald could have been lying, or Hemingway, as we know he was prone to do, could have made the whole story up.

It appears fairly certain that Lois believed that to confirm that she had been intimate with Fitzgerald would have invalidated her moral character, for in the context of the times it would have been an unflattering, unsavory admission. It was important to her to preserve in life her cinematic image of innocence, to insist that her mother was always present when she and Fitzgerald met, and to maintain that the only physical intimacy she had ever had was with her husband. As her son points out, however, the facts speak differently.

The most compelling indicator that the relationship between Lois and Fitzgerald was sexual is the very fact that they were so smitten with each other at a time when she was young, beautiful, and impressionable and his marriage had become unsteady, the memory of Zelda's affair with Jozan still fresh in his mind. The fact, too, that they each wrote stories using each other as literary models—in Fitzgerald's case, extensively so—seems to suggest that their relationship had been more than platonic. Another indicator is the fact that there was an intimate, even flirty tone to some of their correspondence. In his 1935 wedding letter to her, he remarked, as has been noted, that she had played "an important role" in his life. In turn, in her surviving letters she refers to him as "darling" and talks of the unsatisfactory kisses she was receiving from her leading men. Such epistolary evidence lends credence to the belief that the relationship was physical.

More incriminating evidence surfaced in 2003 when Betsy Blair published her memoir, *The Memory of All That: Love and Politics in New York, Hollywood, and Paris,* in which she recalled a childhood visit in New York with her great-aunt Gladys. Her mother had taken her to meet Gladys for tea at the Waldorf-Astoria on Park Avenue, and Blair overheard the two adults talking heatedly about "Scottie," whom the girl assumed was a puppy. She later learned that Scottie was Fitzgerald and that Gladys was speaking of attempting to keep him away from Lois. In later years, Lois maintained that Gladys liked Fitzgerald, which is probably true; but Blair's anecdote does indicate that Gladys also viewed her daughter's relationship with him with a sharp eye.

Additionally, during cocktails one evening in New York around the time of the Ellerslie party, John Barrymore argued with Fitzgerald because he thought Fitzgerald was paying too much attention to Lois. We know of this because Fitzgerald mentioned it in a letter to Charles Green Shaw, with whom he had earlier discussed the episode, but he did not go into detail about what had happened. He wrote that he was concerned he may have given Shaw "a false impression in that Barrymore matter, of having interfered in Lois's affairs. I didn't. We were both pretty tight; he made this remark and I simply called him on it that was all." Along these same lines, if Carl Van Vechten is indeed looking at Scott and Lois critically in one of the Ellerslie snapshots, one must wonder whether, like Barrymore, he was concerned that Fitzgerald's attentions to Lois may have been excessive and perhaps even inappropriate.

Also at the time, in June 1927, a curious piece of artwork appeared in the pages of *Vanity Fair* that seemed to suggest that the relationship between the two had, from the start, been a subject of conjecture. In this elaborate, sprawling two-page illustration, Ralph Barton depicted his version of a Tuesday night at the Coconut Grove, a hot nightclub of the time located at the Ambassador Hotel, where Fitzgerald had stayed during the "Lipstick" adventure. Barton crammed into the picture caricatures of a vast array of personalities connected with the arts of the day, all seated at tables throughout the main floor of the club. At one table, he portrayed writers, and among them he placed several literary personalities Lois either knew or knew of: Carl Van Vechten, George Jean Nathan, Theodore Dreiser, Paul Morand, H. L. Mencken, and Fitzgerald, in the middle of the right edge of the first page of the illustration.

At another table across the room is a group of actors, including a few that had been in Lois's life and career: Douglas Fairbanks Jr. (her co-star in *Stella Dallas* and *Padlocked*), Betty Bronson (a young actress to whom Lois was often compared), William Haines (at a time when the ink was barely dry on Lois's letter to Fitzgerald about his romantic possibilities), and Lois herself, in the middle of the lower edge of the second page. One of the most extraordinary things about the illustration is that Scott and Lois appear to be looking at each other from across the room. Their spatial placement, in fact, and the directions of their gazes leave little doubt that they are seeking each other out. Scott is depicted with his head slightly cocked, his eyes squinted as if focusing on someone in the distance. He even seems to have a bit of a guilty demeanor, and he is unmistakably looking toward Lois. And Lois, whose eyes are not squinted and whose head is positioned facing squarely toward Fitzgerald, is intently looking back at him.

The placement of Fitzgerald and Lois is a small detail in a large, intricate illustration, but it is there, nonetheless, and considering that it dates from 1927, the very year Scott and Lois met, it is almost certainly more than a coincidence. Barton was shrewd, and his positioning Scott and Lois looking toward each other in a room full of famous people indicates that at the very least the artist was hinting that a friendship existed between them. The uncomfortable and uneasy look he drew on Fitzgerald's face and the determined one on Lois's, however, seems to indicate that he was setting forth the premise that even more was going on between them. Also, he did not depict Zelda in his illustration, a glaring omission since she was in her own right famous and recognizable and although uncomfortable in Hollywood would have been at the Coconut Grove right at her husband's side. In fact, in his autobiographical 1928 story "Magnetism," Fitzgerald even wrote of a married couple in Hollywood, whom he based loosely upon himself and Zelda, who frequented the nightclub together. It is not clear whether Zelda was aware of the illustration, but given the popularity of Barton and of *Vanity Fair* and the fact that the picture became so well known that even Stehlisilks manufactured a line of silk featuring it as the pattern, she probably was.

There also seems to be evidence in support of Scott and Lois's having had physical involvement provided by a purported eyewitness to it and by later written references to it both by Scott and by Zelda. The illustrator Arthur W. Brown, who often did work for the *Saturday Evening Post*, was staying at the Ambassador at the same time as the Fitzgeralds during the 1927 Hollywood trip. He claimed that one morning Fitzgerald came into his room with a woman on his arm and said, "Say hello to Zelda." It was Lois he was with, however, not Zelda. Brown asserted that Fitzgerald then asked him to act as his alibi for the day. If Zelda were to ask him where Scott had been, he was to say that Scott had been with him at First National Studios. It is possible that Brown had told his fellow illustrator Barton about the episode, perhaps precipitating the inclusion of Scott and Lois in Barton's *Vanity Fair* drawing.

Correspondence and a taped interview survive from the Fitzgeralds that reference Scott and Lois. Scott wrote to Zelda's psychiatrist in 1932, "Her [Zelda's] affair with Edouard [Jozan] in 1925 (and mine with Lois Moran in 1927, which was sort of revenge) shook something out of us." In a 1937 letter, Scott also mentioned having had an "AFFAIR" with an "ACTRESS (1927)." Fitzgerald also remarked in a 1933 taped conversation at La Paix, his home in Baltimore at the time, that "the girl [Lois] seemed to be more honest and more direct than Zelda." As for Zelda, in addition to her caustic lush-milkmaid description of Lois, which had the feel of having been composed by a scorned woman, she also told her psychiatrist in the early 1930s, "When I knew my husband had another woman in California, I was upset." She further remarked in a later letter, "He left me so much alone that

I was very ashamed of wanting him once.... He was thinking of the actress; he said so." Additionally, she wrote a letter to Scott in 1930 in which she referred to Lois by chastising him for what she termed his "flagrantly sentimental relations with a child."

There are other, miscellaneous points to support the belief that Scott and Lois were involved sexually, even if their validity is open to interpretation. For example, it can be argued that Lois's arranging a screen test for Fitzgerald was a sure sign of their having been intimate, for who would do such a thing except for a lover? One could also say that Fitzgerald's later, openly sexual affair with Sheilah Graham was proof positive that he was capable of having an extramarital affair with Lois.

Still more evidence of Scott and Lois's sexual relationship can be found in Lois's journal, because romance and longing characterize her entries at the time she knew him. Immediately following two undated entries in which she named *The Great Gatsby* and *This Side of Paradise* as being among "Good Books read in 1927" and in which she featured Scott and Zelda in a list of "People interesting" (like Fitzgerald, she enjoyed making lists), Lois penned a series of eight consecutive entries from May 1927 to April 1929 that she addressed to a person she did not identify by name but was most probably Fitzgerald. The first is dated May 9, 1927, only a brief time after she had met him in Hollywood; that is followed by another dated August 27, 1927, in which she speaks of a story the person had written and sent to her. The entry corresponds in time to the publication of Fitzgerald's story "Jacob's Ladder."

In all this journaling, Lois directs her writing to a man about whom she is in a "worshipful state of mind," who is a writer, who discusses literature with her, and who is older than she. She is concerned in these entries that the man not "spoil" himself, hopes that he "might shake every bit of that horrible nonsense away," and notes that "I should love to see you and your talents developed to the highest degree." All these details suggest that she was writing about Fitzgerald. He was an older writer who recommended books to her; and his problems with Zelda, with alcohol, and with writing work that would crown his earlier successes threatened his potential. More specifically, in keeping with the admiration Lois always acknowledged feeling for Fitzgerald, the entries pullulate with adoration and emotional attachment. She speaks several times of love. She refers to letters exchanged between the two of them, and we know she and Fitzgerald were in regular correspondence. She addresses the man as "dear," recalling the terms of affection she used for Scott in her extant letters to him. She even inquires, "Will you like me as a woman?," a sexually charged remark that certainly reflects her youth and his maturity. This journaling is poetic not just for its language, which is lovely, but also because Fitzgerald had traveled west by train to go to Hollywood, where he met Lois, and when Lois began writing these Fitzgerald entries in her journal she was on a train going east, possibly upon the very tracks that had first brought him to her.

Because of its significance to both Lois's and Fitzgerald's lives in the late 1920s, this portion of Lois's journal deserves to be set forth here in its entirety. The following is a complete transcription of these entries. In a few instances, Lois's spelling has been corrected, but her unique style of punctuation has been preserved as written. The gentleman she mentions as having been, for a time, as important to her as Fitzgerald is probably the actor George O'Brien.

May 9, 1927 (NOTES) Eastbound train

I've just climbed upstairs and I'm thinking of you on your trip and of the beautiful letter you sent me—And thinking that very soon we will be near again—I don't *care* for you at all but—well as Christopher Morley said in a lovely little book I'm reading now—if one could put one's feelings into words, they wouldn't be dangerous—That doesn't fit perhaps but I can't analyze and think properly tonight—So few people do analyze—they wander stolidly and unemotionally, except for sex, through life—Never poking at things—and wanting to know why—never dramatizing things to make them interesting—and missing completely that lovely feel of the sea, the night—and the hills—Elementary sensations, you may say, but that feel is a cultivated sense, and I'm quite young as yet—you see—

I want to go to Honolulu—I must be ripe to fall in love or something equally foolish from all indications—Have been so incurably sentimental and romantic lately—Wept my heart out at "7th Heaven" [a Fox film starring Janet Gaynor and Charles Farrell]—want to go to Honolulu—and have taken to writing in the above fashion—or am I wrong again?

Aug 27, 1927—

"The little story is beautiful—The whole spirit is perfect—You have clarified everything for me a great deal—I wrote you a very foolish letter immediately after reading the story which I tore up—I find it difficult to write you—Probably because I sense my literary inferiority so vividly—

I had such a lovely day the day the letter and story arrived—I was just beginning to believe the mail had completely grown out when your grand assurance that it hadn't, arrived. Well, I laughed and cried, and felt beautifully muddled and happy—I never have been able to tell you how enormously I love your work—Maybe I will when I am older and my opinion will perhaps mean something."

Excerpts from a letter I wrote you long ago—I wish I could write to you really. This will have to do.

Your last letter was the loveliest of all—And, sadly enough, I seem to have lost it—It is firmly in my mind though so I don't care.

Oh, dear—dear—dear! I love you so and miss you so—"Something else gone into the past"—*No*—it mustn't be!

Oct. 23, 1927—

I want you so badly!

May third—1928—

It's been a long while since I've written in this little book—But every bit of my life and affection remains the same—dear—you're very vivid in my memory tonight—Have been rereading your sweet letters and reliving our times together. I want to see you, know if you've changed, if I have—I've met only one person who means as much to me as you—He has gone too, though—Why must you both be so far? My understanding always—

August 9, 1928—

How are you, most splendidly foolish one? I wonder where you are? Strange that I shouldn't even know—Somewhere in France—We might be back in 1918—Are you working? How I hope so—I wish something terrible would happen that might shake every bit of that horrible nonsense away from you—My very dear—

I'm growing, dear—*Maybe* you will be pleased with me—And you will be more pleased two years hence—I certainly intend to be *someone* by that time.

Once, a long time ago, you said that I had probably never read a really good book—I didn't have the courage to argue then, being in such a worshipful state of mind, but I *had* read many, though I never absorbed them as deeply as now—Every new thought and feeling, all the marvelous things I'm discovering every day seem to find a waiting cubby hole in my mind—

People are the only disappointment—I will not take second best—It's such a pity, isn't it? But all this is boring, perhaps—It should go in my own diary, (I really intend to start one), this space is *yours* only—Good-by—

Oct. 30—1928

Here I am again, feeling that little ache once more. It has grown so sadly faint and gentle. I want to make it strong again! Where are you, *what* are you? Very, *very* dear—Please don't spoil yourself, please, please. I wish I could stop you, help you. Maybe something has happened though to fix everything. If only it has or will! I should so love to see you and your talents developed to the highest degree.

November ninth.

I'm upset tonight—It makes me think of you, dear. You started it all. Much love always—

Nov. 10—

Dear—dearest dear!

November 20—

I'm so happy—feel so grown-up—complete.
I wish you were here. Will you like me as a woman?

April 5, 1929—

I still think of you and love you, though the hurt has almost become melancholy sweetness now—And I'm still waiting for you to create something. Please don't fail me. Always, always my love. I'm going to be great, dear. You helped me a great deal this evening—I was a bit sad and discouraged. But the thought of your pride and your hope in me was lovely—Good-night.

These journal entries did not surface until after Lois's death. One possible explanation for her never having brought her journals to light in later years could be that she had forgotten having written them, although this theory does not seem sound because she had generally sharp recall and additionally, in one of her letters to Mizener, had mentioned having held on to them. Another explanation might be that she was apprehensive they would be construed as proof she and Fitzgerald had indeed had a sexual affair. On the latter point, she was well aware that a seeming mountain of evidence pointed to the two of them having been more than friends, and she did not wish to add any more substance to the speculation, especially in her later years in Sedona. As Young explains, "She would always shy away from mention of a physical encounter with Fitzgerald, even when it was humorous. Some of the group in Sedona were actors and entertainers. Many of the gatherings centered on careers past and present. She would steer the conversation away from Fitzgerald." Desiring to distance herself from Fitzgerald, then, would have been motive enough for her to hide away her long-ago journaling about him. Another possible theory for her concealment of the journals obviates the question of whether or not she had been sexually intimate with Fitzgerald and goes to the simple issue of her wanting to maintain her privacy. Young points out that her relationship with Fitzgerald "was probably one of the high points of her life and she was not ready to share it."

That insightful remark leads now to the arguments for Lois and Fitzgerald's having been simply friends, an argument of which Lois herself was the main proponent. She always maintained that she and Fitzgerald had never consummated their relationship, even when the world crashed in her door on the subject and refused to take her at her word. She was quick to point out, as she once did to this author, that in the 1920s and 1930s "things were different," and a variety of circumstances supported her position. First and foremost, she insisted unwaveringly that her mother was always present during her meetings with Scott. She pointed out that Gladys was a strong presence in her life at the time and said that the most privacy she and Fitzgerald ever had was when they had their conversations on the stairway at the Mariposa Street apartment building. Even then, Gladys was never far off.

Gladys notwithstanding, Lois also claimed that she was saving herself for marriage. "He never so much as kissed me," she wrote to this author in the summer of 1987. "Of course, no one believes me, but it was a different time." She maintained also that as far as she ever knew, she and Zelda had had a good relationship and that she was totally unaware at the time of any hard feelings Zelda had toward her. She maintained that the positive opinion she believed Zelda held of her demonstrated that she could not have been sexually involved with her husband. She in return had liked and respected Zelda, she explained; and, in contrast to observations made by those such as Louise Brooks, she had only the most flattering things to say about her and in fact wrote to Mizener of her "gorgeousness" and observed to him of the Fitzgeralds,

> They were perfect, as far as I was concerned. Scott, a genius, Zelda
> brilliant, and both possessing just the right amount of gayety [sic] and

gravity, plus being beautiful to look at. They were enchanting—and they enchanted... they traveled on the same golden cloud—It wasn't possible to love just one of them. You loved them both. Or, at least, I did. They were kind of a dream come true to me.

Lois seldom, if ever, uttered a bad word about Zelda and perhaps best expressed her opinion of her when she wrote further to Mizener of the Fitzgeralds, "I can't explain charm. It's an aura about certain people."

Lois also drew attention to the fact that the sentiment of Fitzgerald's inscription to her in her copy of *This Side of Paradise* does not suggest that he is writing to a lover. Written hastily, for part of it is smeared, the inscription includes her full name, "For Lois Moran," thus beginning on an almost formal note, and he then added "from hers devotedly," which was polite and warm but actually, for him, a rather terse sentiment compared to the more effusive inscriptions he was known to have written in other books he inscribed for various people over the course of his career. For example, Carmel Myers, who had been part of the Mariposa/Ambassador clique, received a far more colorful inscription from him in her copy of *The Great Gatsby*.

Lois also explained that there was the issue of her and Fitzgerald's personal morality. Lois, while not strongly conservative, was quick to explain that she had been brought up in Pittsburgh with strong traditional religious values. Even though Gladys had considered that atmosphere oppressive and had fled from it to Europe, enough of it had remained with Lois that she believed, she said, not just in the notion of marriage but also in the notion of marriage before sex. Fitzgerald, she pointed out, had also come from a midwestern background. Raised a Catholic, he had issues, she said, about extramarital sex and would not have cheated on Zelda.

As for the miscellaneous arguments, Lois had rebuttals for those, as well. There was nothing unusual about her obtaining a screen test for Fitzgerald, she said, because she often procured such tests for those she found promising. And even if there is no record of her having taken pleasure in arranging screen tests, the fact remains that Fitzgerald was actually a promising candidate as a screen actor. He was famous; his photograph appeared regularly in popular magazines of the day. He was also handsome and possessed a mellifluous voice that can be heard today in recordings of him reading poetry that were made in Hollywood in 1940 and that suggest he would have worked well in early talkies. A newsreel strip had also been produced of him in the 1920s in which he was glimpsed out of doors writing intently at a desk, and that bit of footage alone revealed him to have had a charismatic screen presence.

In regard to Sheilah Graham, Lois pointed out that Fitzgerald's life was very different at the time he knew Graham than it was when he knew her. When she herself was in his life in the late 1920s, Lois explained, he and Zelda were together and very much in love, and although they quarreled frequently they were devoted to each other. Moreover, their young daughter gave him a sense of family that he held very dear. By the time he knew Graham, however, a little over a decade later, Zelda had been indefinitely institutionalized and was no longer a living, breathing presence in his life. Lois referred to an entry Fitzgerald had written in his 1930s notebooks that read, "I left my capacity for hoping on the little roads that led to Zelda's sanitarium." To make matters worse, Lois said, Scottie was away at school. Fitzgerald loved his family as much as ever and exchanged long and heartfelt letters with his wife and daughter, but the physical void weighed heavily upon him, and it appears that he accepted Graham into life as a kind of surrogate for his family, whom he so very much missed. His feelings for Graham were sincere, but were not on the level of those he had for Zelda, and he would not consider divorce. As Lois had observed to Mizener in 1948, it was never possible to consider the Fitzgeralds as anything but a couple. "I keep saying 'them,'" Lois told Mizener when she was discussing Scott and Zelda, "—which is perhaps a clue to Scott's later life. There was a very definite 'togetherness.'"

As for Fitzgerald himself, Lois believed that he was all too often stigmatized by his own reputation as a celebrated pretty boy who partied and drank and splashed about with Zelda in the fountain at the Plaza Hotel, a genius with words who was flawed by a self-destructive urge to overindulge in a booze-drenched social life. As a result of this view of him, Lois said, many people too readily accepted the proposition that he could have had a sexual affair with her in 1927. In truth, Lois pointed out, Fitzgerald was a man of morals and scruples. He did indeed imbibe, spend lavishly, and live the high life, but at the same time he was devoted to Zelda and Scottie. When one clears away the phony glitter of his public life, Lois maintained, it is plain that Fitzgerald was a decent and conscientious man who in spite of everything always put his family first. According to Lois, what was important is that, when all was said and done, he was hopelessly and completely in love with Zelda and would not have gone as far as to cheat on her.

But Lois's arguments do not outweigh the facts that support her having had an affair with him. As Young believes, the logic of the matter strongly points to the Fitzgerald-Moran involvement as sexual. Fitzgerald and Lois's having been physically involved with each other much better explains Zelda's animosity towards her, why he used her so extensively as an influence in his writing, why she composed such loving journal entries presumably about him, why she wrote short stories in which she created characters based upon him, and why she telephoned him of all people on her wedding day. Young is further correct in stating that his mother would have been embarrassed by admitting to an affair with Fitzgerald, and his assertion that she could not have been more forthcoming in her journals because of the possibility of Gladys seeing them is sound. Gladys, moreover, while concerned about her daughter's relationship with Fitzgerald, could not possibly have monitored her twenty-four hours a day. If Lois and Fitzgerald had wanted privacy, they could have found it. As for Fitzgerald, he was indeed devoted to Zelda and to his daughter, and perhaps he was a tad stuffy when it came to sex, but he was also a tormented, complex, unpredictable human being who at the time was searching for meaning, self-assurance, and love that was fresh and unconditional. It is important, too, to note that after Zelda's hospitalization in the 1930s he did not specifically deny having had a sexual involvement with Lois and in fact bluntly referred to his relationship with her as an "affair."

The strong attraction that existed between Lois and Fitzgerald, two beautiful young people—and Fitzgerald, contrary to what he himself thought, was still a young man—cannot be discounted. Today, lovers of famous writers are unafraid to tell all. Think of Joyce Maynard's 1999 memoir *At Home in the World*, in which she discussed her affair with J. D. Salinger. Mores were different in Lois's day, however. Sheilah Graham got away with revealing the details of her relationship with Fitzgerald because at the time it happened Zelda was institutionalized and Fitzgerald for all practical purposes was a widower, but even she was criticized for telling too much about him in her books. Lois, unlike Graham, possessed the desire neither to discuss her affair with Fitzgerald nor to write books about it, but her reticence does not negate the fact that it had happened.

Now that the sexual nature of Lois's relationship with Fitzgerald has been established with near certainty, it becomes important to trace how she handled the attention she received over the years because of it. Disturbed by the ongoing debate of the exact nature of her interactions with him, she was, by the 1980s, no longer as eager to share her memories of him as she had been in previous days, a somewhat ironic turn of events since she was now, as she had looked forward to being in her August 27, 1927, journal entry, an older woman whose opinion did mean something. As Young points out, "Mother gave many talks on her career, yet the Fitzgerald years were always in the background." Indeed, she began to feel increasingly victimized and even insulted by the public's willingness to unquestioningly accept as fact the supposition that she and Fitzgerald had been lovers. "Mother had come to a point of fantasizing," asserts Young. "After so many years, she had, I think, come to believe her own denials about the Fitzgerald affair." Lois realized that after his death Fitzgerald had become the subject of widespread literary lionization and indeed counted herself as one of his perpetual admirers, once describing herself in a letter to Matthew Bruccoli as a "fellow hero worshipper." She also realized that having known him afforded her fame that was quite unique from, and perhaps even more enduring than, the celebrity she had enjoyed as an actress. And for the most part she was pleased to be part of it all. She became contentious only when she was not taken at her word about what she maintained was the platonic nature of their relationship.

When Lois corresponded with Arthur Mizener in the 1940s and 1950s while he was researching *The Far Side of Paradise*, she had been eager to share her past and wrote him long, detailed letters about Fitzgerald from her home in Beverly Hills. Mizener, a biographer who did not flinch from presenting both the highs and lows of his subject's life, wrote to her, "I think I know a good many of the worst things [the Fitzgeralds] did, and they still seem gorgeous to me," a remark that endeared him to Lois, who came to trust him as a man of integrity. She was pleased when his book was published. In a letter, she tells him she found it a "beautifully written, beautifully understanding story of a great writer and a fine man" and appreciated the brief but meaningful mention that he made of her. Mizener made no reference to Lois and Fitzgerald's having been involved romantically and remarked only that she had been "important to [Fitzgerald's] imagination," an observation that pleased her. She had, indeed, greatly enjoyed sharing with Mizener the memories of pleasant days from her past and wrote to him, "I shall be eternally grateful to you for giving me back my 'shining knight.'" And even years later, in the 1970s, she was still fond of recalling her time with Fitzgerald. In making the notes at that time for the proposed autobiography, in fact, she commemorated the cuisine she and Fitzgerald had enjoyed together at the Mariposa parties by choosing as a name for one of the chapters, which she never actually wrote, "Strawberries, Caviar, and F. Scott Fitzgerald."

By the 1980s, and up until her death in 1990, however, she had developed decidedly mixed emotions about being so closely identified with Fitzgerald and about being better remembered for her comparatively brief relationship with him than for her own career as an actress and her lifelong family commitment to her husband, Clarence Young, and their son, Tim. The basic values she had learned as a girl in Pittsburgh reasserted themselves. As Tim Young explains, in her later years she spoke of wanting to be remembered for having led a "pure and simple life, as she put it, and nothing more." Young goes on that she found Sheilah Graham's books about Fitzgerald "distasteful" because they "cashed in" on Fitzgerald's reputation and because they characterized Fitzgerald as a vastly more unstable man than the one she had known.

The well-known scene in Graham's book *Beloved Infidel* in which Fitzgerald slaps Graham and they struggle with a gun particularly offended Lois. "Mother was horrified by the gun scene," Young says. "She said that the Fitzgerald she knew could be moody and difficult but never violent." Young also recalls that his mother's reactions over the years to the various film versions that appeared of *Tender Is the Night* were typical of her feelings about Fitzgerald. The novel had been made into a television special in 1955, a Hollywood film in 1961 (directed, as had been Lois's *Stella Dallas*, by Henry King), and a television miniseries in 1985, but Lois never evinced the least interest in any of these adaptations. "I cannot remember Mother ever even mentioning the *Tender Is the Night* films," Young recounts. "She had little interest in movies after her career and would not have wanted to dredge up the past by watching films made of Fitzgerald's book."

The ambiguity of her feelings about being closely associated with Fitzgerald became particularly pronounced in 1984, when James Mellow published his biography of the Fitzgeralds, *Invented Lives*, an important and widely read work but one in which the author was not particularly kind to Lois. He described her as having had an "authentic Hollywood smile," which Lois considered a backhanded compliment, and went on to describe her appearance at the Ellerslie party as "prim," terming her outfit and hairdo "prissy." He said little of her career other than to note that when she met Fitzgerald she had been a "protégée of Sam Goldwyn's," a remark that did not set well with Lois because by 1927 Goldwyn was well in her past. Finally, Mellow described Gladys as a "moral watchdog," a remark Lois thought inaccurate because it suggested that her mother was puritanical. Considering that Gladys had taken her to Paris as a way of escaping what she considered the suffocating environment of Pittsburgh, Lois viewed her as having been watchful but never repressive. Moreover, Gladys had liked Fitzgerald, Lois claimed (in contrast to Betsy Blair's later revelation) and, although troubled by his age and the fact that he was married, encouraged her to cultivate his friendship. This was cautious behavior, not puritanical.

Mellow's characterizations of her and Gladys offended Lois, especially because she realized that he had written an otherwise impressive book and had included in it what was probably the most detailed discussion yet published concerning her relationship with Fitzgerald. She knew that many people would know of her for the first time after having read the book, and while she generally maintained that the past was the past, she did resent not having been presented in a more positive light. When she died, Young found among her possessions a copy of the book in which she had used slivers of paper to mark each of the sections that mentioned her. Perhaps as a result of *Invented Lives*, Lois agreed to be interviewed by Richard Lamparski for inclusion in one of his *Whatever Became Of...?* film history volumes, for she knew that he would present her in a far more complimentary manner. The pleasant result of that interview, published in the 1986 tenth edition of the series, assuaged her mixed feelings over Mellow's book.

Because of unflattering episodes such as the publication of *Invented Lives*, Lois became increasingly guarded on the subject of Fitzgerald.

She was far from being a reclusive, reticent Garbo type and was usually happy to talk about her past experiences with him and to acknowledge that she was the model for Rosemary; but if she felt that she was being perceived as having been Fitzgerald's lover she became irritated. "She was very sensitive about it," Young explains. "I once asked her outright if the rumors were true that she and Fitzgerald had been lovers, and she ran from the room in tears saying, 'How could you even think that?'" Young relates further that after her death he "found notes of some of her talks she gave about her career, and they really do not say anything about Scott." Young remembers also that she had been angered when she agreed to be filmed in the 1980s for a Canadian film documentary about Fitzgerald. "She went to Los Angeles to do that," he says, "but she cut the trip short. I remember changing the travel reservations. She came back agitated because she said all they wanted her to talk about was whether she and Fitzgerald ever had sex."

This author also once suffered Lois Moran's wrath by inadvertently pressing too hard on the subject of Fitzgerald. When I first wrote to her in the mid-1980s about my avid interest both in silent movies and in Fitzgerald, she responded by sending me a copy of Matthew Bruccoli's book about Fitzgerald and Hemingway, *Scott and Ernest*. She explained that although she was not an admirer of Hemingway she thought the book would be of interest to me because of its Fitzgerald content. With the best of intentions, then, in 1987 I reciprocated by sending her as a Christmas gift a glossy 8″×10″ photograph of Fitzgerald from his 1920s heyday, a picture I had been excited to find in the archives of the Princeton library. To my surprise, she replied with a note expressing thanks but adding, "Please don't send me any more pictures of him. That was all in the past and he's dead now. I prefer to remember him for what he was, a really nice guy." I should have realized it would have been better to send her a fruitcake. Earlier that year I had written an article about her for *Hollywood Studio Magazine* and had forwarded her the manuscript. In it, I had remarked that she and Fitzgerald had been "enamored" of each other, and to that she had taken immediate exception. "Did you have to say we were enamored?" she complained, adding that she and Tim had discussed the issue and believed that a better way to express it would be say that they "greatly admired one another," which is how it appeared in print. The following Christmas I abandoned all thoughts of giving her a gift that recalled her past and sent instead a cat-shaped teapot and a hummingbird feeder, gifts she received far more jovially.

Young remembers another Christmas episode involving the subject of his mother and Fitzgerald that occurred the same year I sent her that ill-fated photograph. Among Lois's friends in Sedona was a gentleman who made his living playing the piano in various nightclubs and bars. Included in his repertoire were selections from *Of Thee I Sing*, the Gershwin musical in which Lois had starred in 1931. "That Christmas, we all got around the piano," Young explains. "There were poinsettias and tinsel garlands and a Christmas tree nearby, and we were having a great time. We got Mother to sing 'Who Cares?' from *Of Thee I Sing*, and we all chimed in with 'Life is a jubilee' and all those other great lyrics." Something happened, however, to mar the perfection of the moment. The pianist, described by Young as a "friendly drinker with a great sense of humor," stopped the music and openly asked Lois if she had ever been "between the sheets with Scott." Lois, who liked the fellow and considered him a friend, deftly replied, "Oh, let's not bother with all that. Why don't we just get back to singing?" The pianist then improvised a version of the song "Of Thee I Sing," making up the lyrics as he went along. "Of thee I sing of Lois and Scott!" he chortled. Lois was not offended by the incident and appears to have been amused by it, but it was typical of many experiences later in her life that harked back to this one relationship from so many decades earlier.

Another incident in Sedona relating to Lois and Fitzgerald had taken place in the 1970s. Lorraine Bendix, daughter of the actor William Bendix and one-time fiancée of Harold Lloyd Jr., lived there and was active in local community theater. Lorraine wrote some of the plays that were performed there, and she saw potential in writing a drama about Lois and Scott. She was aware of the film that had been made in 1959 of Sheilah Graham's memoir about Fitzgerald, *Beloved Infidel*, with Gregory Peck assaying the part of Scott, and she knew also of the television movie that had been done about him, *F. Scott Fitzgerald in Hollywood*. These works, as Lorraine was quick to discern, illustrated that Fitzgerald's life made for fertile material for a playwright, and his involvement with Sedona's own Lois Moran seemed to have been custom made for her pen. "Lorraine was very outspoken and looked and acted much like Totie Fields," Young recalls, "and with her outgoing personality she approached Mother about the possibility of doing the play." At first, Lois was flattered by the idea and gave it the green light.

But as quickly as the green light had dimmed at the end of Daisy Buchanan's dock in *Gatsby*, so too did this one flicker and fade. After Lorraine had started to write the piece, she showed the first few finished pages to Lois. "Lorraine had great enthusiasm for the project," Young says. As Lois read, however, she realized that "Lorraine was overdoing the Scott gimmick in the show. It was, shall we say, to be a little too much on the sexual side." Lois again felt battered by the subject of her relationship with Scott and withdrew her support for the play. Nothing ever came of it, and Lorraine passed away in the 1980s. The unfinished script has not materialized.

After their relationship had cooled, Lois and Fitzgerald continued to see each other socially, but such visits grew less and less frequent. One such visit was in New York, when they attended the Gene Tunney party. Another, mentioned by Fitzgerald in his notebooks, occurred several years later in 1934 when he was living at La Paix in Baltimore and working on *Tender Is the Night*. Lois, with Gladys, went to visit her old friend there, but to her dismay he was quarrelsome, drinking heavily, and far from amiable. The gruesome and painful meeting typified Lois's later visits with him, which continued until 1935, when she married. In 1948, she wrote an insightful letter to Arthur Mizener in which she ruminated upon her late, haunted visits with Fitzgerald:

> Later meetings with Scott in the early 30s were tortured and miserable. I was still too young to evaluate the reason or reasons—Drinking and worry about Zelda were the obvious reasons—But I don't think they could have been enough to make him so bitter and unhappy and lost—Perhaps it was a "dry" period—the period when nothing seems worthwhile—all faiths are worthless—and you ask yourself 50,000,000 times a day, "Why?" Most of us go through such phases fairly easily—but to Scott, having written so much and so well at an early age, it must have been extremely difficult—and the undermining of his health by too much liquor didn't help any. Psycho and somatic certainly go together. T'would be wonderful if we could know which influences which—I think that Scott needed a "cause or something" to cling to—at that period—some rock or foundation on which to build—He needed to transfer his creative talent to—well—a "cause"—I keep saying. Politics, sociology, economics, whatever—but something that would benefit his fellow-man.

In 1951, she wrote further to Mizener of these later visits: "When I saw him in '33, '34, and '35, he was so different from the man I'd known before, and I was still too young to cope with him. With a little more maturity and wisdom, perhaps I could have helped him. Instead, I just wanted to run."

Lois as Muse, the *Saturday Evening Post*, and the Rejuvenation of F. Scott Fitzgerald

8

*A*lthough Lois and Fitzgerald no longer saw each other after her marriage in 1935, both retained souvenirs of their affair and subsequent friendship. They had their memories, and a few of the letters they had exchanged as well as her journal entries about him had survived intact. More important than all these, though, are the writings that Scott based on Lois, among the first he had done in well over a year, for in those he created the most tangible, if not complex, outcome of having known her. Traces of Lois show up in several of the characters and stories he wrote after having met her, most significantly in three short stories he wrote for the *Saturday Evening Post*, "Jacob's Ladder," "Magnetism," and "The Rough Crossing." Of the greatest importance is *Tender Is the Night*. Most people today have never seen Lois Moran in a movie, but many have read about her, whether they know it or not, in Fitzgerald's perennially popular writings. It is of paramount importance in this consideration of Lois, then, to examine how Fitzgerald drew from her in his works.

Before doing so, however, it is worth pausing to consider those short stories Lois herself wrote while under Fitzgerald's spell. Three such typescripts have been found in her papers of the late 1920s. Each reflects her idealistic view of love and romance and reveals her feelings for Fitzgerald. One of the stories, entitled "Awakening," is about a character named Barbara, an unhappy and morose eighteen-year-old. Gazing at her image in a mirror, she complains, "I have a terrific, aching, longing for something, some intangible, lovely thing, and I can't find it anywhere." A short time later, however, her boyfriend, Bob, kisses her, and she experiences great joy—and guilt. "Yes," Lois writes of the character, "she would probably become a lady of easy virtue, a prostitute—a vampire—sucking men's life blood." Barbara goes on to experience a moment of epiphany while perched upon Bob's lap, a father-daughter tableau that corresponds to Lois's attraction to older, fatherly men. She realizes that what she is feeling is love, not just carnal desire, and, sobbing with joy and relief, she tells Bob, "Oh, darling, I've found what I've always wanted. . . . And I didn't even guess it! Please, dear, please mayn't we—get married?" This story speaks volumes about Lois's frank awareness of her own sexuality, which was tempered by her longing for the sweet, romantic love about which she had so often read in her grandparents' library in Pittsburgh.

A second story, "Fair Lady," reflects her fascination with medieval notions of fairy-tale romance. In this composition, a lonely man in post–World War I Vienna falls in love with a girl in a coffeehouse while being serenaded by a hunchbacked violinist. Her father forbids her to see the man, however, and he is left dejected and hopeless until he sees an ethereal vision of the girl coming toward him in his room. In an act of cathartic cleansing, he sinks to his knees, "weeping, weeping for lost beauty and lost romance." This is a story clearly influenced by *Peter Ibbetson*, the George du Maurier novel Lois so admired about love transcending the boundaries of the physical world, but its theme of forbidden love relates to her affair with Fitzgerald.

The third story is untitled but contains the most obvious connection between Lois and Fitzgerald. In it, Lois's heroine is horseback riding along the seashore with the man she loves as she silently ruminates upon her relationship with him. Lois's description of the gentleman conjures up Fitzgerald immediately. "She loved his serious kind eyes," she wrote, "the long, slightly drooping figure, his sharply cleft chin and upper lip." The reader's suspicions that she is writing about Fitzgerald are confirmed when she goes on to explain that the man is a gifted writer, noting, "He could create. He wrote beautifully—wrote heartbreaking, intangible lovely things." The girl berates herself for not being able to create as does he, but she takes solace in being an inspiration to his work. The following passage seems to have been written by Lois as an autobiographical contemplation of her own significance to Fitzgerald and is similar to descriptions Fitzgerald wrote of his own Lois-themed characters, especially of Jenny in "Jacob's Ladder":

> She radiated life, in its purest most idealistic form—that was why he loved her. She was the one justification of all he wrote. He felt the need of some tangible ideal, someone to give him renewed courage and love of life, of people, and he found that radiant quality in her. He never tired of trying to express her vibrancy—it ran through every phrase he wrote and filled his work with a barely suppressed ecstasy.

The story ends with the happy couple riding off into the sunset. This piece is obviously about Fitzgerald and contains the most pronounced sexual undercurrents of Lois's three stories. Zelda most likely never saw it—one can only wonder what new act of destruction she may have effected in retaliation if she had. Indeed, in it Lois had created a thinly disguised description of her relationship with Fitzgerald, and it betrayed the romantic feelings she probably had for him. Interestingly, it also revealed her awareness even then that she was in turn an inspiration to him in his writings, apparently the only extant contemporary reference that indicates she understood the part she was playing in Fitzgerald's work. Lois and Fitzgerald, most probably, discussed the subject of Lois as muse, but if any letters were written between them on that specific subject, they have not survived.

Lois's stories were not published, and one cannot help but wonder whether she had intended them to be. She wrote in her journal on February 12, 1927, "Wrote a lot of rambling nonsense in the afternoon to Scott—Hope he will think it some good—afraid I will never be a writer though—I had better stick to acting." This entry notwithstanding, however, she did put a word count on the untitled story, which seems to indicate that she intended it to be published. Moreover, while she was correct in assessing that these stories would probably not have made it to the *New Yorker*, any number of popular and film-oriented magazines would have printed them based on the value of her name alone. It seems, then, that she opted not to have them appear in print. One is reminded of Tim Young's remark that she wanted to keep her relationship with Fitzgerald as a special thing reserved just for herself. Could she have hidden these stories away because she feared that they could too easily have been construed as being about Fitzgerald? With *Vanity Fair* printing its Ralph Barton illustration in which the two are looking toward each other, and with Zelda burning clothes and tossing expensive jewelry out of train windows, Lois had good reason to anticipate that at least those who knew her would make the connection with Fitzgerald.

Fitzgerald, on the other hand, wrote three stories of his own that were influenced by Lois, and, ever the literary exhibitionist, accustomed to using his personal life as material for his work, he had no qualms whatsoever about publishing them. The strongest and best known of these pieces is "Jacob's Ladder." Had he never created Rosemary in his famous novel, Lois would still be remembered in connection to him for this story alone, for it is a well-crafted piece, filled with some of his most poetic language, and she was the inspiration for one of its main characters. The story is a melancholy tale of romantic longing told in the framework of Hollywood film production, and he liked the result well enough that he later incorporated much of it into *Tender Is the Night*, as he told Lois in his 1935 letter. Fitzgerald often, as he put it, "stripped down" his stories for material to include in his novels. In this case, *Tender Is the Night* was the better for it, but in consequence, "Jacob's Ladder" was for years one of his most neglected works. Since he felt that too much of its content had gone into *Tender Is the Night*, he opted not to include the story in his 1935 short story compilation *Taps at Reveille*, so it remained virtually forgotten until it was republished years later in a posthumous collection of his short fiction. It originally appeared in the August 20, 1927, *Saturday Evening Post*, and even at the time the magazine recognized that it was of such high quality that it merited a pay increase for its author.

Fitzgerald's plot for "Jacob's Ladder" was one he would revisit several times. It concerned a thirty-three-year-old man who falls in love with a sixteen-year-old girl. The Lois connection can be seen in this detail alone, especially because he wrote it only a short time after having met her, but in this early work the man is not married. He tackled that more ambitious plotting in the later two stories and in *Tender Is the Night*. Here, he narrowed his story to concentrate on the emotions that an unmarried man experiences when faced with the prospects of aging and love. In this respect, it is apparent that in some respects "Jacob's Ladder" was a kind of preparatory exercise for him in the writing of *Tender Is the Night*, and the story has long been a point of reference for those tracing the compositional process of the novel.

When retold, the plot of "Jacob's Ladder" seems a simplistic and uninteresting reworking of the Pygmalion story. However, in Fitzgerald's hands it is engaging. He begins the story as the older man, Jacob Booth, meets the younger woman, Jenny Delehanty, at the sensational murder trial of her sister, and from this vivid beginning he never loses the reader's interest. As Jacob comes to know Jenny better, he realizes that although she is uncultured and lacks social grace, she has a marked natural potential to become a film actress. A man of independent means who is well connected socially, he changes the girl's name to Jenny Prince, introduces her to the right Hollywood people, and watches from the sidelines as her movie-star career ascends. He has little to do with her life once she becomes a film celebrity, but he visits her, helps her to avert a scandal, and eventually falls in love with her, sharing a kiss with her in a taxi and at one point even glimpsing an ethereal image of her coming toward him in a hotel room. But Jenny, while grateful to him for the opportunities he has made possible for her, does not reciprocate his romantic feelings and is more intrigued by a Latin film actor named Raffino. Nonetheless, she offers to marry Jacob; but he knows it could not be a happy union because she has told him outright that he does not "thrill" her. Still very much in love with her, he lets her go for good when she tells him she has fallen in love with the director of one of her films. Dejected, at the story's end he wanders into a theater that is showing one of her films and takes a lonely seat in the darkness, now just another one of her fans left with the image of her he would see on the screen.

Fitzgerald drew upon a variety of real-life details in writing "Jacob's Ladder." For example, when Jacob travels from New York and visits Jenny in Los Angeles, he stays at the Ambassador, the hotel at which Scott and Zelda had stayed in 1927. In a film Jenny is making at the time of the story, she plays a dowdy girl who nonetheless inspires the local football hero. Jenny steals the picture, a situation that recalls Lois's film persona. Jenny also notes that this was the first film in which she has had sex appeal, another indicator that Fitzgerald was writing with Lois's innocent film persona in mind but also one that hints at the sexuality he had awakened in her only a short time earlier. Further, Jenny's attraction to her director echoes Lois's own fondness for many of her directors, especially Allan Dwan. The director to whom Jacob introduces Jenny, moreover, has a studio on Long Island, a plot detail that may be Fitzgerald's nod to sequences in Lois's film *Just Suppose*, which had been filmed there. There is also an episode in the story in which an actress has trouble with her stockings, bringing to mind the famous ribbed stockings that Lois wore in *Stella Dallas*. And, too, the scene in the story in which Jacob sees a supernatural vision of Jenny recalls a similar incident in Lois's own story "Fair Lady," although one cannot be sure who was borrowing from whom on this point, or whether the appearance of this scene in both stories was only a coincidence. Of surer origin is Fitzgerald's unabashed use of Lois's telegram to him and Zelda after they had left Hollywood.

In the story, Jacob sends a very similar telegram to Jenny: "New York desolate. The nightclubs all closed. Black wreaths on the statue of Civic Virtue."

In terms of the story's reflecting Fitzgerald's feelings for Lois, the theme of love between an older man and a younger woman remains intact, and it is in this respect that it most clearly borrows from aspects of his relationship with her. One sentence captures the sense of aging and desolation Fitzgerald was experiencing and the part that Lois helped to play in soothing that pain. Jacob, Fitzgerald writes, was "living more deeply in [Jenny's] youth and future than he had lived in himself for years." Fitzgerald further evinced his fondness for Lois in two beautiful descriptions that he created for her alter ego in this story. He first notes of Jenny, "Her face, the face of a saint, an intense little Madonna, was lifted fragilely out of the mortal dust of the afternoon. On the pure parting of her lips no breath hovered; he had never seen a texture pale and immaculate as her skin, lustrous and garish as her eyes." He followed this description with another rapturous passage from which Lois appears to have borrowed in her previously quoted description of the girl she based on herself in her untitled story: "She was radiant. A communicative joy flowed from her and around her, as though her perfumer had managed to imprison ecstasy in a bottle." Fitzgerald could not have written such descriptions openly about Lois, but he was able to weave them into his fiction. Curiously, at the story's beginning Fitzgerald characterizes Jenny as ignorant and socially inept, attributes that by no means could have been applied to Lois. Perhaps he intended these aspects of the characterization as smokescreens.

Lois most probably was aware of her influence upon "Jacob's Ladder" at the time Fitzgerald wrote it. In his 1935 wedding letter to her, he referred to it as something with which she would be familiar, and the very fact that he would have mentioned it to her at all shows that the story held significance for them. Also, Lois's Fitzgerald-themed journal entry the same week the story appeared seems to have been more than coincidence. It is as if she saw the story in the *Saturday Evening Post* and was prompted to nostalgia in writing that she missed Fitzgerald and did not want her affair with him to be something in the past. In later years, Lois said little about the story, but this was because much more was made of the part she played in *Tender Is the Night*, a more important and better-known work. However, "Jacob's Ladder" does remain an important prelude to *Tender Is the Night*. That the young girl is an actress who has yet to develop onscreen sex appeal is the most obvious Lois-inspired detail that shows up in both writings, but there are other, smaller points that appear in each of the two, as well, such as a scandal threatening the actress's career, her having a love scene with the older male character in a taxi, and her having a romantic interest in a Latin film actor.

In "Magnetism," published in the March 3, 1928, issue of the *Saturday Evening Post*, Fitzgerald again explored the theme of an older man becoming smitten by a younger girl, and again he did so using the film world as a setting. However, this story differs from "Jacob's Ladder" in that the hero is married and the girl more readily recognizable as Lois—smoother and more refined than Jenny. Also, the hero of "Magnetism" is not in love with the girl, but, rather, the girl is in love with him. The main character, George Hannaford, is a thirty-year-old movie star married to another movie star, Kay Tompkins. Their marriage is happy until George takes notice of a young, up-and-coming eighteen-year-old actress named Helen Avery. Though he is not unfaithful to Kay, the advent of Helen creates turbulence in his marriage, resulting in a triangular structure that parallels Fitzgerald's own life.

However, George does not fully reciprocate Helen's feelings for him, a detail that differs from Fitzgerald's feelings for Lois in real life. "It hadn't been love," Fitzgerald writes of George and Helen. Fitzgerald seems especially intent upon making this point, perhaps as a means of expiating any guilt he may have been feeling for his actual emotional and sexual involvements with Lois. He returns to autobiographical truth when he writes that there was an unmistakable spark between the older man and younger girl. One is reminded of Scott and Lois's Mariposa chats when he writes, "He hadn't said a word to Helen Avery that Kay could have objected to, but something had begun between them." Fitzgerald also summons Lois when he writes of George and Helen, "He had felt that they both tolerated something, that each knew half of some secret about people and life, and that if they rushed toward each other there would be a romantic communion of almost unbelievable intensity." Fitzgerald suggests more specifically that Helen is a version of Lois when he writes a scene in which Helen is elated to have won a part in a film based on a novel she had admired, a situation that had occurred several times in Lois's own career with pictures such as *Stella Dallas*, *The Reckless Lady*, and *The Prince of Tempters*. In short, Helen is, like Lois, an actress who is young, who reads, and who has a crush on a man the same age as Fitzgerald.

"Magnetism" is the least engaging of the three stories in which Fitzgerald based characters on Lois, but it does hold the reader's interest in that he seems to have written it, especially in terms of the three main characters, as an autobiographical exercise. Moreover, Fitzgerald wrote it in a Hollywood setting just a short time after his own sojourn there. So obviously inspired by real life was the story that Fitzgerald, in addition to making it clear that George does not love Helen, also includes a passage in which George expresses guilt over his attentions to the girl, thereby further lessening the impact of any recriminations he himself may have faced as a result of his self-reflective, even confessional story. He also puts into Helen's mouth, speaking to George, a strongly worded line—"Oh, we're such *actors*—you and I"—that can be interpreted as invalidating the importance of the George-Helen association and by inference his own involvement with Lois. The dominant theme of the story is not George's relationships with the two women, however. Rather, "Magnetism" seems a study of George's relationship with himself and how he handles fame and "magnetism" in his life away from the public, a situation to which Fitzgerald could well relate. In all these respects, "Magnetism" was a very personal story for Fitzgerald. In terms of Lois's influence upon it, Helen Avery is more polished and accomplished than Jenny, but the underlying story of her involvement with an older man remains the same.

In "The Rough Crossing," published in the June 8, 1929, issue of the *Saturday Evening Post*, Fitzgerald fused elements from both "Jacob's Ladder" and "Magnetism," creating as a main character a married man in show business who experiences an intense infatuation with a younger girl. The focus of "The Rough Crossing," however, is decidedly on the marriage instead of the infatuation. It is also a darker, more intense story in which Fitzgerald drew his characters with the unflinching realism that he would utilize so masterfully in *Tender Is the Night*. It is perhaps technically the best-written of the short fiction he wrote in which he based characters upon Lois; but, at the same time, he here presents the Lois-based character, Betsy D'Amido, with a certain amount of asperity and recrimination. Fitzgerald writes the male character, Adrian Smith, more as a victim of the young girl's ultimately insincere wiles than as a seducer, and he makes sure, as he had done in "Magnetism," that the character he so clearly based on himself says to the girl that he feels "terrible" about their involvement.

Fitzgerald may have feared that this story, like the other two, would all too easily be seen as autobiography; therefore, he seems to have deliberately kept it vague as to just how far the involvement between Adrian and Betsy goes. Furthering his more critical portrayal of the girl character, Fitzgerald also greatly diminished her importance in the story. It is the wife, Eva, who is the central female character, and Fitzgerald creates her with careful detail, which is interesting because this was the last of his major Lois-based short stories and, if the story mirrors real life, shows that as time went by Fitzgerald had become less admiring of Lois, and more appreciative of Zelda. The unflattering characterization here of Betsy prefigures unpleasant elements he would incorporate into Rosemary in *Tender Is the Night*. Fitzgerald also drew upon real life—Zelda's throwing her watch out a train window—for the story's most electrifying moment, when Eva throws an article of jewelry from the ship.

To judge from this story, in Fitzgerald was still very much aware of Lois, as was Zelda. Looking at "The Rough Crossing" as a reflection of Fitzgerald's life at the time, one comes away with the realization that the Fitzgerald marriage was still bruised because of Scott's affair with Lois. At the time it was written, Scott and Lois were still in contact, as evidenced by her 1929 journal entries; his marriage to Zelda continued to be tumultuous; and in 1928 the Fitzgeralds had sailed back to America after visiting Europe, a telling fact considering that "The Rough Crossing" is set on an ocean liner. There is even a well-known photograph from the period of Scott, Zelda, and Scottie standing on the deck of a cruise ship all looking unhappy, Scott in particular, and the tone of "The Rough Crossing" is indeed melancholy.

In "The Rough Crossing," Adrian Smith, a stage director, embarks upon a cruise with his wife Eva. The trip begins pleasantly, but Adrian soon meets a pretty, tennis-playing eighteen-year-old girl, Elizabeth "Betsy" D'Amido, who for a time bewitches him: "Her youth seemed to flow into him, bearing him up into a delicate, romantic ecstasy that transcended passion. He couldn't relinquish it; he had discovered something that he had thought was lost with his own youth forever." Betsy tells Adrian that she loves him, and they kiss. In the meantime, Eva becomes seasick. Confined to her cabin, she is nevertheless intensely aware of the situation developing between her husband and Betsy. Fitzgerald, typically, is not specific as to how far the flirtation between Betsy and Adrian goes, though the implication is that the kissing was the extent of it. Eva is upset and hurt by Adrian's interest in Betsy and complains to Adrian, "Oh, the younger set. And you just having the time of your life—with a child," a line Zelda may have had in mind in her 1930 letter to Scott in which she accused him of having had "flagrantly sentimental relations with a child"—Lois.

The trouble in the Smiths' marriage is symbolized by an intense storm that drenches and shakes the ship mercilessly. Fitzgerald uses this metaphor powerfully in the story's most dramatic and unnerving moment. A party is held on the ship that most of the passengers cannot attend because of seasickness, but Eva, certain that Adrian and Betsy have arranged an assignation, forces herself to go. Still seasick, she drinks too much. Inebriated, depressed, and losing sight of Adrian, physically and emotionally, she wanders onto the storm-swept deck and in an act of rage and hurt removes the prized pearl necklace Adrian had given to her and flings it into the dark ocean. The next day the Smiths have a bitter argument, but when Eva disappears into the storm Adrian goes after her, and they are thrown together by an enormous wave that crashes down onto the ship. The story ends as the passengers leave on a boat train. Adrian and Eva are bewildered by the strange course their marriage had just taken and agree that the whole episode had to have been nothing more than a bad dream. Adrian promises to replace her pearls in Paris. Betsy's last appearance in the story is when she strolls by and tells them that after weathering such a storm she hopes she will be recognizable to her fiancé. Then "she passed gracefully along the corridor and out of their life."

The parallels between this story and Fitzgerald's life are readily apparent. Fitzgerald, fresh from a cruise, utilized a ship and storm motif to boldly tell his story of a marriage between two handsome and urbane people that enters rough waters when the husband begins paying his attentions to a young girl. Adrian and Eva are clearly Scott and Zelda, and Betsy, moreover, is reminiscent of Lois—young, vivacious, and athletic (one is reminded of the many Hollywood publicity photos that were issued of Lois playing tennis, as well as of her friendship with the tennis celebrity Bill Tilden)—and when she professes to Adrian, "I fell in love with you the minute I saw you," it evokes the depth of feeling Lois expressed in real life about Fitzgerald. In "The Rough Crossing," however, Fitzgerald sympathizes with the wife, and the girl is seen at the end of the story as insincere and manipulative, telling Adrian that she has a fiancé and therefore their involvement had meant nothing to her.

Betsy's display of coldness makes the reader inevitably wonder whether in making her so unlikable Fitzgerald was somehow indicting Lois for some wrong. Perhaps the obscure incident he mentions in his 1935 letter to her—the one in which she had put him "on the spot," presumably about his drinking—had already occurred, and he was using the character Betsy as a conduit for his anger toward Lois. Then, too, in hardening his depiction of the young girl, he could have been placating Zelda. It is possible that in vilifying the character he was indirectly condemning himself for having himself been attracted to a girl such as Lois, who was so much younger than he, but this explanation is unlikely: Adrian bemoans that he feels bad about the developing relationship, thus expiating much of the censure he would otherwise have received. There is another reading of Betsy, however. It is possible that her abrupt exit was actually an act of caring, of tough love. She knows she has been involved with a vulnerable man, endangering his marriage, and wishes to atone for it by feigning an engagement and a callous demeanor, thereby distancing him and placing him back into his marriage. This problem with this approach to Betsy, however, is that nothing is set forth earlier in the story to suggest that she had the maturity or sensitivity to effect such a selfless act. It seems more probable that Betsy was just as she appeared, a shallow girl who uses Adrian as the object of a brief infatuation on a trip and nothing more. The ethereal qualities of the Lois-based characters in "Jacob's Ladder" and "Magnetism" have here been stripped away. What is left is a girl who, although physically attractive, is flawed in character.

In these stories, Fitzgerald blended details from his own life and fantasy to create three very different tales that each featured the interactions of an older man with a younger woman. At a time in his life when Fitzgerald considered himself ancient, his thirties, he created male characters who were the same age and who were undergoing the same emotional difficulties. Today, we can recognize that Fitzgerald was going through a prolonged midlife crisis and that, as is typical of many men in that situation, it had become extremely important to him to be thought of as attractive and successful by a younger woman. In life, Lois fulfilled this need for Fitzgerald, and she was important enough to him that within two years of having met her he had published the three high-profile *Saturday Evening Post* stories that featured her. As literature, the writings sparkle with his graceful language and style. When the stories are approached as autobiography, though, they reveal a fascinating secondary significance and shed light as to where Fitzgerald was in his mind and life as the 1920s were ending.

On this last point, the most apparent fact that emerges from the stories is that the Lois-themed character becomes less important, while the Fitzgerald-based character becomes stronger and more centered upon his life and, in two of the stories, his marriage. As each of the three stories appeared, the Lois-based characters became less and less attractive, degenerating from the Madonna-like Jenny in "Jacob's Ladder" to the hardened, manipulative Betsy in "The Rough Crossing." At the same time, the male characters Fitzgerald based upon himself became stronger in their own identities and less enchanted with the Lois-based characters. At the end of "Jacob's Ladder," Jacob descends into a dark, brokenhearted world because Jenny does not reciprocate his feelings for her; but by the end of "The Rough Crossing" Adrian Smith has a new level of self-respect and strength as he calmly watches Betsy walk out of his life in the clear light of day.

Between 1927 and 1929, Fitzgerald seemingly had overcome some of his personal angst in regard to Lois, and by the time he completed his third and final Lois-themed story one might conclude that she had outlived her literary usefulness to him. In actuality, however, it had only just begun. In *Tender Is the Night* he went on to create a longer, more complex, and more detailed characterization based on Lois, that of Rosemary Hoyt. As for Lois, she no doubt recognized herself in Fitzgerald's short fiction and was pleased and flattered to be a part of it. At the time, however, she could not have known the importance her affair with Fitzgerald would in later years come to assume in her life. In the 1920s, her priority was to achieve recognition for her own accomplishments and ambitions. It would have been inconceivable to her then that in 1934, only a few years after the appearance of "The Rough Crossing," Fitzgerald would set into motion a major part of her legacy by modeling a lead character after her in one of the century's best-known novels, thereby creating, to the detriment of the memory of her work as an actress, an indelible place for her, not in Hollywood history, but in literary mythology.

Before delving into *Tender Is the Night*, however, it is necessary to augment the discussion of Fitzgerald's Lois-inspired short fiction. In addition to the three *Saturday Evening Post* stories already discussed, Fitzgerald also incorporated Lois more briefly into several of his other short works: five additional *Saturday Evening Post* stories, "The Bowl," "The Love Boat," "At Your Age," "The Swimmers," and "A Freeze-Out"; a 1927 nonfiction essay that appeared in *College Humor*; and *The Last Tycoon*, the unfinished novel on which he was working at the time of his death. Lois's presence in these works is minimal but nonetheless interesting. "The Bowl" (January 21, 1928), the most significant of the secondary Lois-themed stories, was about a football player who copes with ambiguous feelings about the game as well as with being engaged to the wrong girl. Although he has a love-hate relationship with football, the sport really is his passion in life. However, he convinces himself to abandon football and instead pursue his relationship with the girl, who does not approve of his being a football player because her brother had died after being injured in a football game. The young man eventually returns to the sport and realizes that the girl is wrong for him. At the story's end, having broken his ankle and broken up with the girl, he meets Daisy Cary, a young film actress who is as passionate about her career as he is about football. She commiserates with his injury and tells him that she, too, once suffered physically because of her work: she was making a film when she had a fever but nevertheless had to dive repeatedly into a canal on the set, which led to pneumonia. The two are smitten with each other, and the story ends with the implication that they will make a happy couple because they understand each other's love of what they do. As brief as Daisy Cary's appearance was in the story, she was undoubtedly based on Lois: she is a film actress who is dedicated to her work, and the canal scene parallels a similar episode in Lois's life that had occurred while she was filming the lake sequence in *The Prince of Tempters.*

The other secondary *Post* stories each concerned an older man who eases the angst of his life by idealizing younger women. Given the fact that Fitzgerald wrote them in the late 1920s and early 1930s, a period when Lois was still much on his mind, it is probable that he was again mirroring his own relationship with her in this fiction. In "The Love Boat" (October 8, 1927), Bill Frothington, a man in his late twenties, is married but looks back to a girl he met at a high school dance, Mae Purley, as representing the happy youth that he feels he has lost. In "At Your Age" (August 17, 1929), Tom Squires, age fifty, wishes to restore youth to his life before it is too late and becomes engaged to a young debutante, Annie Lorry. He comes to see, however, that the age difference would prevent them from being happy and breaks off the engagement. In "The Swimmers" (October 19, 1929), Henry Clay Marston, a thirty-five-year-old living in Paris, suffers a breakdown when he discovers his wife with another man. While he is recovering, he goes to the shore, where he meets a nameless, clean-scrubbed, all-American girl of about eighteen who, by teaching him to swim, helps him reclaim balance in his life. This story seems particularly autobiographical: the wife's infidelity recalls Zelda's affair with Jozan, and the girl's age and athleticism are suggestive of Lois. In "A Freeze-Out" (December 19, 1931), Forrest Winslow falls in love with a beautiful younger girl, Alida Rikker, whose purity of character entrances him; he marries her even though she is of lower social standing.

Fitzgerald made what was perhaps his only overt in-print statement about Lois in an essay he authored about his alma mater for *College Humor.* "Princeton" appeared in December 1927 and consisted of musings about the school's history. In one passage, he notes that although Princeton had changed over time, undergraduate appreciation for the fairer sex had not, and he mentions Lois's visits to the campus as proof. "There is less singing and dancing," he wrote of Princeton in the mid-1920s. "The keg parties are over but the stags line up for a hundred yards to cut in on young Lois Moran."

The Last Tycoon, published posthumously in 1941, was based on Fitzgerald's experiences in Hollywood. It is narrated in the first person by a young girl, Cecilia, whom some believe Fitzgerald based upon Lois. In fact, he based her dually upon his daughter and his friend Budd Schulberg. However, an episode in the early pages of the book does recall one from Lois's life. In an airplane, Cecilia is chatting with the stewardess, who tells her of an actress and her mother whom she had encountered on a westward flight two years earlier. It was the height of the depression, the stewardess tells Cecilia, and the actress was so preoccupied with finances that she confided to the stewardess, "I know what mother and *I* are going to do. We're coming out to the Yellowstone and we're just going to live simply till it all blows over. Then we'll come back." Lois had in fact said just this on numerous occasions. Fitzgerald referred to her Yellowstone theory in his notebooks; and in October 1931, she expressed her belief in the value of fleeing to the wilderness in a letter to Don Tressider, then president of Stanford University, about her view of the depression and her place in it. "Conditions certainly are horrible," she wrote. "Mother think[s] that 1932 will be a terrible year and that we will all be safer in the mountains or ranches or in the Valley." Fitzgerald's reference to Lois in *The Last Tycoon* was undoubtedly the last he ever made of her in his fiction.

...is Moran and F. Scott Fitzgerald at ...erslie, spring, 1927. Carl Van Vechten ...be glimpsed peering behind Fitzgerald; *far left* is Ernest Boyd.

Lois photographed in Paris by Fontaine in 1925. Her habit of looking upward was a trait Fitzgerald admired.

A 1920s postcard folder depicts Mary Pickford and Douglas Fairbanks Sr. at Pickfair, their famed home where Lois met Fitzgerald at a party in early 1927.

...ght: The Ambassador Hotel on ...lshire Boulevard in Los Angeles as ...ooked at the time Scott and Zelda ...zgerald stayed there while he was in ...vn to write "Lipstick" for Constance ...lmadge.

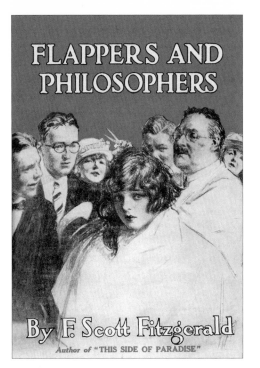

The original dust jacket by W. E. Hill for Fitzgerald's *Flappers and Philosophers*, 1920. Lois filmed a scene in *Publicity Madness*, 1927, that uncannily resembled this by then well-known illustration.

Carmel Myers, like Lois an intelligent screen actress and a friend of the Fitzgeralds, occupied a bungalow next to them at the Ambassador in 1927.

Fitzgerald was attracted to Lois's intellect. She is glimpsed here engrossed in a book at her Beverly Hills home at 517 Elm Street.

Top left: A photo depicting Gene Tunney in his first, championship-winning fight against Jack Dempsey in Philadelphia on September 23, 1926. Lois attended a party in his honor with Scott and Zelda at the Ritz Hotel in New York in early 1927. Fitzgerald could hardly be separated from the pugilist.

Top right: John Barrymore occupied a bungalow adjoining the Fitzgeralds' at the Ambassador in 1927. At the time, he quarreled with Fitzgerald over Fitzgerald's attentions to Lois.

Scott, Zelda, and Scottie Fitzgerald in Paris, Christmas 1925.

Lois Moran celebrates Christmas in Hollywood, ca. 1927–1928.

Ralph Barton's June 1927 *Vanity Fair* illustration that depicts Fitzgerald, *right side of the first page, middle*, and Lois, *bottom of the second page, far right*.

Lois and Ben Lyon in the swimming scene in *The Prince of Tempters* that Fitzgerald drew from in "The Bowl," 1928, and *Tender Is the Night*, 1934.

Right: Lois and Carl Van Vechten photographed together in 1927 in a newspaper clipping that survives in one of her scrapbooks. She disliked his 1928 novel *Spider Boy* but otherwise was captivated by the writer and amateur photographer, who was present with her at the Fitzgeralds' 1927 Ellerslie party.

Lois's custom-made bookplate of the 1920 She affixed the label to books in her personal library by the likes of Fitzgerald, Van Vechten, Hemingway, and T. S. Eliot.

Lois as photographed by her friend Carl Van Vechten in 1932.

ois and Ronald Colman in *Stella Dallas*. cenes such as these likely prompted itzgerald to use this title for the film for hich Lois's fictional counterpart, Rosemary oyt in *Tender Is the Night*, is famous: *addy's Girl*.

Gladys, photographed by Chidnoff in New York, who was not necessarily as approving of Lois's relationship with Fitzgerald as is popularly believed.

ctress Betsy Blair, Lois's cousin, who, as a hild, overheard Gladys complaining about ois's involvement with Fitzgerald.

F. Scott Fitzgerald in the 1920s. At the time, his good looks contributed to his fame.

LOIS MORAN, Fox star—
The next time you see
her in a close-up, notice
how lovely Lux Toilet
Soap keeps her skin. She
says: "Even the finest
French soap could not
leave my skin more won-
derfully smooth than
Lux Toilet Soap does."

Photo by C. Hewitt, Hollywood

F. SCOTT FITZGERALD

—because, as the most brilliant of America's younger novelists, he was the first to discover and portray an enchanting new type of American girl. Because, at the age of 23, he woke up to find himself famous as the author of *"This Side of Paradise."* Because no other man of his time writes so sympathetically, skilfully, and fascinatingly about women.

Neither Lois nor Fitzgerald were immune to the advertising craze of the 1920s. *Above*: Lois endorses Lux Toilet Soap. *Right*: Fitzgerald endorses Woodbury's Facial Soap.

Left: Fitzgerald, *right*, in 1927 as a Hollywood tourist, poses on a film set with Richard Barthelmess, who most likely was filming *Out of the Ruins*, a war film released in 1928.

Lois swathed in glitter and fur in the late 1920s, epitomizing Fitzgerald's description of Rosemary Hoyt's "starry-eyed confidence" in *Tender Is the Night*.

Lois Moran, photographed at Paramount by Eugene Robert Richee in 1927. The photograph was inscribed to the author in 1988.

Tender Is the Night, Beautiful Fairy Tales, and the Shadow of Rosemary

9

*F*rom the time of the earliest Fitzgerald scholarly research, going back as far as the first biography (Mizener's *The Far Side of Paradise,* 1951), biographers have agreed that Fitzgerald's unquestioned inspiration for the character of Rosemary Hoyt in *Tender Is the Night* was Lois Moran. Researchers have discussed the biographical details of Fitzgerald's relationship with Lois as the basis for Rosemary; and Lois herself, while maintaining that *Tender Is the Night* was only fiction, did confirm, whenever she was asked, that she was indeed the model for the character. "Rosemary was an accurate portrait of me at the age of seventeen, though the circumstances were changed," she remarked, before she had become jaded on the issue, in a mid-1950s interview done for a program about Fitzgerald for NBC's radio series *Biography in Sound.* "For instance, I never met Scott in Europe. We met in America. And the emotional content was perhaps lifted or built into a bigger thing, but on the whole it was a very fine portrait and I'm kind of proud of it."

Lois's own acknowledgment of having inspired Rosemary and the biographical particulars have generally formed the foundation of any discussion of her influence upon the novel; but while this approach is in itself sound and convincing, it does not address a major facet of the genesis of Rosemary: exactly what characteristics, traits, and personality details did Fitzgerald observe in Lois that he incorporated into Rosemary, and in what ways did Lois and the character differ? While Fitzgerald did not create Rosemary as a mirror image of Lois, he drew extensively from his association with her in writing in the details of the character. A phenomenally observant man with a penchant for grilling his acquaintances for details about their personal lives, he scrutinized Lois as if she were a specimen under the lens of his literary microscope. An examination of the process of the book's composition demonstrates how Fitzgerald came to base characters in it both on people he knew in real life, even himself.

Fitzgerald labored for years on *Tender Is the Night*, and he had high ambitions that the work would stand as his masterpiece, greater even than *The Great Gatsby*. In fact, he had the initial idea for the new work less than a month after the publication of *Gatsby* in 1925, and he spent the next nine years in agonizing writing and rewriting, numerous revisions, and multiple manuscripts to create *Tender Is the Night*. He originally intended the story to be about a character called Francis Melarky, a young American who murders his domineering mother while they are traveling through Europe. From 1925 to 1930, he wrote five drafts of the Melarky version of the story. In 1929, however, he began to change it to reflect events that were occurring in his own life. After going to Hollywood in 1927 and meeting Lois at Pickfair, he began to introduce new film-related characters into the story that were in large part the products of his own experiences in the film colony and observations of the people in it. These characters included Lew Kelly, a film director; his wife, Nicole; and a young actress named Rosemary. Recalling "The Rough Crossing," Fitzgerald wrote chapters about the director and his wife traveling aboard a ship and encountering the young actress. He abandoned this story line in 1930, however, and returned to the Melarky plot.

Soon events in his personal life again influenced the course he took with his project, for in 1930 Zelda suffered an emotional collapse and was hospitalized in Switzerland. Fitzgerald was deeply affected by the calamity and began to feel a strong urge to write about it rather than about the Melarky story. He first penned a story, published in the *Saturday Evening Post*, entitled "One Trip Abroad," in which a young American couple, Nelson and Nicole Kelly, journey to France to study music and art. There they enter into a life of dissipation and are eventually hospitalized in a Swiss clinic. Fitzgerald was slowly veering away from the Melarky plot, with its theme of matricide, and developing something that was much more a product of his personal experiences and emotions. As Lois remarked in the *Biography in Sound* interview, "I suppose that was a conflict with Scott. There were other people and yet this great urge to write. Consequently, he used all his friends in books. Although lightly disguised, it was pretty easy to recognize everybody." Fitzgerald also drew elements from Gerald and Sarah Murphy, with whom he was the best of friends on the French Riviera, as models for certain characteristics of the married couple.

Fitzgerald determined to give up the Melarky aspect of the novel once and for all when, back in America in February 1932, Zelda suffered another breakdown and was hospitalized at the Phipps Psychiatric Clinic of the Johns Hopkins Hospital in Baltimore, Maryland. Now Fitzgerald decided that the story would be about a mentally ill woman, a character based upon Zelda but for whom he retained the name Nicole. Writing such a character was difficult for him, but it proved cathartic and helped him to cope with his own personal difficulties. Nicole's husband, Dick Diver, is a once-promising psychiatrist who has been broken by personal and professional disappointments—a character Fitzgerald based to a great extent on himself. Like Fitzgerald, Dick feels overwhelmed by a sense a failure and is convinced he is old even though he is only in his thirties. Fitzgerald also continued to develop the character of the actress, Rosemary, and began basing her more specifically upon Lois.

Through a process of continual work and revision, Fitzgerald authored initial manuscripts for the story that he called "The Drunkard's Holiday" and "Doctor Diver's Holiday: A Romance." He eventually found a far more striking title for his project in a phrase from "Ode to a Nightingale," by his favorite poet, John Keats. Because he needed money, and because his publisher, Scribner's, wanted to do some advance publicity for the book, Fitzgerald consented to have *Tender Is the Night* appear first in serial form in *Scribner's Magazine*. Thus, from January to April 1934, a period during which Lois was still in the public eye, Fitzgerald's story appeared in magazine installments, and it came out in book form shortly thereafter. In terms of Lois, it seems entirely appropriate that the story was originally published serially, for two of her biggest films, *Stella Dallas* and *Padlocked*, had been based on best-selling books that had first appeared as magazine installments.

The story opens on the French Riviera in the summer of 1925. A seventeen-year-old movie actress, Rosemary Hoyt, arrives there on vacation with her widowed mother, Elsie Speers. At a beach near a resort hotel, Rosemary encounters a group of older, worldlier people that includes a married couple of great warmth and beauty, Dick and Nicole Diver. Soon, the girl forms friendships with several of the people she meets at the beach, especially with Dick, a psychiatrist in his thirties to whom she is attracted. She and Dick slowly begin to carry on a flirtatious but platonic relationship, and after attending a dinner party given by the Divers, Rosemary, utterly charmed by him, falls in love. Dick gradually begins to reciprocate when he sees and is impressed by her film *Daddy's Girl*. Feeling middle-aged and past his prime, he comes to crave her youth and vitality, qualities he feels are so terribly lacking in his own life. The two eventually share a kiss in a taxicab in Paris, but the bliss Rosemary begins to feel is upset by two events. First, in a subplot involving Abe North, one of her acquaintances from the beach, a man is found dead in her bed, and it is only through Dick's quick thinking that her career is saved from scandal. Secondly, a short time later she witnesses Nicole, in a bathroom in a Paris hotel, swaying back and forth near the tub and ranting psychotically at Dick, one of our first clues we have that all is not well with Mrs. Diver.

Fitzgerald then takes the reader back in time to 1919 and relates how Dick, a young and promising American psychiatrist, has been called in on the case of a wealthy mental patient, Nicole Warren. Slowly, Dick becomes more and more involved with Nicole and her family, especially her father, who admits to having had an incestuous episode with Nicole, and the aloof Baby, Nicole's sister. Dick falls in love with Nicole and they marry. Although blessed with two children, their marriage is otherwise plagued by Nicole's relapses and Dick's slow sublimation of his own personality and ambitions into the easy lifestyle provided him by the Warren money.

Fitzgerald next moves his story back to the present day. The Diver marriage is more tumultuous than ever, and as it disintegrates Dick becomes increasingly involved with Rosemary, telling Mrs. Speers that he loves her daughter and obsessing over the girl. Dick encounters Rosemary in Rome, where she is making a film, and in her hotel room they consummate their relationship. The experience is an empty one for Dick, however, and he begins to feel disillusioned with the girl. The relationship between him and Rosemary weakens and is particularly compromised when Rosemary tells him that she plans to marry a Latin film actor, Nicotera. He retaliates in his way by presuming to give her acting advice, in marked contrast to his first bedazzled reaction to her when he had seen *Daddy's Girl*, and gives too much credibility to a gossipy story Rosemary's devoted friend Collis Clay tells him about a supposed sexual indiscretion she is said to have had with an undergraduate aboard a Pullman train. In the meantime, Nicole, who knows of Dick and Rosemary's relationship, gradually becomes stronger psychologically and less dependent upon Dick; she eventually falls in love with a soldier of fortune named Tommy Barban. The Divers divorce, Nicole marries Tommy, and Dick leaves life in Europe, including Nicole and Rosemary, behind him and returns to America, where he becomes an itinerant small-town doctor. Fitzgerald does not specifically state what becomes of Rosemary, but one assumes that she marries Nicotera and continues her career as a film actress.

To describe Rosemary's appearance, Fitzgerald employed lush language in which he drew upon some basic facts about Lois. Like Lois, Rosemary has a physique toned by swimming. Like Lois, Rosemary was also a dancer, a pursuit that has resulted in a "body calculated to a millimeter to suggest a bud yet guarantee a flower" and in her carrying herself "like a ballet-dancer, not slumped down on her hips but held up in the small of her back." Moreover, Fitzgerald writes, Rosemary is known for the "unguarded sweetness of her smile," the "dazzling" quality of her skin, and, as Dick tells her, for being a girl "that actually did look like something blooming." Such portrayals vividly recall what had been written about Lois by the press and by studio publicists, but Fitzgerald's description of Rosemary rivaled any that had ever been written of Lois:

> [She] had magic in her pink palms and her cheeks lit to a lovely flame, like the thrilling flush of children after their cold baths in the evening. Her fine forehead sloped gently up to where her hair, bordering it like an armorial shield, burst into lovelocks and waves and curlicues of ash blonde and gold. Her eyes were bright, big, clear, wet, and shining, the color of her cheeks was real, breaking close to the surface from the strong young pump of her heart. Her body hovered delicately on the last edge of childhood—she was almost eighteen, nearly complete, but the dew was still on her.

Another important aspect of Lois's life that Fitzgerald utilized for literary purposes was that he instilled in Rosemary, at her first presentation in the novel, Lois's age and her maturity level as he perceived it when he first met her at the Pickfair party in 1927. Rosemary is seventeen, has never had a drink, and is innocent of and naive about the world, a fact the character would be the first to deny but that Fitzgerald conveys to the reader when he has her childishly exclaim "Heavens!" to express surprise or shock no less than twice in the first ten pages. Furthermore, as Fitzgerald points out, she "had yet to attend a Mayfair party in Hollywood." It is not too great a leap to infer that Mayfair, a popular Los Angeles hotel, is here intended as a reference to Pickfair.

Fitzgerald further details Rosemary's age and experience in terms of her devotion to her mother, whom he here calls Elsie Speers, and in this respect he is clearly and directly writing about Lois, who so adored her own mother and said as much in press interviews, her journals, and conversation with friends. Indeed, anyone who knew Lois at the time knew of the strong bond between her and her mother, and Fitzgerald exploited this relationship fully in his tale by creating in Rosemary a maternal devotion so intense that it may even have gone beyond its real-life model and bordered on parody. From the book's first pages, Rosemary is constantly thinking of her mother, whose photograph she carries with her and whom she calls "Mother, darling" (Fitzgerald's apparent reference to the terms Lois used to address Gladys, "Mother, dear" and "Angel face"), and she never makes a move not sanctioned by her parent. Mrs. Speers "always had a great influence" upon Rosemary; the girl views her as "forever perfect" and is portrayed by Fitzgerald as "falling in love with her mother's profile against a lighted door." She even tells the film director Earl Brady, a secondary character in the novel, "I couldn't do without her." And, like Gladys, Mrs. Speers has also a strong hand in her daughter's business matters and career decisions. The relationship between Rosemary and Mrs. Speers is best seen in a small but meaningful scene at the book's beginning. Rosemary, at the beach on the French Riviera, wonders whether her mother, napping at the hotel, will be able to sleep in the heat of the day. This strongly suggests the frequent naps that Gladys had to take because of her headaches and Lois's concern for her comfort in this regard.

It is no surprise that Fitzgerald modeled the character of Elsie Speers after Lois's own mother and did so in precise ways. Like Gladys, Mrs. Speers comes from the American midwestern middle class, is a doctor's widow, is her daughter's "best friend," and capitulates the child "onto the uncharted heights of Hollywood" after having taken her to

Paris, where Rosemary, recalling Lois's tenure at the Paris Ballet, had "obeyed the sure, clear voice that had sent her into the stage entrance of the Odeon...when she was twelve and greeted her when she came out again." At the same time, just like Gladys, Mrs. Speers "was not recompensing herself for a defeat of her own. She had no personal bitterness or resentments about life."

Fitzgerald instilled other biographical details and personality traits of Lois into Rosemary as well, and sprinkled his narrative with specifics about Rosemary's life and career that correspond strongly to those of Lois. For example, Rosemary went to school in Paris, where, we are told, she made herself ill drinking too much lemonade, experiences that appear to draw upon the time Lois lived there and the fact that she frequently consumed grenadine, a sweet children's drink, when she visited the cafés with her friend Michael Knox. Rosemary also enjoys having dresses made—in the novel, she runs into Nicole at a dressmaker's—and she likes to shop for clothes when she is happy, such as when the character, in a buoyant mood, purchases a pair of espadrilles, facts that recall Lois's own predilection for having dresses made for herself, especially by Charles Le Maire. Another Moran-based particular is seen in an Italian hotel room, when Rosemary receives a telephone call from someone who once knew a second cousin of hers. Fitzgerald may have inserted this episode, which does not forward the plot and seems out of place in the narrative flow, as a way of including some reference to Lois's family and acquaintances back in Pittsburgh, who continued to follow Lois's career for years after she and Gladys had parted from them. Yet another, and particularly obvious, Lois detail that Fitzgerald wove into Rosemary was Lois's delight in wearing those wristwatches, which she all too often seemed to lose and which so annoyed Zelda Fitzgerald. Fitzgerald uses this detail ingeniously, combining it with Lois's adoration of Gladys, to create one of the most inspired moments of the story, for it is when Rosemary goes to the desk in her Paris hotel room to write a letter to her mother and discovers the watch she thought she had lost that she becomes aware of the corpse in her bed.

It is important also to note that Fitzgerald took pains throughout the novel to inform the reader that Rosemary had a strong work ethic, for which the real-life Lois was well known. Like Lois, Rosemary was a product of her American middle-class background and placed a high priority on work: "Rosemary had been brought up with the idea of work." One is reminded of the interviews Gladys gave early on in Lois's career in which she spoke of Lois's realizing from a very young age that she would need to work. Rosemary "knew little of leisure but she had the respect for it of those who have never had it," and she sees in Dick attributes she saw in herself: "She felt the layer of hardness of him, of self-control and of self-discipline, her own virtues." Such passages are reminiscent of the long hours Lois put in on studio sets, where she learned to take naps between takes, and the instances when, in writing in her journal after a day's shooting, she was so exhausted she would spill ink onto her desk. They also recall the vigorous physical routine she followed.

The subject of work segues into another area of Lois's life that Fitzgerald found fertile for use in creating Rosemary: her film career. Rosemary is, after all, a freshly minted movie star, exactly what Lois had been when Fitzgerald first knew her, and it is in this context that some of the strongest parallels between the literary character and the real person can be drawn. By the time he was engrossed in writing *Tender Is the Night*, in the late 1920s and early 1930s, Fitzgerald was unquestionably aware of *Stella Dallas* and of the immediate stardom it had brought to Lois. He seems to broadly refer to the process by which Samuel Goldwyn had signed Lois for *Stella Dallas* when he explains:

> Mrs. Speers had spent the slim leavings of the men who had widowed her on her daughter's education, and when she blossomed out at sixteen with that extraordinary hair, rushed her to Aix-les-Bains and marched her unannounced into the suite of an American

producer who was recuperating there. When the producer went to New York they went too. Thus Rosemary had passed her entrance examinations.

Lois had been catapulted to fame by one film, *Stella Dallas*, and Rosemary has also achieved renown via a single movie, a picture entitled *Daddy's Girl* in which she had earned much adulation by enacting an innocent and inexperienced child, much like Laurel in *Stella Dallas*. Fitzgerald's calling the picture *Daddy's Girl* plays upon multiple elements. Most obviously, it relates to the plot of the novel in that it rather starkly refers to the incestuous relationship Nicole had with her father. It also carries connotations of Lois's life and career. The title alludes to the parent-child themes of *Stella Dallas*; it suggests Lois's own fond remembrances of her father and stepfather; it brings to mind Lois's attraction to older men; and it conjures the mystique of unaffected youth for which Lois had become famous in her films. Rosemary's performance in *Daddy's Girl* also recalls Lois's in *Stella Dallas*. Fitzgerald describes Dick Diver seeing a screening of *Daddy's Girl* in a lovely passage that could easily, if a bit too obviously, refer to Lois in *Stella Dallas*:

> There she was—the school girl of a year ago, hair down her back and rippling out stiffly like the solid hair of a tanagra figure; there she was—*so* young and innocent—the product of her mother's loving care; there she was—embodying all the immaturity of the race, cutting a new cardboard paper doll to pass before its empty harlot's mind.

Also along the lines of *Stella Dallas*, Fitzgerald made use of Lois's contract with Goldwyn, which had required her to remain "unmodern and unsophisticated." In the sequence in which Rosemary discovers the corpse in her hotel room, Dick is acutely aware that if he does not intervene "no power on earth could keep the smear off Rosemary—the paint was scarcely dry on the Arbuckle case. Her contract was contingent upon an obligation to continue rigidly and unexceptionally as 'Daddy's Girl.'" In calling the contract into play in the context of this potential scandal, Fitzgerald brilliantly exposes the extreme limitations such a morality clause could place on an actress, for it puts Rosemary at risk of losing her career because of a situation for which she is not responsible and over which she has no control. Such restrictions certainly plagued Lois, who was well aware of the expectations placed upon her by both Hollywood and the public to maintain her "child wonder" image, although unlike Rosemary she never had to deal with a scandal that threatened her career.

Fitzgerald also wrote into Rosemary's character the inevitable sense of constriction that had resulted from being overly identified with a single character, the one she enacted in *Daddy's Girl*. Such typecasting had also branded Lois. Just as Rosemary is always thought of as being the star of *Daddy's Girl*, Lois was all too often thought of as the girl from *Stella Dallas*. In this context, Rosemary utters in the novel a sentiment about the public's perception of her to which Lois herself probably gave voice a thousand times. Early in Rosemary's career she tells her mother, with some pleasure and conceit, that people recognized her wherever she went because of *Daddy's Girl*, but as the story progresses and years pass she becomes increasingly resentful of being identified so ceaselessly for a single picture. She explains to Earl Brady, "Nobody wants to be thought of forever for just one picture." In a moment of Fitzgerald's dead-on observation of detail, Brady, at the time Rosemary encounters him, is directing an actress on how to wear her stockings—an episode Fitzgerald borrowed from "Magnetism"—in an almost certain reference, as in that previous story, to the ribbed stockings Sophie Wachner designed for Lois to wear in *Stella Dallas*.

Because of the success of *Daddy's Girl*, Fitzgerald tells us early on, "Los Angeles was loud about Rosemary," a remark that recalls the laudatory articles published in 1926 about Lois in that city in the *Los Angeles Times* and the *Los Angeles Herald Examiner*. By the novel's end, however, Rosemary has become a bit disillusioned with Hollywood, much as Lois did in the later years of her own career, and she is making a picture entitled *The Grandeur That was Rome*, a synthetic Hollywood epic of lesser quality than *Daddy's Girl* but that purports to give her sex appeal, in contrast to her *Daddy's Girl* image. Lois was also attempting to develop an image of sex appeal when Fitzgerald knew her. In the book, however, Rosemary is not even sure that she will be given the chance to be sexy, complaining to Dick rather resignedly, "I have a good part in this one if it isn't cut." Rosemary's distaste and frustration with a single, popularly held conception of her was very similar to how Lois came to feel as, year after year, she perceived that Hollywood and the public continued to think of her more as Goldwyn's "Fragile Cameo" than as a capable and adult actress.

During the time of his infatuation with Lois, Fitzgerald took note of many other details of her career, and he deftly wove these observations into his creation of Rosemary. As has been mentioned, Rosemary tells Dick that when she was making one of her films she had contracted pneumonia, even though her mother was on the set, when filming a scene in which she was required to dive repeatedly into a Venetian canal. This episode in Rosemary's fictional career echoes four aspects of Lois's real one, all of which Fitzgerald was probably aware: (1) it recalls a love scene in *The Prince of Tempters* that takes place in a lake; (2) it draws upon the ear infection ("swimmer's ear") Lois suffered in 1926 and about which she wrote in her journal; (3) it parallels Lois's strong work ethic, which would have impelled her to continue filming even when it would make her ill; and (4) it refers to the role of Gladys in Lois's life, for Fitzgerald, in including Mrs. Speers on the set when Rosemary films the canal sequence, is alluding to Gladys's constant presence on Lois's film sets (although there is no evidence that Lois ever became ill, because her mother would not countenance her being overworked during filming).

Another detail from Lois's life that Fitzgerald utilized in *Tender Is the Night* was her financial acumen. Rosemary, born to the American middle class, appreciated the money she earned as a film actress and realized that although her income was substantial, it came from her own hard work and was dependent upon her remaining in the movies. It was, therefore, Rosemary understands, a wealth that differed from the old money of Nicole's family, the Warrens. This distinction, the difference between what Fitzgerald famously termed the rich and the very rich, was central to much of Fitzgerald's work, but here it also spoke of Lois's own financial sensibilities. Neither she nor Gladys ever forgot that it had only been through the benevolence of their wealthy relative Edith Darlington that they had been able to leave Pittsburgh, nor did they lose sight of the fact that although their lifestyle in Pittsburgh had been far from impoverished, it could hardly compare to the comfortable, though not ostentatious, manner in which they now lived. There is a scene in the book in which Rosemary is astonished to see how freely Nicole spends her money, and it would be fair to assume that Lois would have had a similar reaction, for although she was not miserly she was careful and cautious about having funds for the future. This awareness of and need for financial security led her and Gladys to invest in the stock market, a fact the press of the day frequently reported, and it does seem probable that Fitzgerald was drawing upon it in his specific reference to Rosemary's finances in the book.

Yet another portion of Lois's life that Fitzgerald found to be of use was the nature of her contractual arrangements in the film community. At the time he wrote *Tender Is the Night*, he had had enough exposure to the workings of Hollywood to grasp how unusual it was that Lois was, when he first met her, a freelance actress in an industry driven by long-term studio contracts, and structuring Rosemary's career along similar lines was an irresistible notion. Consequently, in the novel Rosemary is a freelance actress who is considering projects at various studios, including First National and Famous, real studios at which Lois herself had worked. It cannot be mere coincidence that Fitzgerald here chose to name two studios with which Lois was actually affiliated.

Attuned to every nuance of Lois's career, Fitzgerald was also aware of one of the more problematic aspects of her work as a film actress: the criticism some reviewers leveled at her for what they saw as her lack of sincerity in love scenes. Though she dismissed such criticism as irrelevant, Fitzgerald did not seem to take her at her word, for in the novel he notes, rather pointedly, that Rosemary had felt "aversion...in the playing of certain love scenes in pictures." Also, when Rosemary embarks upon her love affair with Dick, she at first thinks of it as some great scene from one of her films, which would seem to indicate that she lacked utterly the kind of romantic experience that would have enabled her to enact convincing love scenes on film. Fitzgerald was better able than anybody else at the time to judge Lois's romantic capabilities, and in it appears that he sided on this issue with the critics, a point that also comes into play late in the book when Dick does the unthinkable in presuming to give Rosemary acting advice.

Scholars generally believe that Fitzgerald based the character of the director, Earl Brady, whom Rosemary meets at his studio in Monte Carlo, upon Rex Ingram, an important silent-era director who had never made a film with Lois but who did in real life have a studio at La Turbie on the Riviera. The Brady/Ingram theory seems plausible: the film Brady is directing stars a Latin lover type called Nicotera, who is reminiscent of Rudolph Valentino, the legendary actor who had achieved fame in Ingram's hugely successful film *The Four Horsemen of the Apocalypse* in 1921. However, the no-nonsense, even brusque Brady, who is nonetheless quite fond of Rosemary, also brings to mind two other directors with whom Lois actually had worked and who Fitzgerald must have known were her good friends, Allan Dwan and Herbert Brenon; and, further, Fitzgerald could have inserted the Nicotera character not so much to support Brady's being Rex Ingram, but as an acknowledgment of Lois's grief over Valentino's death. Fitzgerald may have used the Monte Carlo locale for Brady's studio as a reference to the fact that much of Lois's film *The Reckless Lady* was set place there.

Fitzgerald appears also to have chosen certain proper names in *Tender Is the Night* because they bore relevance to Lois's life and work. For example, his choice of the name Rosemary might suggest that he knew of Lois's work in *The Road to Mandalay*. Additionally, he may have chosen to call Rosemary's later film in the novel *The Grandeur That Was Rome* as a way of referring to real-life details. On one level, the title recalls the fact that parts of Lois's early film *Feu Mathias Pascal* had been filmed in Rome. Additionally, *The Grandeur That Was Rome* seems to be a reference to *Ben-Hur*, a sword-and-sandal epic that was one of the biggest of all silent films. The Fitzgeralds had met Carmel Myers on the set of *Ben-Hur* in 1924, and Lois had made a vivid impression on the public and the press at the film's New York premiere.

Fitzgerald also carefully notes that, for all of her fame and success of the world of motion pictures, she is at heart unhappy with them, and he remarks of her in a memorable observation which he took pains to word precisely in the galleys, "She was In the movies but not at all At them." Such detachment from her profession leaves Rosemary feeling lonely, an aspect that Fitzgerald furthers throughout the novel when he writes "Actors and directors—those were the only men she had ever known," and "Rosemary was a romantic and her career had not provided many satisfactory opportunities on that score." The former observation was not true of Lois, for she was certainly acquainted with many people besides actors and directors, but the latter does have the ring of truth, for Lois was indeed a romantic.

Elaborating on Rosemary's dissatisfaction with her career, Fitzgerald notes that she views spending time with the Divers as a "return from the derisive and salacious improvisations of the frontier," and even a rainstorm in Paris causes her to think of "full gutters in Beverly Hills," an indication of her opinion of life in California. Here Fitzgerald utilizes one of the most blatantly autobiographical details of his relationship with Lois. Because of her emotional dissatisfaction with her peers in the film community, Rosemary announces that she has arranged a screen test for Dick so that he could come to California and star with her in a film.

It can be seen that Fitzgerald, in borrowing details from Lois's life in writing Rosemary, did so to this point respectfully and more or less accurately. Why, then, would Lois herself, especially in the later years of her life, have been so careful about distancing herself from the book? She was in general gracious and even-tempered about the wave of Fitzmania that overwhelmed her for so many years, but it is also true that she came to resent being so closely associated with Fitzgerald and with *Tender Is the Night*. She stated in the *Biography in Sound* interview in the 1950s that she was "kind of proud" of Rosemary having been based upon her, but by the 1970s and 1980s, perhaps as a result of the overexposure she believed had befallen her because of Fitzgerald (not to mention a few rereadings of the book), she had become considerably more reticent on the issue. In fact, even though Fitzgerald incorporated many complimentary and flattering reflections of Lois into Rosemary, he also created in her negative traits that have lead many readers of the book to dislike the character and, by association, Lois; and the issue of Rosemary's sexual involvement with Dick, and whether or not it was similar to the affair between Lois and Fitzgerald, continues to be a source of debate and conjecture among Fitzgerald buffs and movie historians.

Many readers of *Tender Is the Night* come away from the novel unsure whether Rosemary is a sympathetic character. While Fitzgerald presents great detail about her career, life, and certain personality traits, and in so doing effects a fairly positive portrayal, he includes cutting, even jarring particulars about the character, especially in regard to her sexual ethics, which surface mainly in her relationship with Dick and do not resonate favorably with the reader. Indeed, a variety of Rosemary's actions do not reflect positively upon her integrity as a person.

Immaturity, ego, and self-absorption are the most apparent personality flaws Fitzgerald creates in Rosemary. Young, famous, and adored, she is frequently selfish and even shallow. Because of her profession, she often sees life cinematically, as a member of some unseen audience watching the events of the story unfold as if in a film. This gives Fitzgerald an inspired narrative device, for it allows him to present events as seen though her eyes—which are, additionally, the eyes of an American watching events unfolding in Europe, giving much of the novel a distinctly American flavor in spite of its European locales. But Fitzgerald is not entirely impressed with Rosemary's cinematic outlook and the self-absorption it creates in her. For example, when Rosemary encounters the group of new people at the beach on the French Riviera, he observes, "Her immature mind made no speculations upon the nature of their relation to each other, she was only concerned with their attitude toward herself." She is pleased when one of the women tells her, "We know who you are. You're Rosemary Hoyt...and we all think you're perfectly marvelous and we want to know why you're not back in America making another marvelous moving picture." This episode is not flattering to Rosemary, because when she relates the story to her mother she does so with a "glow of egotism" that wins her few points with the reader. Indeed, she all too often sees life from the perspective of a film star who thinks too much of herself and too little for herself and who is overly concerned about what others think of her. She is, Fitzgerald writes, "untrained to the task of separating out the essential for herself" and has "never done much thinking." For this reason, the sweetness she projects is suspect. She tells Dick, echoing Helen Avery's line in "Magnetism," "Oh, we're such *actors*—you and I," and Fitzgerald describes her as a "little wild thing" that is "absorbed in playing around with chaos." From these details, the reader cannot help but conclude that Rosemary is callow, superficial, and unable to separate herself from the role playing inherent to her career.

Rosemary's insincerity can be glimpsed in four small but telling details. First, she reacts one-dimensionally to that initial kiss in the Paris taxi: "Suddenly she knew...that it was one of her greatest roles and she flung herself into it more passionately." Second, she persists in calling Dick "youngster"—not a term of endearment considering his midlife crisis and fear of growing older. In that context the reference becomes a rather mean-spirited reminder that she is considerably younger than he and hence has a certain power over him. Third, the unpleasant way she treats her admiring friend Collis Clay gives one pause. Fitzgerald may have based Collis on Sonny Selwyn, a devoted friend of Lois and the nephew of Edgar Selwyn, who produced the stage version of *Stella Dallas*. Collis, a boy Rosemary met at Yale, is rather dim and gossipy, but he sincerely adores her and has seen *Daddy's Girl* four times. Her demeanor toward him, however, is, in keeping with the conceit Fitzgerald has established in her character of condescension and disdain. Fourth, when she entertains Dick in her hotel room in Italy, she accepts phone calls from Nicotera, does little to keep Dick from thinking they are having an affair, and makes a doubly offensive remark to Dick about her relationship with the Latin lover: "Do you want me to play around forever with half-wits like Collis Clay?" With this remark, not only does Rosemary needlessly insult Collis, who although not the sharpest tool in the shed is still her friend, but she also implies that the blatant sexuality of a Latin lover, and its implied carnality over intellect, is enough to make her happy. Her calling Collis a "half-wit" is ironic—it applies more to her than to him.

Sex, indeed, is the subject that most turns Rosemary ugly. She is fully aware that Dick is married to Nicole. She knows, too, that Nicole is emotionally unwell, because she had witnessed one of her unbalanced episodes with Dick in the bathroom in the Paris hotel. And, however young and inexperienced she may be, she surely knows that Dick is vulnerable. Yet, she has no qualms about entering into an affair with him. Moreover, she does so in a manner that is not always dignified, in one scene literally begging him for sex and telling him that if she becomes pregnant she could go to Mexico for an abortion, as had another girl at the studio. Moreover, during the affair with Dick, she readily flaunts her relationship with Nicotera, even intimating that she might marry him. In her defense, Rosemary may have been too young and too inexperienced to know better, but Fitzgerald brings even this detail into question. Collis Clay tells Dick a story that had long circulated: Rosemary had been aboard a Pullman train car with an undergraduate and had gone into an unoccupied room with him; they shut the door, and he asked her if he could pull down the blinds because it was hot. A conductor discovered them, however, and, suspecting inappropriate behavior, broke them up. This story suggests that Rosemary is more sophisticated than she lets on and should be able to better gauge her behavior.

Fitzgerald further delineates Rosemary's unsavory character flaws by placing them in the context of her relationship with Nicole. Echoing the way Zelda viewed Lois, Nicole does not like Rosemary, "pointedly" refers to her "as a child," and regards her with suspicion and disdain. Her opinion of Rosemary is subjective, however, so to enhance it Fitzgerald makes carefully thought out use of a concrete plot detail. Like Zelda, Nicole is fully aware of the relationship between her husband and the young actress. In the novel, however, there is no question that it is a sexual one, and, in an important detail, Fitzgerald alters the sequence of events so as to have Dick become involved with Rosemary before Nicole has her affair with Tommy Barban (i.e., Edouard Jozan). In reality, Lois entered Fitzgerald's life after Zelda's involvement with Jozan. By placing the affair between Dick and Rosemary before Nicole's infidelity, Fitzgerald implicitly indicts the two characters, and by association both himself and Lois. He seems to be saying that their interaction may be viewed as understandable cause for Nicole's adultery and thus overtly calls Rosemary's character into question. He further diminishes her likeability when he suggests to the reader that she is the cause of Nicole's second nervous breakdown when Nicole says to Dick, "Things were never the same after Rosemary." Moreover, in one of the more graphic details of the novel, he notes that Nicole wonders if the bedsheets had been bloodied after

Dick has had sexual intercourse with Rosemary, an unsettling image that, in the context of adultery, is in its very ugliness a further taint upon Rosemary, whose image as a sweet and pure girl is now further compromised.

Dick sees in Rosemary "all the world's dark magic; the blinding belladonna, the caftein converting physical into nervous energy, the mandragora that imposes harmony." His relationship with her is actually more cacophony than harmony, however, for while he is intent upon keeping knowledge of the affair from Nicole, he becomes increasingly "swayed and driven as an animal" and becomes sexually obsessed with the girl, often remembering the alleged Pullman car episode. Rosemary, who does not reciprocate the depth of his feelings and rather coldly calculates her options when Nicotera enters into the picture, could ennoble herself by dissuading his attentions. But she does not, and it is this inaction that is most damaging to her character and the reader's sympathy for her. The reader tires of her long before Dick does—presumably, this was Fitzgerald's intention—but when Dick finally reaches "the end of his dream of Rosemary," he strikes back by presuming to give her acting advice, in contrast to his awed reaction when he first saw her in *Daddy's Girl*. Dick's criticism of her capacity as an actress slashes away at the very element that makes Rosemary most appealing. His final, embittered denunciation of her, uttered to Nicole, does not help matters: "Rosemary never did grow up."

Lois could not help but have been initially stung by the many flaws that Fitzgerald wrote into this character. "Mother would sometimes talk about when she first read the book," recalls Tim Young.

> She liked most of it, but there were also things she didn't like. The sexual involvement between Dick and Rosemary didn't set well with her because she always claimed that she and Fitzgerald had never had a physical involvement. Also, Rosemary didn't turn out so nice in the end, and this bothered her. She was a sensual person, but she was never the selfish, sex-crazed starlet that Rosemary was. She took a lot of the book personally, for a time.

Gladys shared some of her daughter's initial reservations about the work because she believed that Fitzgerald had insulted her own physical appearance. "She thought the book was perfectly wonderful," Lois recalled to this author in 1987, "but she was upset with Scott for referring to her 'faded pink cheeks,' since she [Gladys] was in her early thirties at the time." And when the book was first published, Lois was irritated to find herself the subject of teasing by certain New York intellectuals, especially at one soirée given by the critic Alexander Woollcott. She recalled to Mizener in 1951, "I have a recollection of a party at Alex Woollcott's where I was ribbed a good deal about being Rosemary and no one seemed to give a damn about the book's worth. George Kaufmann, whom I love, teased me most, in a gentle way, though."

Lois and Gladys, however, soon came to take a more philosophical approach to the novel. Rosemary did indeed possess a number of distasteful qualities and Mrs. Speers was faded looking, but Lois remembered that Fitzgerald, first and foremost, was a writer of fiction, an author who drew upon his own life in his works but who also changed and manipulated characters and events to suit the needs of his stories. "You must remember," she wrote to this author in 1987, "that authors take certain characteristics of a person, then shape them according to the story's needs." Gladys came to a similar realization, and not long after the book's first appearance both she and Lois ceased to take any offense from it. Neither held a grudge against Fitzgerald for the not always flattering details he wrote into the characters he based on them. "Mother believed that it would have been silly for them to have held on to any anger she and Grandmother may have felt about a book," observes Young. Indeed, in time Lois even came to feel indignant about the novel's having been so easily dismissed when it appeared. Recalling the Woollcott party at which the book was not treated kindly, she fumed in a letter to Mizener in 1951, "It makes me mad to think that all the supposedly bright, brilliant folk there could so easily pass over a talent such as Scott's, no matter what the era was."

By the time that she wrote these words, Lois had come to a better understanding of Fitzgerald's psychology when he wrote the novel. She realized it would have been impossible for him to suffuse *Tender Is the Night* with the brightness and levity that had characterized portions of *This Side of Paradise* and *The Beautiful and Damned*, as well as many of his short stories. He had progressed to a point in his life and career in which his outlook had grown grimmer and less idealistic, a view the book inevitably reflected. Indeed, one comes away from *Tender Is the Night* a bit shaken by the keen, razor-sharp literary dissection he performed on its characters. "I know *I* would never have wanted to be in it," Young says. Many were based on people Fitzgerald knew, as Lois pointed out in her *Biography in Sound* interview, and no one, least of all he and Zelda, came away unscathed from their literary impersonations.

One of the points Lois made to support her belief that Fitzgerald's creation of Rosemary's negative qualities was not based upon her was the fact that one of the most incriminating aspects of the character, her supposed indiscretion with the undergraduate in the Pullman car, had actually been used by Fitzgerald in another work on which she is presumed to have had no influence, a 1929 short story entitled "Basil and Cleopatra," before he assigned it to Rosemary in the pages of *Tender Is the Night*. Another point Lois made along these lines was that in his working notes for the novel, Fitzgerald set out the plan that Rosemary was to be a positive character. He wrote, "Her career is like Lois or Mary Hay [an actress and the wife of Richard Barthelmess]—that is, she differs from most actresses by being a lady, simply reeking of vitality, health, sensuality."

Because Lois kept perspective about the role she played in *Tender Is the Night*, she was usually happy to acknowledge that she was the model for Rosemary, to a point. Her feelings about being too closely associated with Fitzgerald and with the book were mixed, and she was ill at ease with living in, as Fitzgerald phrased it in the novel, "the shadow of Rosemary," of being perceived as a living version of the literary character. "To Mother the present was sacred," observes Young. "She did not want to be pigeonholed for an old book or a past romance." Lois said as much herself when she warned this author in 1987 of the folly of "preoccupation with the 1920s" and in a 1971 letter to Matthew Bruccoli in which she wrote, "Someday it would be a joy to write about Scott," but added, "Do not bury thyself in the past."

These cautionary remarks notwithstanding, it is a fact that Lois, as Fitzgerald's friend and probable lover, fueled his imagination and provided a source for a substantial amount of material that he incorporated into his work. At the time she knew him, she was not aware of the extent to which he used her as a model for characters and details in his writing, but today we can readily discern her influence. We know her as Rosemary Hoyt, of course—that fact appears in most books written about Fitzgerald—but she also appears to us in the forms of Jenny Delehanty (later known as Jenny Prince), Mae Purley, Daisy Cary, Helen Avery, Betsy D'Amido, Annie Lorry, and Alida Rikker, not to mention unnamed characters in "The Swimmers" and *The Last Tycoon*. "There she was," wrote Fitzgerald in *Tender Is the Night* when Dick Diver first glimpses Rosemary on the silver screen. Today, we may say the same, for she is there, to us, sometimes delicately wafting, sometimes boldly advancing, in, out and around the elegant words of his prose like a variously sparkling, variously sullied, but always interesting apparition born of his keen clinical-quality talent for observation, superb memory for detail, and acicular, expressive literary artistry. He sometimes portrayed her with the delicacy of a kitten ("The Swimmers," "The Bowl"), sometimes with the throttle of general infantry (*Tender Is the Night*, "The Rough Crossing"), but it was generally apparent when he had her in mind. Lois's legacy was thus threefold: she was, as she wished to be remembered, a devoted wife and mother; she was an actress in the movies, theater, and television;

and she was, no matter how she felt about it in later years, muse and lover to one of the greatest of twentieth-century American authors.

In the last years of her life, she was keenly aware that she had been the model for Rosemary and other Fitzgerald characters, and she knew that this made her a kind of living legend. While it is true that often she found such attention intrusive, it is also true that generally she dealt with it graciously. She expressed the dichotomy of her feelings on the subject in the late 1980s, when I sent her a photograph that I asked her to inscribe, a 1926 Paramount studio portrait of her taken by Eugene Robert Richee. In my request, I commented that the way she looked in that photograph—young, wistful, and quite beautiful—must have been the way Rosemary looked in the book. Her response was perhaps as concise a summation of her view of the Fitzgerald/*Tender Is the Night* phenomenon as she ever made: "*Tender Is the Night* was only a fairy tale," Lois Moran wrote, "though a beautiful one."

✆ Book III ✆
"Brickbats and Bouquets"

Lucky me. Was in New York at just the right time
(the early '30s) when everybody was fresh and bright.
They were all young when I knew them,
though I was the youngest.

Lois Moran, 1988

Mother was like that. She did everything in style.

Tim Young, 2004

Going "Clarabow," Anita Loos, and Stardom as a Fox Featured Player

10

*I*n 1935, F. Scott Fitzgerald wrote to Lois that her acting career had been "galvanically" successful, and he was correct. By the mid-1930s she had retired from motion pictures and her stage appearances had become increasingly sporadic, but she could look back upon an expansive body of work dating to 1924 that included dozens of films and several theatrical productions. However, in 1927, the year she met Fitzgerald, she regarded her position as a screen and stage star as a work in progress and had no desire to revel in past accomplishments. That year, in fact, marked the beginning of perhaps the most ambitious period of her career. She was at last decisively able to expand upon her range as a performer and to splinter from that long-ago, Goldwyn-imposed "Fragile Cameo" image.

She achieved this progression under the auspices of William Fox, the one studio mogul able to convince her to sign a long-term studio contract, and his chief of production, Winfield Sheehan. At Fox Films, then one of the biggest and most promising studios, she speedily evolved from having played young innocents in previous films such as *Stella Dallas*, *Padlocked*, and *God Gave Me Twenty Cents* to enacting more mature, glamorous characters in flashier productions such as *Publicity Madness*, *Love Hungry*, and *Don't Marry*. Fox and Sheehan cast her in a wider variety of roles, and during the next several years she appeared in a broad range of films that resulted in a diverse filmography.

Lois had sensed that her career was upon the brink of change in the fall of 1926, on the evening that *God Gave Me Twenty Cents* had opened the lavish Paramount Theater in New York City. As a guest of honor, she had been one of the first attendees to visit the building's lofty observation tower, from which could be experienced the unique sights, sounds, and sensations of the city from on high. Gazing out over the lights, her hair windswept and cheeks flush with evening chill, and perilously balancing a cellophane-wrapped bouquet of pink roses that had been presented to her, she experienced a second epiphany from the heights. That evening, as she had done when seated in the balcony during the premiere of *Stella Dallas* at the Apollo in 1925, she arrived at a realization. Then, shy and demure next to her mother, she had realized that she could be a movie star; now, taking in the grandeur and sparkle of the city, she realized that she *was* a movie star—and that she liked it. She was developing ever stronger poise and style, and as her sense of self became more defined, so, too, did her ego and her resolve that she welcomed fame and success. In 1928 she recorded a sentiment in her journal that fully reflected this outlook. "By God," she wrote thickly in fountain pen, "I must accomplish all my dreams, make them real!"

She made progress in furthering her film ambitions when in late 1926 she filmed *The Music Master* for Fox, her first picture for that studio, although at this point she followed her pattern for signing for one picture only; her decision to enter into a long-term contract still lay several months in the future. Her choice of *The Music Master* was a good one, for it had been an enormously successful stage play in 1900, so much so that as late as 1926 it was fondly remembered and the project of creating a film based on it viewed as an undertaking of importance. A parent-child drama in the vein of *Stella Dallas* and *The Reckless Lady*, *The Music Master* was a sentimental tale of a father who by chance is reunited with his long-lost daughter, played by Lois. Lois approached the picture as one of the most significant opportunities of her career, and she was reassured that her friend Allan Dwan, who had directed her in *Padlocked*, would again be guiding her. *The Music Master* was also her first costume film. Lavishly gowned by Emery J. Herrett in 1900-era hats, jewelry, and long trailing skirts accentuated heavily with beads and lace, she had seldom looked more beautiful; Fox even retained the official photographer of the Ziegfeld Follies, Alfred Cheney Johnston, to compose still photographs of her. Inspired by the picture's sparkle and opulence, she gave one of her finest performances.

Charles Klein had written the original play, and David Belasco had produced it on the stage. For the movies, Charles's son, Philip Klein (Charles had died in 1915 in the sinking of the *Lusitania*), prepared a competent scenario. The plot concerned Anton von Barwig, a destitute music teacher, played memorably on the stage by David Warfield and in the film by the character actor Alec B. Francis, who recognizes one of his students, Helene Stanton (Lois), as his long-lost daughter when he observes her holding a doll just like one his daughter had. Problems ensue, however, because the girl is engaged to Beverly Cruger (Neil Hamilton), a dashing socialite, and her adoptive father (Charles Lane), when confronted with the truth by the teacher, pleads for secrecy as to her parentage so as not to jeopardize the marriage. All ends happily when the girl determines the truth and both she and her groom are so happy by the news that they invite the music master on their honeymoon.

Lois enjoyed filming this tale of sentiment and old lace, and she garnered excellent reviews for her work in it. Critics, impressed that she had resisted becoming lost in the contrivances of the plot and the lavish visual trappings, praised her. Roscoe McGowen wrote in the *New York News* that she "comes through triumphant with a natural and believable performance." John S. Cohen Jr. said in the *New York Sun* that she "gave a thoroughly fine performance. Of all the budding group of screen actresses, Miss Moran is by the far the best bet." And Herb Cruikshank wrote in the *New York Morning Telegraph,* "Lois shines with new luster. . . . Without doubt she is the most promising of our younger feminine screen players." Among those who disagreed was the critic for the *New York Telegram*, who wrote that Lois "pales into insignificance."

The film did excellent business, and Fox, keenly observant and aware of Lois's potential, lost no time in offering her a long-term contract. By working at Fox Films, he explained to her, she would be able to work with the many excellent actors he had under contract and would in addition be able to expand her range. Pleased by the high-quality film she had just made, she listened to Fox's arguments carefully, then conveyed her polite regrets and explained that she was still uncomfortable with a commitment of such magnitude. She and Gladys continued to believe that Lois's career would best proceed with the two of them personally selecting projects, and Fox, most likely wishing to keep his options open, told her that she could return to his studio at a later time if she so desired. Lois was resolute in her decision to continue freelancing, but her choice of her next two pictures would alter her thinking.

Lois believed that appearing in *The Music Master* had been advantageous to her career—she described it in her journal as "sweet, gentle, slow-moving, but charming"—but she also worried that she was typecasting herself by appearing again as a daughter in a family melodrama. It was time, she concluded, to radically update her image. Victoriana was passé, the 1920s were roaring about her, and she wanted her screen persona to keep up with the times. Unfortunately, she followed through on this sensible line of thinking within the framework of continuing to freelance. She and Gladys were out of their depth in selecting modern Jazz Age pictures, and their next two choices showed it. In stark contrast to earlier quality dramas such as *Stella Dallas* and *God Gave Me Twenty Cents*, they in early 1927 chose two mediocre sex pictures that were, comparatively, poorly received and did not challenge Lois as an actress.

The Irresistible Lover, the first of these two films, was made for Universal-Jewel and paired Lois with Norman Kerry, a popular actor.

Directed by William Beaudine, this farce, Lois's first comedy, revolved around a promiscuous bachelor named J. Harrison Grey (Kerry) who mends his ways when he meets the lovely Betty Kennedy (Lois). But she, put off by his libidinous past, does not reciprocate his feelings. After her brother (a young Arthur Lake, in advance of his success in the *Blondie* films) intervenes, however, she eventually falls in love with Grey, and they are wed.

Neither Lois nor Kerry could overcome *The Irresistible Lover*'s insipid plot, which seems more suited to an episode of *Love Boat* than to a film starring a major up-and-coming actress. A glossy production that had been supervised by Carl Laemmle Jr., it had the potential to be an above-average comedy but failed to achieve the level of merriment to which it aspired. Lois and Kerry, faced with such mediocre material, failed to spark as a screen pairing.

The reviews reflected the picture's inadequacies. Critics lambasted the commonplace plot, and Lois received the most unflattering notices of her career. Regina Cannon complained in the *New York American* that "her role is not worthy of the clever girl's talents," and Palmer Smith lamented in the *New York Evening World* that "she appears to be wasted in this feature." In spite of the reviews, Lois suspected that the film would do reasonably well at the box office, which it did.

The next picture Lois and Gladys chose was a drama for Paramount entitled *The Whirlwind of Youth*, a project that appealed to her for a number of reasons. It would allow her to film again at the studio where she had made *Padlocked* and *God Gave Me Twenty Cents* (Famous Players–Lasky had become Paramount); it was based on a popular novel, *Soundings*, by Hamilton Gibbs; and it would give her the opportunity to appear in another picture with a plot that reflected modern tastes and mores. She also liked the director Paramount had selected for the feature, Rowland V. Lee, an actor turned director who could boast a large list of directing credits. Lois was further pleased by the cast, a lineup that included Donald Keith, a young aspiring actor; Vera Veronina, a scorching young German screen siren appearing now in her first American film; and Alyce Mills, a sensitive, comely screen performer.

Like *The Irresistible Lover*, *The Whirlwind of Youth* was a film preoccupied with sex, but it was a softer picture that gave Lois better moments as an actress. She played the eighteen-year-old Nancy Hawthorne. (The casting was age appropriate: Lois celebrated her eighteenth birthday on the set.) Nancy is a naive girl who falls in love with a male jazz baby, Bob Whittaker (Keith). The quintessential "It Boy," Bob has no interest in Nancy, however, and instead dallies with a variety of other women, including a torrid Spanish *señorita* (Veronina) and an English flapper (Mills). All Nancy can do is to look on heartbroken from afar, especially when the characters end up in Paris. World events intercede, however, when World War I breaks out. Bob becomes an army officer, Nancy becomes a nurse, and the two meet again behind the front. In these new circumstances, Bob, having matured a bit, realizes he loves Nancy, and all ends well.

The Whirlwind of Youth was not a strong film for Lois. She played an emotionally expressive character that she liked, but overall the picture, in spite of its colorful World War I ending, was beset by a weak script, although it did do fairly well at the box office. Critics were mixed in their reviews of her performance, but she was pleased by what *Variety* had to say: "[Lois] sustains the picture. She is an optical treat and can do her stuff before the lens, in and out of close-ups."

Lois was fond of neither *The Irresistible Lover* nor *The Whirlwind of Youth*. These pictures had proven moderate financial successes, but she believed it would be career suicide for her to go on making watery films of this type. Times had changed for freelance performers, however, and offers for more substantive roles were not coming in. The studios had commenced loaning contract players to one another, a less expensive enterprise than retaining freelance actors, and had additionally signed on an increasing number of feature players. Such studio changes meant that freelancers were no longer in demand as they once had been. Jerry Hoffman reported in the December 12,

1926, *New York Morning Telegraph*, "There are a few artists, these in a great minority, who have been successful free-lancing during the past season or two. Most of these will find during the coming year that jobs will not be as frequent." Lois remembered Aileen St. John-Brenon's impassioned *New York Telegraph* column from 1926 beseeching her not to sign with a studio, but she also realized that freelancing had now become a luxury she could no longer rely on to net her choice roles. She had hoped a project with John Barrymore might materialize, and the idea of his starring with her in a film was the subject of an article in the *Boston Advertiser* provocatively entitled "Lois Moran Lures John." Plans fell through, however, and she was left feeling more dejected than ever. William Fox's offer of a studio contract came to her mind, and, early in 1927, believing she had nothing to lose, she journeyed to New York to meet with him.

Fox was still eager to sign Lois. Wearing his trademark white sweater, an article of clothing he believed symbolized his success, he met with her in his enormous office, imposingly accentuated with stained-glass windows. Driven and shrewd, he was resolute in adding Lois to his stable of screen performers and, as he had done after *The Music Master*, only this time with even more vigor, he quickly pointed out to her the advantages his studio could offer her. Fox Films, he told her, was one of the busiest and most prolific of all studios, yet it was not so big that he and Sheehan could not give each of its contract players individual attention. His was a well-respected studio, he went on, and he had under contract many highly regarded performers, including Madge Bellamy, Olive Borden, John Bowers, Louise Brooks, June Collyer, Dolores Del Rio, William Farnum, Charles Farrell, Janet Gaynor, Neil Hamilton, Buck Jones, Edmund Lowe, Victor McLaglen, Tom Mix, and George O'Brien. He also informed her that he was willing to pay $2,000 a week, a sum that would allow the Morans to live very well indeed in the 1920s. Lastly, he played a trump card he had not possessed earlier. He tempted her with a project he deemed suitable for her first film under contract, an imaginative satire on the advertising business written by Anita Loos entitled *Publicity Madness*.

Lois anguished over what to do. A year before, she would not have considered becoming a contract player; however, she now understood that circumstances had changed for freelancers. She was also well aware that selecting her own films had become increasingly onerous. Gladys, moreover, was eager to pursue her own interests and wanted more time to devote to her new passion, investing in the stock market. Lois weighed all these factors and gave thought to the arguments Fox had presented to her. After deliberating, she telephoned Sheehan with the news that she had decided to accept Fox's offer and sign on with his studio. Both Sheehan and Fox were elated and, in publicizing the addition of Lois to the Fox family, they stressed the high ambitions they had for strengthening her ability as an actress and for starring her in more demanding roles.

In a February 1927 article for the *New York Sun*, the columnist Cedric Belfrage commented on the future that Fox believed awaited Lois at his studio:

> The salary equal to that of two prime ministers which she receives each week is not so pre-eminently an immediate cause of satisfaction as it is a very solid promise of what the Fox people have in mind for her. The money talks in money's usual plain spoken way of great starring roles and great stories ahead for its recipient. It would, as Miss Moran observed when she signed her contract, be unnecessary to pay so much for just another wide-eyed bathing beauty or a mere target for kisses and custard pies.

In the spring of 1927, Sheehan promptly put *Publicity Madness* into production at Fox Hills, Fox's Hollywood studio. After her sojourn in New York, Lois would be returning to Hollywood.

Lois's spirits soared as she reported to the set of her first film for Fox under her new contract. Albert Ray had been assigned to direct the picture, and because he had previous experience directing comedies, Lois felt confident that he could guide her through this film.

Her costar was Edmund Lowe, a charismatic leading man who had made a name for himself in the role of the cocky Sergeant Quirt in *What Price Glory* in 1926, and she was pleased to have the opportunity of appearing with him. She was also happy to be enacting a story by Anita Loos, whom she knew from the mock film of *Camille* in which she had recently appeared and whose wit and intelligence she liked and respected. Lois believed that making *Publicity Madness* would be one of the most felicitous events of her career. She was not disappointed.

Loos had originally written the film as a vehicle for Douglas Fairbanks Sr. entitled *His Picture in the Papers*. As *Publicity Madness*, the film revolved around an underappreciated soap salesman named Pete King (Lowe). Fired from one concern, he gets a job as a promotion man for a rival soap company that is doing badly and in need of drastic action. Pete devises two high-handed publicity schemes to improve the company's sales. He first changes the name of the soap from "Uncle Elmer's Saturday Night Soap" to "Violet Soap," after the owner's plain daughter (Lois), with whom he falls in love. He goes on to issue soap wrappers, ads, and park statues showing Violet in a bathtub under which are the words "You Should Have Violet in Your Bath." He gives the real Violet a complete makeover, including taking her to a barber to have her hair bobbed.

Pete then concocts a contest. He offers a prize of $100,000 to the first aviator who can fly across the Pacific from California to Hawaii and testify that Violet soap was the secret of his success. He believes his aviation challenge will be impossible to meet. However, forty-nine flyers enter the contest. He then enters the contest himself, sure that he can win, to save the company from having to pay the prize money. He embarks on his flight with Violet, and what ensues is madcap. The engine goes dry and Lowe is forced to lubricate it with Violet soap, and when Violet espies the shores of the distant Pacific island she leaps out of the cockpit and dances on the fragile wings. They come in last, but that does not matter. The soap company has derived terrific publicity, and when Pete and Violet make it to shore they are married.

In writing this frenetically paced tale, Loos took penetrating aim at one of the most noteworthy phenomena of the 1920s, the exponential growth of the advertising industry. So pervasive was advertising, in fact, that even Scott Fitzgerald, whose own father, like Pete King in the film, had been a soap salesman, worked briefly as a copy writer at an advertising agency, and Zelda remarked of the time in her 1932 novel *Save Me the Waltz*, "We grew up founding our dreams on the infinite promise of American advertising. I still believe that one can learn to play the piano by mail and that mud will give you a perfect complexion." Lois herself did several product endorsements in the 1920s and 1930s for companies as diverse as Lux soap, the Golden State Limited railroad, and Spur Ties and Garters. In *Publicity Madness*, Loos lampooned the extremes to which some companies would go to create innovative advertising, and in creating the airplane race she was apparently satirizing the Dole Pineapple Company, which had offered a purse of $25,000 to the first person who could fly their product from the West Coast to Hawaii (no one did).

Lois got along smashingly with Lowe, an older, urbane man who reminded her of the dapper Adolphe Menjou, and together they created a fresh onscreen chemistry, especially in the airplane sequence, for which they wore jaunty custom-designed aviation outfits. One cannot help but think that, like William Powell and Myrna Loy, they would have made a fine Nick and Nora Charles in *The Thin Man* films of the 1930s and 1940s. The film even featured a terrier that resembled Asta, the much-adored pet of the Charles household in the Powell-Loy films. Lois and Lowe would go on to be teamed in three other films, making him the most frequent costar of her career. Lois also liked working with Albert Ray and appreciated his deft handling of comedy.

Upon the release of *Publicity Madness*, critics shared in the merriment and gave the film sparkling reviews, best exemplified by that of Radie Harris, who wrote in the *New York Telegraph* that the picture was a "highly diverting farce": "Lois, Edmund, and Anita prove a happy triumvirate and their combined efforts afford perfect light hearted entertainment." Lois's own notices were particularly complimentary, critics praising her beauty and flair for comedy. The critic for the *New York World* best summed up the critical reception afforded her for her portrayal of Violet: "Somewhere an imaginative motion picture showman with a Ziegfeldian flair for painting, powdering, dressing and lighting his leading women has taken hold of Lois Moran, the heretofore shy and serious minded player of Little Eva parts in the movies, and has transformed her into a captivating ingénue, a bright and vivid and irresistible cutie."

Appearing in *Publicity Madness* gave Lois a sense of accomplishment. She had faced up to what was perhaps the greatest challenge to the well-being of her career thus far—signing a long-term studio contract—and she had weathered the trauma well and made a winning film. With the contract hurdle behind her, she devoted more time to her personal life. She continued to live at home with Gladys and Betty, but that was not uncommon; as other actresses, such as Claire Windsor, Louise Fazenda, Billie Dove, Mary Pickford, and the Gish sisters, either lived with their mothers or maintained residences for them nearby. Gladys went on as head of the family, watching out for her daughter's best interests, and *Liberty* magazine even observed that Lois "is guarded as religiously as a college quarterback before the big game." Lois herself wrote in her journal in February 1927, "Mother and I have such a lot of fun. Work then reading and cooking, discussing or dissecting people and things." Gladys gave an interview to *Photoplay* at the time in which she spoke of the strong bond shared between herself and Lois: "When I wake up and am worried about her being in an automobile accident (her father was killed that way), I send her a thought message and in five or ten minutes she calls me up and tells me that she's all right." She added that her relationship with her daughter was based on mutual respect. "Mother love is bunk," she said. "It's only for sentimentalists. I like Lois as she likes me—as a person."

Gladys, however, had developed new interests of her own by this time. Lois's earnings enabled her to pursue an avid interest in investing in the stock market, and, no longer required to pore over potential scripts for Lois, she began devoting more and more of her energies to ticker tape and stock exchanges. "She was not as astute at the game of the stock market as she thought she was," explains Tim Young, but stocks and bonds became her obsession, and the press often reported that the Morans were among the wealthiest people in the film colony.

Lois left monetary matters to Gladys and concentrated on Betty's upbringing. She taught her adopted sister dancing and how to curtsey, watched over her diet and recommended books to her, and most particularly made sure she was applying herself to her piano lessons. "She has lots of cute personality and is very quick," Lois observed in her journal. "I like her—Children certainly benefit from being forced to stand alone—Betty particularly—She could very easily be spoiled by other treatment." Betty had by this time announced her ambitions of herself becoming an actress.

Back at Fox, Lois's spirits soared. Feeling happy and successful, she began production on *Sharp Shooters*, her second film under her Fox contract. An unusual picture with a plot reminiscent of that of *Madame Butterfly*, *Sharp Shooters* costarred George O'Brien, fresh from Murnau's *Sunrise*, the pinnacle of his film career. A handsome, well-built, and capable actor whom publicists labeled "The Chest" and who today would have little problem giving the likes of Schwarzenegger and Stallone a run for their money, O'Brien would become Lois's friend and eventually, for a time, the subject of her romantic longings. Boris Karloff and Randolph Scott also appeared in the film in small, uncredited roles.

"Oh, I do everything in this one," Lois explained to the *Los Angeles Times* when *Sharp Shooters* hit theaters later in the year. Sheehan chose for her second contract film a colorful tale that would present her in a worldly manner yet would also pack an emotional wallop and complement her talents. Lois played Lorette, a French girl who falls in love with an American sailor named George (O'Brien). George, however, is a womanizer: "I'm going to buy some of this cologne so as I can sprinkle it on my women and be able to tell 'em apart in the dark." He is called the sharp shooter because he has a magnetic effect on so many different women. Lorette is naive, speaks little English, and does not understand George's fickle ways. In fact, she believes he will marry her, and when he departs for New York she follows him. When she encounters him there, however, he is with a new girlfriend (Gwen Lee) and pretends not to know her. His buddies (Noah Young and Tom Dugan) are appalled by his callous behavior and insist that he marry her. He does so, reluctantly, and the marriage begins turbulently. He eventually comes to his senses, however, and realizes he loves her, and the story ends happily.

Critics greeted Lois's performance in *Sharp Shooters* favorably. John S. Cohen Jr. of the *New York Sun* found her "thoroughly charming." The *New York Times* remarked that she was "more captivating than ever before," and Regina Cannon wrote in the *New York American* that she excelled at her "lily in the ash can" role and had succeeded in "throwing to the four winds her reputation as interpreter of unsophisticated roles."

Sharp Shooters proved a milestone for Lois both professionally and personally. Professionally, it was the clearest evidence yet that Fox and Sheehan were remaining true to their goal of changing her image. At the opening of the film, for example, when Lois meets O'Brien, she is seen dancing in a revealing, suggestive costume. This episode seems to have been purposely created to showcase Lois in a new light, for she could have met O'Brien in any number of more pedestrian ways. A scene showcasing Lois performing a modern dance in a skimpy costume was sure to help eradicate the memory of Laurel in *Stella Dallas* and to display the new Fox player in a modified, provocative way. It also showcased her range as a dancer. Fox and Sheehan intended *Sharp Shooters* as a vehicle to present Lois to audiences with a different look, for in it she appeared more made-up and glamorous than she had in most of her previous films. The character Lorette was, granted, very much like Mary in *God Gave Me Twenty Cents*, but the presentation, not the plot, was the novelty in this new picture.

Personally, *Sharp Shooters* was the first of three films in which Lois would appear with O'Brien, who in life had the same effect on women as did the character he played in the film. Lois had never encountered such a virile man's man. His blunt physicality contrasted with Fitzgerald's lyrical intellectualism, and over time she became smitten with him and the bold kisses he delivered in many of his scenes with her. The following year, in October 1928, she wrote a detailed description of him in her journal:

> All in all our George, with whom I have a peculiar sort of understanding, an instinctive one of which we seldom speak, is a lovable, nice, dear with a secret little twinkle in his eye of which I am extremely fond, and is probably the finest actor in motion pictures today. I will be interested to see how he will fare in the talkies. He has a pleasing voice, methinks. I love him very much.

Lois's ending of this discussion of O'Brien with an expression of "love" is significant, because it suggests that he was one of the most noteworthy objects of her affections after Fitzgerald.

Indeed, as the months of the acquaintance passed, and as she matured into womanhood, Lois's attraction to O'Brien was increasingly based on the physical. As evidenced by her journal entries, she began to think less of his personality and more of his body. In one entry she wrote in late 1928, she echoed the short stories she had written when she had known Fitzgerald the previous year: "I do love him to kiss me. Suppose I'm just a sensuous little beast!—Kissing is so ridiculous, really—Rather sloppy—to tell the truth. But nevertheless I don't mind so much when he administers his embraces." In a later entry she was intoxicated by O'Brien: "Still upset about the gentleman—It's fairly easy to dismiss him from my mind with a book, thank goodness—Otherwise I should be a rather pleasantly unhappy young lady, without doubt."

Lois confided to O'Brien the way she felt about him. He, however, did not reciprocate her romantic feelings, as he seldom became involved with his leading ladies, and instead stressed the importance and value of their friendship. "Thank goodness we've talked it over and I shan't be upset anymore," she wrote, attempting to mask her bruised feelings. "Hooray! He said that we were *really* friends, weren't we, and why shouldn't we tell another anything we please? He *always* understands—the very, *very* dear person." Later, Lois would compose a couple of brief entries that reveal her in reality to have been less forgiving of O'Brien's romantic rejection of her.

After *Sharp Shooters*, Lois went on what may be called a Fox assembly line. Sheehan, who was fast becoming a personal friend, continued to select her films with care, but by 1928 the appearance of each new Moran film ceased to be the event the release of many of her earlier pictures had been. Lois had feared that this lessening of stature might occur under a studio contract, but she now reacted to it differently than she had anticipated. She recognized that life was easier for her with the studio selecting her films and that she was enacting a variety of characters in different and engaging films. Late in her tenure at Fox, in the early 1930s, she would find herself bitter over the later poor films Fox assigned to her, and most of what would be written about her in later years would dismiss her work for him as mediocre at best, but throughout the rest of the 1920s she happily directed all of her creative energies to any picture in which she appeared. She soon became comfortably established as what Sheehan termed a "Fox featured player," and she enjoyed her career as never before.

Love Hungry, Lois's next film, was an ordinary picture in which she would not have considered appearing in her freelance days. Under the studio umbrella, however, she enacted her part in it with gusto. In the film, directed by Victor Heerman, she played Joan Robinson, a jaded chorine who must choose between marrying for love or for money. After debating for the length of the film, she finally decides upon love and weds Tom Harvey (Lawrence Gray), the attractive but impecunious object of her true affections. "I don't want money," she proclaims. "I just want love!" Surprisingly, Lois received generally excellent reviews for her work in this mediocre film. The *Philadelphia Evening Ledger* remarked, "Lois Moran, sweet as ever, makes another step into comedy. She baby faces her way into another huge success." In a *New York Times* review entitled "The Triumphant Poor," Mordaunt Hall observed, "It looks very much as if she really enjoyed the scenes, and frail though is her part, she lives up to what's wanted without ever stepping out of character." Quinn Martin, however, disagreed. Writing in the *New York World*, he lamented that Lois was straying further and further away from her *Stella Dallas* days and had digressed into becoming "a typical Hollywood agitator of the most conventional pattern." *Love Hungry* did satisfactory business, especially after it enjoyed a lavish premiere at the Fox-owned Roxy Theater in New York.

Lois had better opportunities in her next film, *Don't Marry*, a glistening comedy that in a way echoed her own early life in Pittsburgh. This film, which featured her *Music Master* costar Neil Hamilton, dealt comically with the struggle between progressive 1920s thinking and the more conservative values of earlier generations. One reason Gladys had left Pittsburgh was that she believed her relatives there were staid, restrictive, and behind the times; so a film dealing directly with the subject of new values versus old was of great interest to Lois. *Padlocked* had explored the issue heavily and dramatically; *Don't Marry* did so humorously but did so just as intensely. The film particularly recalled Lois's years in Pittsburgh in that it featured a young lady rebelling against what she sees as Old World puritanism with the help of a farsighted elder. Of course, Lois, under the auspices of Gladys, had done the same with the help of her aunt.

James Tinling, a relatively new but resourceful director who would be important to Lois's career in the coming months, directed the film. Lois played Louise Bowen, a modern young flapper whose old-fashioned aunt rules her existence because she controls the girl's inheritance until she marries. "I won't have you smoking and wearing one-piece bathing suits," the aunt tells her. Louise, feeling that she cannot stand these restrictions anymore, goes to see a wily elderly attorney. He is not in, so she consults with his nephew, Henry Willoughby (Hamilton), a cynical young gentleman who dislikes modern women and whose motto is "Don't Marry." "I came to see you about a divorce," she tells Henry. "I'm not married, but I want you to find me a husband and arrange for a quick divorce so I can get rid of my family." Henry is shocked. "I'll do nothing of the kind," he says. "You modern women are all alike. Selfish. Willful." He decries modern girls as "smoke-eaters" and "gin-garglers" and tells Louise, "That's the most indecent proposition I've ever heard. There ought to be a special jail for women like you!" Louise rushes out in a fury, determining that Henry shall be the very man she will marry—just so she can divorce him.

To accomplish her aims, she gains the support of the elderly General Willoughby, Henry's uncle (Henry Kolker). Together, they plot a scheme in which Louise will disguise herself as her cousin Priscilla, a sweet, old-fashioned girl. As Priscilla, Louise sets her cap for Henry, wearing long dresses, demurely playing a harp, riding about in carriages, and brandishing knitting needles. She even registers horror when Henry smokes a cigarette. Henry becomes infatuated with Priscilla, and they become engaged. Louise, in the guise of Priscilla, then begins a campaign of praising Louise and the modern girl. Soon, the campaign is successful and Henry begins to care more for Louise than for the prudish Priscilla. By the end of the film, Henry has opted for Louise, Louise has fallen for Henry, and divorce is the farthest thing from either's mind.

Lois delighted in playing Louise Bowen and her "cousin" Priscilla. Steadily strengthening her abilities as a comedic actress, she drew upon the experience she had gleaned from *Publicity Madness* to make *Don't Marry* a fluffy, merry affair for all concerned. She realized that several of the characters she had heretofore played, most recently

Helene Stanton in *The Music Master*, were more akin to Priscilla than to Louise, and she thus saw the project as a means of poking some fun at her own peaches-and-cream image, which she was now attempting to put behind her. She even wore a modern bathing suit in the film, something she and Gladys had refused to do when considering *The American Venus* the previous year. "Mother liked *Don't Marry*," recalls Tim Young. "Whenever she saw Neil Hamilton playing Commissioner Gordon on the *Batman* television series in the 1960s, she thought of working with him on this picture."

Fox publicists hilariously proclaimed *Don't Marry* as a saga of "How a Modern Miss Made a Flaming Youth of Her Straight-Laced Boyfriend." The public, anxious to see Lois in another new kind of picture, attended in droves, and as word spread that the film was amusing, box office returns rose. Critics, realizing that *Don't Marry* was unique, devoted many column inches to the film and to Lois's new image. "Lois began to emerge from her chrysalis of innocence about three pictures ago, so to speak," wrote George Gerhard in the *New York Evening World*, "and now she is a full-fledged butterfly." Leonard Hall, writing in the *New York Telegram*, agreed: "What the film does do is project an entirely new Lois Moran. Gone is the startled fawn effect we knew in her first films. The lily has turned into a rose and Lois is a big girl now." Hall concluded, "Lois, one of the last of the sweet and simple, is going modern—even clarabow—on us. She smokes cigarettes, she wears practically no bathing suit and she kisses boys." A writer at the *Philadelphia Public Ledger* agreed with Hall's comparison and described Lois's performance as the work of an "embryonic Clara Bow." These comparisons of Lois to Bow are noteworthy: after all, Lois's detractors had complained that Bow should have been cast in her role in *Padlocked*.

O'Brien and Hughes,
the Coming of Sound,
and Christmas in Yosemite

11

*R*evamping Lois's image had been a shrewd maneuver, for the public was now following her career with a fervor not seen since the *Stella Dallas* days. Credit for the creation of the new Lois can be given to Lois herself, for it was she who first understood the importance of preventing her screen persona from becoming stale, but it must be shared with Winfield Sheehan. A blond, blue-eyed Irishman who had worked his way up through the ranks of the Fox organization from secretary to chief of production, the equivalent of Irving Thalberg's position at MGM, Sheehan contributed much to the changing course of Lois's career. He was more interested in stories than in stars and was willing to feature his players in pictures that challenged preconceived notions other studios and the public may have held about the actors. It is perhaps telling that he referred to his actors as "featured players" rather than as "stars," because to him actors existed in support of the story at hand and not the other way around. Lois found his approach logical, and, as was usually the case with older men whom she respected, he soon became her personal friend.

Sheehan, in fact, grew fond both of Lois and Gladys, and it was not long before he was a frequent dinner guest of the Morans. In 1928 Lois made note in her journal of one of these evenings: "It was nice to see him. He's a real friend, understanding and loads of fun. We have had so many good times together. He stimulates me mentally in addition to teaching me many interesting things about all phases of business, motion picture and otherwise." Sheehan was particularly welcome on this occasion because he had brought gifts. She excitedly wrote that he "had practically a whole music store sent out in response to my request for a few sheets of the more popular New York hits."

Confident that Lois could be an asset to many types of films, Sheehan next cast her in a crime drama entitled *The River Pirate*, a picture that gave her little to do but was nevertheless important because it would be one of Fox's first features to use Movietone, an early sound process. Fox introduced Movietone to audiences at the same time as Warner Brothers began using its sound process, Vitaphone. At first Fox used it in one- and two-reel comedies and in newsreels. One of the first moguls to discern the potential of sound, he took a passionate interest in adding Movietone to his feature films as well and determined that limited use of the medium in *The River Pirate*, for both sound effects and dialogue, would be a judicious means of setting into motion the process of welding sound and silent film. The result was clumsy, but it was progress. It also featured certain sequences that were, for dramatic purposes, tinted attractively in blue. Based upon a popular magazine serial and book by Charles Francis Coe, the film was directed by William K. Howard. Those appearing with Lois included Victor McLaglen, who, like Lois's previous costar, Edmund Lowe, was best known for his role in *What Price Glory*, and Nick Stuart, a popular young actor. Donald Crisp also starred.

Coe had created in *The River Pirate* a mixture of jail breaks, thievery, and romance, elements Sheehan hoped would guarantee a successful film. The picture opens as Sailor Frink (McLaglen) meets Sandy (Stuart) in jail. Sandy has been falsely imprisoned, and Frink takes a paternal interest in him. When he is released on parole he returns to the prison to break Sandy out, in a dramatic sequence featuring Movietone sound effects. After the jailbreak, Frink and Sandy become gangsters who rob warehouses along rivers. Calling themselves

River Pirates, Frink and Sandy become successful in their enterprise, although a detective called Colfax (Crisp) seeks to arrest them. After Sandy is wounded in a heist, he is taken to the hospital, where he meets another patient, Marjorie Cullen (Lois), who by coincidence is Colfax's ward. Later, when Frink goes out on a job alone, Marjorie tells Sandy that the police are on to the pair and are planning a raid. Marjorie and Sandy go to tell Frink, and just as they arrive the police show up. Frink speaks up and clears Marjorie, but he and Sandy are arrested. The film then switches gears arrestingly as an elderly gentleman appears holding a copy of the book *The River Pirate* and takes a seat. In the Movietone talking portion of the film, the man tells the audience how the drama ends. Sandy is released and marries Marjorie, he says, and Frink reforms and is released from jail in time to be the best man at the wedding.

Lois knew that she was little more than window dressing in *The River Pirate*. As she explained to Radie Harris in a September 1928 *New York Morning Telegraph* interview, "It's really all Nick's and Victor McLaglen. I am just in it to lend romantic interest." She did not mind her relatively minor role, though, because she relished working with the two actors, especially McLaglen, who was undoubtedly the most intense character actor with whom she had appeared since Jean Hersholt in *Stella Dallas*. McLaglen was not traditionally handsome. A writer at the *Warren (Pa.) Tribune* called the casting of Lois and him "Beauty and—and—Victor McLaglen." Nevertheless, the actor was a burly, no-nonsense performer who took immediate charge of his scenes with a bravado that came through strongly on film, even though some claimed that in *The River Pirate* one could read his lips and see that he was uttering obscenities. His dynamic in the film was with Stuart, and Lois saw right away that their father-son relationship in the picture echoed many of her own parent-child dramas, particularly *The Road to Mandalay*, but she was more than happy to be on the outside of the central relationship this time around. She watched McLaglen, studying the acting technique that allowed him to dominate a film and would in 1935 win him a Best Actor Academy Award for *The Informer*. She believed she came away from the film with more insight into her art. She also liked working with Stuart, and although her feelings for this youthful masculine actor did not approach those she had for O'Brien, there was enough onscreen chemistry between them that Sheehan would later cast them in another important picture, *Joy Street*.

When released, *The River Pirate* was hindered in its popularity by the fact that it had to compete for business with another, although differently plotted, waterfront film, Josef von Sternberg's *The Docks of New York*, which appeared at the same time. *The River Pirate* was additionally beset by the very mixed reviews critics afforded it, particularly in regard to the Movietone ending and to Lois's performance. Critics either loved or hated the Movietone ending, and Lois's notices for were among the poorest she had yet received, but she had anticipated lackluster reviews because her part in the film was so weak. The *New York Journal* felt that she was "badly miscast as Marjorie," and a reviewer at *Screen World* remarked, "I had a sneaking feeling that this brilliant little Moran girl should have been cast in a role 'teenth degrees bigger than the part she played."

Like Fox, Lois recognized the potential of sound film and believed that *The River Pirate* had been beneficial to her career, even if her performance did receive uneven reviews. Her enthusiasm for the Movietone did not go unnoticed, and Fox and Sheehan would go on to cast her in several of the studio's subsequent sound efforts, including such high-profile films as *Behind That Curtain* and *Joy Street* as well as the expensive musical *Words and Music*. Lois's success in adapting to the sound process was rooted in more than just her ready support for its promise, however, because she continually and tirelessly applied herself to the task of perfecting her vocal skills. Since those far-off days when she had appeared on stage as the fairy sprite Lalita in Connelly's *The Wisdom Tooth*, she had never abandoned her dream of becoming a theatrical actress, nor had she lost sight of her goal of becoming an accomplished singer. Even after signing her Fox contract, in fact, she nurtured her ambition of eventually achieving success upon the stage. Her vocal and stage efforts of this period demonstrate that the theater was seldom absent from the film actress's thoughts, and it is one of the great ironies of her career that her efforts in this regard helped her film career immeasurably, for by honing her voice and diction she was able make the transition in movies from silence to sound with far greater ease than many of her peers.

Lois approached her vocal and stage goals in two ways. First, she continued studying with a voice teacher and applied herself diligently to improving her vocal strength and clarity. One evening in 1928, she danced with the actor Walter Pidgeon at a party. Pidgeon, who himself was a fine baritone although he rarely sang in his films, encouraged her to sing into his ear, and when she did so he told her that she had a fine voice but it was limited and she should take lessons. He referred her to an Italian former opera singer, Otto Morando. Morando agreed that she had potential and agreed to give her lessons. Serving her orange juice, crumpets, and tea between her vocal exercises, he worked with her to expand the range of her voice and achieved results quickly. She wrote in her journal in 1928, "I really love singing—If I can only make something of my voice!"

Lois continued to look into stage work, although at this time little came of most of her efforts. The most noteworthy episode in this regard was her attempt back in the fall of 1926 to net the much-coveted role of Tessa in the Broadway production of a hugely successful British play, *The Constant Nymph*, which the producer, Basil Dean, had coauthored with Margaret Kennedy. The plot concerned a young girl who falls in love with a self-absorbed composer. Lois had read the part for Dean but did not win it. "He [Dean] says that I have great talent but that I don't have enough technique for the part," she lamented in her journal, continuing, "Oh how I wish I had had some experience on the stage."

In 1928, another noteworthy theatrical possibility came Lois's way. Henry Kolker, who had appeared as her co-conspirator in

Don't Marry and who was also a director and a writer, was planning to stage a Christmastime production of J. M. Barrie's *Peter Pan* and wanted Lois to enact the lead. Lois, who had long dreamed of playing the ethereal Peter, remembered the wealth of material she had read in her grandparents' library in Pittsburgh about how wonderful the legendary actress Maude Adams had been in the role in the original production. She also knew that because the play had been filmed in 1924 with her friend Betty Bronson, this new stage production might be the only chance she would ever have to play the role. "How I should adore it," she wrote in her journal. "Perhaps there is a chance of my doing it." Unfortunately, nothing ever came of the project. Lois never did realize her ambition of playing Peter Pan.

Although neither *The Constant Nymph* nor *Peter Pan* worked out for Lois, she did realize some actual stage experience during this period. From time to time the Writers' Club in Los Angeles staged what it called "playlets," brief plays that were produced for the enjoyment of its members. These playlets attracted little attention from the press and the public, but film actors enjoyed appearing in them, and the *Baltimore Morning Journal* called them "the particular pride of the screen colony." In the fall of 1927, several Hollywood screen stars appeared in Writers' Club playlets, including Lois, who reunited with Belle Bennett in a production entitled *U.S.A.*, which also featured Bryant Washburn. Lois had to fit the playlet into her demanding Fox schedule, working on the project at night, but she was happy to be appearing onstage and was elated to be acting again with Bennett, especially as Bennett possessed a rich background in stage and vaudeville and could offer advice about the craft of theatrical acting.

At Fox Hills in the summer of 1928, Winfield Sheehan appears to have experienced some degree of remorse over having assigned Lois such a lackluster part in *The River Pirate*, because the next two films he chose for her were full bodied and afforded her far more multifaceted opportunities as an actress. Both of these pictures costarred her once again with George O'Brien, both featured larger-than-life plot lines, and both were silents that utilized Movietone sound effects. Sheehan's decision to pair her again with O'Brien proved cunning, because the screen electricity between them was enhanced by Lois's deepening feelings for O'Brien in real life. The wild stories of the films served as vivid backdrops that added flair and color to the emotional interaction of the two stars.

Like *The River Pirate*, *Blindfold* was written by Charles Francis Coe. The new film was based on Coe's story "Fog." The plot concerned a rather plain-looking young reporter, Mary Brower (Lois), whose world is shattered when a group of diamond thieves kills her brother, a policeman, on her engagement day. Her fiancé, Robert Kelly (O'Brien), is also a policeman and sets out to avenge his lost comrade's murder. In his search for the murderer, Kelly is shot by the same gang, a turn of events so devastating to Mary that she lapses into shock and suffers the "fog" or "blindfold" of amnesia. The leader of the gang, the suave, nefarious neurologist Dr. Cornelius Simmons (Earle Foxe, an accomplished character actor), realizes that he can use the girl to further his various schemes. He convinces her that she is one of his gang, and before long she becomes a glamorous, bejeweled femme fatale—of sorts, as her main gown in these sequences is a rather mannish mock tuxedo style accentuated with a carnation resembling a man's boutonnière—who aids the doctor in his schemes. Mary's new life as a confidence woman continues until Kelly locates her and helps her regain her memory. Using Mary as bait, Kelly then devises a trap whereby he can arrest the doctor and his gang. The ruse succeeds, and Dr. Simmons's gang is disbanded.

Both Lois and O'Brien relished their roles in *Blindfold*. Lois explained to the English film weekly *Picture Show* in 1929, "I was quite thrilled at the prospect of reveling for the first time in screen wickedness." She counted Mary Brower as one of the more flamboyant parts she played in film and wrote in her journal in October 1928, "*The Fog*, retitled *Blindfolded* [sic] is good and I am also quite good and decidedly different in it from any other part I have ever played."

During filming, however, she had to contend with the fact that she did not care for the picture's director, Charles Klein, perhaps the first director she had actively disliked. Klein, not to be confused with the Charles Klein who wrote *The Music Master*, was an intense German filmmaker who had a flair for visuals but not, Lois believed, for characterization. When production of the film, which initially retained Coe's original title *Fog*, began in July 1928, Lois wrote in her journal, "Making an extremely interesting picture *The Fog* directed by Charles Klein a splendid director," but by the time shooting was completed in October she wrote, "Charles Klein is clever as a photographer being extremely interested in effects but I do not have confidence in his ability as a director of drama and acting. He is absolutely cold and ununderstanding. Perhaps I am mistaken. Time will show. Personally he is repulsive to me."

Lois's belief that Klein was not properly directing her did not diminish her enthusiasm for the film, however, and she dealt with the problem constructively. Rather than locking horns with the director or initiating messy confrontations on the set, to which she was not temperamentally inclined, she sought advice from outside the studio and asked her many friends for their opinions as to how she should enact her role. She was elated when she received what she considered profound guidance from one of her most admired acquaintances, the famed master photographer Edward Steichen, whom she knew from a series of unembellished, elegant camera portraits he had taken of her, some of which had and would be published in the pages of *Vanity Fair*. "He gave me a good analysis of what I have always instinctively felt," she wrote in her journal in August 1928, "—that all people have, even though it may be hidden deep deep in them, all the characteristics of the human race." Steichen advised her to apply this concept to her acting. "So in order to play a part that seems absolutely impossibly foreign to one," she wrote, "one only has to dig deep and feel these long-covered characteristics and push them forward gradually till they grow and grow. . . . Then one can *live that* person—that is how I have instinctively done some things I suppose—And why I have always contended a good actress could play any part." With Steichen's words in mind, she strove to keep her part in *Blindfold* grounded in realistic and believable human behavior. While Klein was given full directorial credit when the film appeared, Steichen's imprint was also there, in that his philosophies guided Lois in her portrayal of the psychologically complex Mary.

As for O'Brien, he liked playing the simpler part of the macho policeman Robert Kelly not only because it was well suited to his talents but also because his own father, Dan O'Brien, was chief of police in San Francisco and helped him in the interpretation of the character. O'Brien appreciated that Kelly in the story sets out to find the killer of his fellow officer and believed that the plot of *Blindfold* positively depicted policemen and the code of honor to which many adhered. "My dad and I looked forward to this day," he told *Picture Show* when work on the picture started, "for it's an opportunity to show our friend the policeman in the sympathetic light he deserves."

Lois collected stellar reviews for her performance in *Blindfold*, notices that made up for the poor ones she had received for *The River Pirate*. Raymond Ganly, writing in *Motion Picture News Review*, believed that her performance was "deft" and that she was most effective in two scenes in particular: the one in which Mary reacts to the news that her brother has been killed, and the one in which the character bends over the fallen body of her lover and at that moment lapses into amnesia. *Variety* admired that she "did some acting especially in the fainting scenes" and that she could play the amnesia sequences so convincingly. The *Los Angeles Times* remarked, "Lois Moran does an...able piece of work in the somewhat difficult, almost dual, role she is called upon to fill."

Lois's next film, *True Heaven*, was based on "Judith," a story by C. E. Montague that was, as Lois described it in her journal on October 31, 1928, the day production began, "a spy story in which, as a German secret service agent, I disguise myself as a trench prostitute to get information from an English officer. Great fun." O'Brien played the officer. Directed by James Tinling, who had previously directed her in *Don't Marry* and would later again do so in *Words and Music*, *True Heaven* gave Lois the opportunity to enact a story that was by turns war melodrama and absurd romance, a picture that sacrificed credibility in order that its stars could enact one outlandish situation after another. It was an excellent showcase for Lois and O'Brien.

At the time of its release, columnists reported that the two actors were now an established team whom the camera liked and who would be appearing in even more films together. The pairing of "The Chest" and "The Fragile Cameo," they reported, had worked. Fox announced that they would be appearing together in another picture, *Speakeasy*, but that film was ultimately produced with a different cast and the two did not appear again together in film. O'Brien went on to marry the actress Marguerite Churchill in 1933 and became a successful cowboy actor in various Westerns of the 1930s and 1940s. The fact that *True Heaven* was Lois's last film with him, however, did not detract from the fond feelings she generally had for it in later years.

True Heaven was set during World War I. It concerned a young German spy in the Mata Hari mold called Judith (Lois) and a British officer, Lieutenant Philip Gresson (O'Brien), from whom she at first attempts to wrest state secrets and with whom she subsequently falls in love. The film opens with Judith in a Belgian bar freely dispensing caresses to the officers, a flashy, suggestive entrance that recalled Lois's risqué introduction in *Sharp Shooters*. When she notices Gresson, she sets her wiles upon him and manages to get some secret information. However, a bombing raid (realistically depicted) sends everyone in the cabaret into the cellar. Judith realizes she has fallen in love with the young officer, but soon her superiors send her back to Germany, and she vanishes without his knowing the reason.

A short time later, Gresson is sent on a spy mission of his own, to Germany, where he masquerades in a Prussian officer's uniform. Behind enemy lines, he once again encounters Judith. They share a night of romance and ecstatic avowals, and she confides to him her hope that soon the world will be at peace and enjoy true heaven. When morning dawns, however, she agonizes over what to do. She has been deeply instilled with Loyalty to the Kaiser and the Fatherland, and she finds herself in the torturous position of having to choose between her country and her lover. She opts for the former and turns Gresson over to her commander. He is immediately sentenced to execution, and Judith, now regretting what she has done, pleads for his life. Her plea is unsuccessful. Gresson is placed in front of a firing squad, and his death seems certain. Just at that moment, however, news of the Armistice arrives, and he is spared. He forgives Judith, telling her that as a soldier he understands her action, and the film concludes as the two embrace joyfully.

Lois had fun during the production of the film as she had on no other, mainly because of her increasing infatuation with O'Brien. By now she was also at ease at the Fox lot and liked the crew so much that it was not uncommon for her to arrive on the set bearing cupcakes she herself had baked for them. Moreover, she believed that James Tinling was doing a fine job as director, in refreshing contrast to the unsatisfactory experience she had had with Charles Klein when filming *Blindfold*, and she wrote in her journal, "Jim is showing great originality and talent in the directing of the film." Throughout the production, she made additional notes in her journal on how well she believed everything was going. Most significantly, she noted of O'Brien, "George certainly is grand to work with."

The tone of Lois's journal entries suggests that during the production of *True Heaven* her interest in O'Brien was at its height, as was also, perhaps, her burgeoning sexuality, more so than earlier with Fitzgerald. During that October and November of 1928, O'Brien seems to have been a powerful source of joy for her. She made a number of entries in her journal that reveal her to have been conflicted and a tad lovesick over the man she called "the gentleman." "Quite upset again," she wrote on November 9. "Afraid I will never truly fall in love though (Don't be silly, Lois). I'm just very attracted to him and also very fond of him but would never think of him seriously. I do love him to kiss me though.... A few kisses isn't being untrue to one's ideal, do you think? I used to say it was before ever having experienced one—How one's ideas change."

On December 6, the day she concluded work on the picture, she wrote:

> I did exceptionally good work during this last month, I think. Of course, I was tremendously interested in the story and picture but this other excitement helped, too. I had the same feeling during November and December last year [probably referring to the filming of *Sharp Shooters*], too, if I remember correctly. And about the same person. Just the silly desire to have him kiss me, knowing all the time that I didn't love him. I suppose it's well for me that he doesn't feel the same.

Neither Lois's affectation of a hard-boiled attitude on the subject of O'Brien nor her professed lack of interest in whether he reciprocates her romantic feelings is convincing. Of all the actors she had worked with, she wrote entries of a romantic nature only about O'Brien. On December 2, she even penned in her journal, referring to him, "Here I am, crying about that fool again!" Moreover, the final two mentions she makes of him in her journal smack of a woman scorned. While fan magazines trumpeted her and O'Brien as one of the great new screen pairings, later that December she wrote that "George is too afraid to disclose himself," and in January she penned what was for her the ultimate dismissal: "George O'Brien would be great if he had intelligence." The feelings she had referred to as "this other excitement" had run their course, even though her new O'Brien-as-clodhopper attitude appears rooted more in emotional self-defense that in fact.

Such personal involvements between Lois and O'Brien, or the lack thereof, did not detract from *True Heaven*'s release being generally enjoyable for her. There was initial confusion that the film was a rehash of another similarly named recent war picture, *Seventh Heaven,* which had starred Janet Gaynor and Charles Farrell, and the picture had additionally to compete with such weighty films as *Wild Orchids* with Greta Garbo, *The Godless Girl* with Lina Basquette, and *The Canary Murder Case* with William Powell and Louise Brooks; but as word spread that *True Heaven* was a different kind of film with its own merits, theatergoers went to see it in healthy numbers. Lois, moreover, received generally good reviews for her portrayal of Judith. The *Los Angeles Times* printed a particularly laudatory assessment of her performance: "An extraordinary performance by Lois Moran is the chief distinction of *True Heaven*. Possessing a charm and a grace at the outset which make her always easy to look at, Miss Moran has gained steadily in dramatic stature since she burst, in surprised freckle-faced innocence, upon photoplay fans in the easily recalled *Stella Dallas*."

The most valued feedback she received for *True Heaven* came from Tinling. Midway through the film's production, the two chatted on the set about her performance. "He thinks it will be the first time I have truly been *awakened* since *Stella Dallas*," she wrote in her journal on November 19. "Perhaps he's right." Tinling believed that the romantic portions of the picture would enable Lois to achieve an emotional openness that he believed had been lacking in her films subsequent to *Stella Dallas*, and she agreed with him. "I know I feel tremendously different, really," she wrote, "stirred and moved to the very depths." She added a summation of the emotional progression she believed she had achieved in her films thus far:

> The past few years have been very busy and uncertain where my emotions were concerned—I suppose it was the process of growing up—I have *always* given my best to pictures, though, never could act half-heartedly. But now I feel that I *understand*. My sympathy for people and things is much greater. I'm cruelly youthful no longer.

Principal filming of *True Heaven* began to wrap during the Thanksgiving season of 1928. O'Brien flew to San Francisco to be with his family during the holiday. Lois remained in Hollywood. Still lovesick over O'Brien, and missing him while he was away, she attempted to assuage her bruised emotions by attending parties. Charles Chaplin, who had appeared with her in Ralph Barton's spoof of *Camille* in 1926, gave one such soirée at his home. Lois chatted amiably with the famed "Little Tramp" and made the acquaintance of the novelist, social historian, and political activist Waldo Frank. Then considered one of America's premier intellectuals, Frank was most renowned for having written a book in 1919 on revitalizing American culture entitled *Our America*. Lois delighted in talking with him at the party—to her, this powerfully cerebral man was more intriguing even than Chaplin—and she described him in her journal as "most interesting."

Another Thanksgiving gathering Lois attended was not as pleasant for her, however. On the evening of November 24, she attended a party that her friend Bebe Daniels gave for Marion Davies. At this social event, she met up with two celebrated gentlemen of the day, the director Marshall Neilan and the wealthy aviator, filmmaker, and playboy Howard Hughes. Neilan had directed Hughes's 1926 film *Everybody's Acting* and had been the first director on a film Hughes was currently making, *Hell's Angels*. Lois was initially happy to chat with the two men, but by the time she arrived home early the next morning she was upset because one of them made what she considered to be an inappropriate advance. "Learned another lesson today," she wrote angrily in her journal that evening, "namely that men who appear to be 'big brothers' aren't always 'big brothers.'" She had gone to the party depressed over O'Brien and had felt vulnerable and trusting when she encountered Neilan and Hughes. "Feeling rather sad and low," she wrote,

> I permitted one of the aforementioned to put a sympathetic arm about me and perched in a big armchair with him in front of the fire—With the result of 1st a flaming embrace quite as warm as any fire, 2nd the prompt crossing off of my calling list that gentleman's

name.... His kiss seemed to me like one of bad experiences, the gorrey [*sic*], nervous kind—strange, I never thought of that man as such a silly fool! *Men* are so stressful at times.... I've learned a grand lesson, though—No more sitting on men's laps for *me* unless the sitter has *very very* proper credentials or happens to be *the* one.

Lois never specified whether it was Neilan or Hughes who had so offended her, no doubt believing that to do so would have been bad form. However, given her predilection for aviators, and judging from the many accounts we have today of his wild youth in the film colony, Hughes was most likely the man in question. Moreover, she gave an interview the following year in which she mentioned Neilan in passing but in a friendly context that did not suggest she had any animosity toward him. In his 2001 biography, *Hughes: The Private Diaries, Memos, and Letters*, Richard Hack describes Hughes during this time as "morally corrupt," preoccupied with seeking out young actresses for sex.

After recording the experience in her journal, Lois did not again speak of the incident. Says Tim Young:

> You would think that this kind of encounter with a man as famous as Howard Hughes would have been something Mother would have talked about, but this probably was one of those long-ago events that she put in the back of her mind when she left Hollywood. The past, even when it involved someone like Howard Hughes, was not something Mother usually thought much about.

Interestingly, Craig Broadway, the grandson of Lois's chauffeur, Howard Pierce, remembers his grandfather's mentioning that he had driven Lois to visit Hughes earlier in the 1920s. Perhaps relations between her and the millionaire had been friendlier before the botched pass at the party for Davies. Shortly after her marriage, she again saw Hughes when she and her new husband hosted a shipboard party for him and the actress Billie Dove. No doubt she ceased to place much importance upon the incident once she was safely betrothed.

The advent of the Christmas holidays proved happier for Lois. Fox, increasingly anxious to make use of the Movietone sound process, in which he had substantially invested and which by this time had evolved to the point where it had even been used in a Chicago hospital to create the first filmed surgical procedure, determined with Sheehan that a musical would provide them the ideal means with which to promote their sound product. They thus set about spending huge amounts of money on and casting many of their contract players in a lavish production filled with short comedic and musical numbers that would emulate the spectacular sequences produced onstage as the *Ziegfeld Follies*. They called theirs the *Fox Movieland Follies*, and they selected Lois, owing to her voice, dancing, and stage background, to be one of the picture's primary stars. Additionally, they chose Harlan Thompson to write the book; and they retained the talented showmen Con Conrad, Sidney Mitchell, and David Stamper to write the score and special numbers. They assigned Marcel Silver, a French filmmaker new to Hollywood, as the initial director. Production on the film's various numbers began as early as 1927, though it was not until 1929 that a feature-length compilation was released. One of the first sequences Lois filmed was an exotic musical number entitled "The Belle of Samoa," in which she donned a South Sea Island grass skirt and sang and danced with a chorus of some sixty island girls.

Filmed in November 1927, *The Belle of Samoa* gave Lois ample opportunity to showcase her musical talents, in addition to being the first film in which she spoke. She worked hard, preparing much of her own choreography, and on the evening of November 4, the day during which most of the shooting had been accomplished, she wrote with satisfaction about the experience in her journal. "How I did enjoy it all!" she penned. "I liked particularly the feeling of power one has up on a large stage with many spot-lights on one and a great audience out front whom one can amuse or bore at will—There is such a sense of freedom, abandon, and strength." In addition to the musical scenes, Lois also filmed dialogue sequences with the veteran comedy team

Clark and McCullough, who started in vaudeville and whose films of the 1930s today enjoy a minor cult following. She had to think fast in order to keep up with the rapid delivery of the quick-witted comedians. "C. & M. are extremely clever," she recorded in her journal, "and seem to write all their own lines. Thank God I wasn't born a vaudeville comedian. Don't think I could have stood the strain." A bit later, she further noted, "Rehearsed again with Clark & McCullough today and received a grand lesson in vaudeville technique. Everything moves so quickly and, if well-done, very spontaneously. They are extremely clever."

Only a two-reel film of approximately twenty-five minutes, *The Belle of Samoa* nonetheless attracted a good deal of attention. *Variety* noted that she "displayed some hitherto uncovered charms" in the film, and Ed O'Malley, writing a short time later in a *Filmograph* article in which he discussed her transition from silent to sound pictures, observed:

> She hearkened to the "mike" and immediately found him a most ardent suitor. Almost overnight she leaped into talkie heights through the medium of a little two-reeler comedy, *The Belles* [sic] *of Samoa*, from the chrysalis to the butterfly—the new Lois Moran. She had everything—grace of form, nimbleness of limbs, sweetness and distinctness of voice, glitter, fire and alluring beauty.

Lois again acted in material for the feature-length *Movieland Follies*—which Fox by this time had renamed the *Movietone Follies*, in deference to his patented process that made it all possible—during that winter of 1928, now under the direction of Tinling (Silver had returned to France). Filming of the *Follies* overlapped with that of *True Heaven*, but Lois did not mind the exhausting schedule because she enjoyed the work and, in the case of the *Follies*, was elated that the Movietone process lacked what she called in her journal "the horrid scratch that the Vitaphone gives to voices." As *Picture Play* reported at the time, "Lois is having the time of her life working in the Fox

Follies." The primary number she now filmed was a large-scale Art Deco production number in which, donning an ostentatious feathered dress, she sang and danced with a troupe of handsome young men and an entourage of glittering chorus girls. The intense work left Lois, as she noted in her journal, "terribly tired." Nonetheless, she wrote of the number, "Methinks it will be darling," and described it all as "gorgeous fun."

As all this footage was being completed, Fox and Sheehan found themselves in a quandary: they had shot much more material than could be contained in a single film. In addition to Lois's sequences, they had numbers from a wide variety of other actors, including Sue Carol, David Rollins, Lola Lane, Dixie Lee, and an abundance of singers, dancers, and choruses of show boys and girls. They resolved the issue by dividing the footage into two separate films. As the *Los Angeles Times* reported, "When Fox had completed its Fox Follies, it discovered that there was enough material in the production for two pictures. So it thriftily removed the numbers of Lois Moran...and has put them away in the vault to be used in another musical comedy which some of the gifted writers signed by Fox will shortly begin to compose." In 1929, Fox released its two films: *The Fox Movietone Follies of 1929*, which featured Sue Carol as the principal actress, and *Words and Music*, which featured Lois as its star.

Lois finished filming her sequences on Christmas Eve, 1928. She had remained at home for Thanksgiving, but for Christmas she desired a non-domestic environment and determined that Yosemite would provide a diverting setting for the holiday. "The valley is very beautiful this year," she wrote excitedly in her journal, enjoying the respite from the demanding shooting schedules that characterized her life in Hollywood. The light dusting of snow that fell upon Yosemite that winter invigorated her; and, free of the demands of her day-to-day life at the studio, she skied, skated at a nighttime carnival, and embarked upon a sleigh ride through the valley under the moon while two college girls behind her sang "Black Bottom." "I am fast acquiring the knack of being able to 'ecstasize' myself," she wrote in her journal. "I mean it has become easier for me to gain real enjoyment from beautiful things."

Lois returned to Los Angeles in time to attend a New Year's Eve party given by Winfield Sheehan at the Mayfair Hotel. Refreshed and happy, she looked forward to 1929, believing that the "Fragile Cameo" had proven herself durable and that the new year would bring her continued success and personal growth. A few weeks previously, confident that at Fox she would soon achieve a film triumph that would rival that she had enjoyed with *Stella Dallas*, she had written in her journal, "I can hardly wait for my big success! Somehow I feel it can't be long in arriving." Additionally, she felt certain that in the coming months she would better understand her emotions and her relationship to the opposite sex, aspects of her life that because of O'Brien had become increasingly important to her during the previous year. "It seems I've always been in a muddle emotionally," she wrote in her journal. "A pleasant muddle, nevertheless—It's fun to think about now that I seem to be wading out of it—To be truthful, I'll probably find myself in a much deeper one before long; but who cares—Bigger and better muddles for me—they make life interesting."

"Understanding, Love, Observation, and Imagination"

12

"Steichen told me wonderful things tonight," Lois Moran wrote in her journal in August 1928. "How to make life *rich*, and *how* to be great or strive to be." Lois trusted the judgment of her friend, whom she believed "radiated a grand something always" and whose advice had guided her so winningly during the production of *Blindfold* earlier that same year, and she listened intently to everything he said to her. That summer evening, the photographer explained that the elements one needs in order to live a happy life are understanding, love, observation, and imagination. Lois took his words to heart and resolved to live her life in accordance with this wisdom. She had embodied naturally the personality elements that Steichen outlined, but she never before had been self-conscious of them. Now that she was, she set about applying these qualities to the way she viewed her friends, and she recorded the results in her journal. It is evident from these entries that she began to regard people more critically.

One of the first people Lois attempted to understand and observe after Steichen offered his advice was the powerful editor and drama critic George Jean Nathan, whom she and Gladys had for years known socially. Lois had initially been awestruck by the imposing Nathan, but as time went on she changed her opinion of him, coming to view him as a pompous, intellectually limited social climber. "He is brilliant but up to a certain point only," she penned in her journal in October

1928. "Unfortunately for his peace of mind, he realizes this and trying to fool himself and others assumes a slightly pompous air and quite a little conceit." Nathan, apparently, was not aware the change in Lois's opinion of him, because in later years he would speak fondly of her.

Other acquaintances whom Lois began to view more critically, all in 1928 journal entries, included *Vanity Fair*'s managing editor, Donald Freeman; the novelist Carl Van Vechten; and the violinist Fritz Kreisler. She admired Freeman, and her friendship with him helped ensure that her photograph would appear in his publication several times throughout the years, but she thought he was slumming. "Donald is wasting himself," she wrote. "His environment seems to be spoiling him—that terrific New York atmosphere would spoil anyone who wasn't terribly strong." She addressed another journal entry to Van Vechten, referencing his recent Hollywood novel *Spider Boy*: "Carl, your *Spider Boy* was a disappointment, one would think you were small, petty, almost turned Hollywood, if you understand the expression." Of Kreisler, she remarked, "He is no longer an inspired violinist, though a great man and a fine artist."

In spite of her increasingly censorious views of certain men in her life, the prospect of romance was on Lois's mind in the late 1920s and early 1930s. In the autumn of 1928 she referred to herself in her journal as "a silly romantic little fool." She was frustrated in her love life, however, because she was divided in her thinking on the subject of the opposite sex. On one extreme, she maintained that she was a romantic and that her utmost pursuit in life was to marry, settle down, and have a family. "I long for a dark head on the pillow beside me," she wrote in her journal in 1932. On the other extreme, she was at heart a suffragist, the kind of woman who would later be called a feminist, who was not above criticizing men when she felt belittled as a woman. "Men, as a general rule, are so damned selfish," she complained in her journal in 1928:

Just pampered darlings. Women are the real cause because they make such fools of themselves over the male of the species. There is not much to do about it, except to be just as selfish as they are, use them as a silly amusement (as they employ women). . . . Personally, if a man treats me as a mental inferior, I practically go up in smoke.

In spite of her mixed feelings, Lois generally enjoyed her relationships with men. In the aftermath of her affair with Fitzgerald, she blossomed sexually and was infatuated with several men in the years before she met Clarence Young in the autumn of 1934. There was no scarcity of real-life love interests for her at the time: her admirers included, among others, Douglass Montgomery, Neil Vanderbilt, and George Abbott. Montgomery was a young, amiable film actor, best known today for having played Laurie in the 1933 screen version of *Little Women*, who charmed her in the early 1930s. "Perhaps I should marry him, if he'll have me," she wrote in her journal in 1934. "I should like to get the marriage germ out of my system. We would probably divorce in a few years and both be a lot better from the experience." Vanderbilt was a newspaperman and writer whom she met in early 1934. Lois described him in her journal as "by far the most interesting man I've met in the last year or so—a liberal and a radical who really knows what he's talking about." Abbott was a renowned Broadway producer, writer, and director with whom Lois carried on an ongoing flirtation and to whom she referred as her "flame" in one journal entry in 1934.

As for her career, between 1929 and 1931 was the wrong time for her to be at the Fox studio. At the end of the 1920s, William Fox ambitiously set out to become the most powerful of all film moguls, but his schemes backfired in 1929 because of the stock market crash, government antitrust actions initiated against him, and an automobile accident that disabled him for two months. Morale at the studio was badly shaken, and in 1930 he was forced to sell his shares in the company to a group of bankers. It seems more than coincidence that in the midst of this turmoil the quality of Lois's films at the studio began to drop. The career maladies she had feared might result from signing a studio contract gradually came to pass as one weak picture after another was handed to her. There was little she could do other than to do her best with the mediocre material. Sheehan was himself so embroiled in the studio's business disputes that he was not of much help to her. She became less confident and arrived for work each day at Fox Hills in increasingly downcast spirits. The movies she made during this period were by no means a totally bad lot, but many of them were haphazardly conceived and scripted. There were exceptions, such as *Behind That Curtain*, but as a whole this group of films marked a pronounced decline in her career.

Fox publicists made much of the studio's Movietone sound process and announced to the press in 1929 that Lois, because of her voice training, would be among the elite group of the studio's first actors to appear regularly in sound features. One of the first of these films was *Making the Grade*, a silent film with roughly 10 percent Movietone dialogue that again teamed her with Edmund Lowe, but with much weaker results than had been achieved with their earlier *Publicity Madness*. Directed by Alfred E. Green from a George Ade short story, *Making the Grade* concerned a man (Lowe) who strives for success when he returns to his hometown. Lois played the role of Lettie Ewing, the manager of an exclusive tearoom who had been Lowe's childhood sweetheart and whom he now seeks to win back. The film, complete with a trite happy ending, had the feel of a standard, assembly-line studio romance, prompting *Variety* to remark that overall it was only "fair for the average house program." *Variety* did like Lois's "small but appealing role," however, and *Filmograph* found her "very sweet."

Fortunately, two far more worthwhile films followed *Making the Grade*. The first was *Joy Street*, a silent with synchronized Movietone sound and musical effects. It was a youth-oriented party film with a plot that traced the life of Marie Colman as a schoolgirl turned flapper, a story to match what Lois described at the time in her journal as her own "very buoyant" nature. Raymond Cannon was the director, and the film featured Nick Stuart (Lois's costar in *The River Pirate*), Rex Bell, John Breeden, José Crespo, Sally Phipps, and Lupita Tovar, making her film debut in a career that is today most remembered for the 1931 Spanish version of *Dracula*.

Lois delighted in enacting a roaring Jazz Age heroine who was more what columnists of the day referred to as a "nicotine type" than a sweet, innocent lass and who promised to, as Ann Sylvester phrased it in *Picture Play*, "out-Crawford Joan in *Our Dancing Daughters*" (Crawford had famously epitomized the flapper in that 1928 film). In an interview she gave to Sylvester for *Picture Play*, Lois demonstrated some of the new skills she learned while making *Joy Street*. Reported Sylvester:

> Proudly she reached for a cigarette. With the poise of an addict, she flared the match on the bottom of her shoe, and inhaled deeply. No faking—a real, down-in-the-lungs puff. The wide eyes narrowed to a glint of—you know what I mean. The lips parted into a cynical half-smile. Slowly, carefully, she exhaled. It was the last of the kiddie motif. "Don't tell anybody," she whispered, "but it took me a week to learn that."

Joy Street was a popular film at the box office and proved a boon to Lois's sagging spirits at Fox. The *Los Angeles Times* called it "a daring story of modern youth and its 'whoopee-making' proclivities," and the *Hollywood News* quoted William K. Howard, the director of *The River Pirate*, as remarking, "Lois has made the transition from sweet girl ingénue to sophisticated leading woman without losing any of her charm. There is a wonderful difference between the Lois Moran of *Stella Dallas* and the sophisticated leading lady of *Joy Street*."

Her next film, *Behind That Curtain*, a talkie that became a career highlight, further cheered her. Based on a novel by Earl Derr Biggers, the film is primarily remembered today for an early screen appearance by the sleuth Charlie Chan, here played by the Korean actor E. L. Park a short time before the Swedish actor Warner Oland made the part his own in a series of films made in the 1930s, and because it included Boris Karloff in a brief role in his first talking film as a servant who mutters platitudes about the desert. It more properly should be remembered, however, for a fine plot full of twists and turns and for showcasing Lois in a spellbinding, vastly underrated performance. Irving Cummings, who crafted a well-mounted production, directed the film. Modern audiences are sometimes put off by the technical creakiness of this early sound undertaking, but the patient viewer is rewarded by a worthy film.

In *Behind That Curtain*, Lois had the opportunity, rare in her later pictures, to enact a three-dimensional role of substance, grit, and emotional complexity. She plays Eve Mannering, a young London heiress who unwittingly marries a philandering murderer (Philip Strange, a young Fox hopeful whose career never blossomed), turns to an old acquaintance (Warner Baxter, who had played the title role in the film version of *The Great Gatsby* in 1926) for love and guidance, and becomes swept up in a thriller that takes her to India, the Persian desert, and San Francisco. As the troubled Eve, she faced an onslaught of difficulties and handled them with intelligence and dignity. Her training both as a dancer and as an actress in silent pictures allowed her to use her face and body with extraordinary effectiveness, most especially in scenes in which she constricted the muscles of her body to help her convey anguish and frustration. Additionally, many critics praised Lois and Baxter for their precise onscreen diction, a rare and difficult achievement in those infant days of sound productions.

It is not an exaggeration to say that Lois dominated *Behind That Curtain* as only a star actress could have. The film historian Don Miller observed, "In *Behind That Curtain*, she [managed] to partly overcome the stilted screenplay and situations largely on her own merits." Today, the film is often a disappointment to mystery fans because Charlie Chan plays such a small part in it, although Biggers had featured the character more prominently in the novel, and many Boris Karloff admirers are unhappy because his character was onscreen for such a short time, but neither of these factors detracts from the fact that in this film Lois effected some of her most confident and convincing acting.

At the time of its original release, *Behind That Curtain*, which opened the grandiose San Francisco Fox Theater, garnered generally excellent reviews, in particular the write-up afforded it by *Variety*. In its review after the film had played at the Fox-owned Roxy in New York, it gushed, "It is big box office from the first iris to the last camera flower. It is on a par with the best Fox has put on Broadway and far superior in meaty earning qualities to many of his recent average." The periodical was liberal also in its praise for Lois's performance: "Lois Moran shows more promise as a young actress of emotional ability in *Behind That Curtain* than in any picture in which she has yet appeared." The production of the film had been arduous, however, because of difficulties that arose with some of the location filming. In Death Valley, where the desert scenes were filmed, the heat became so intense that cast and crew were forced to sleep under wet sheets. In San Francisco, excited crowds made the filming of outdoor street scenes so difficult that diversionary tactics had to be devised in order to complete the shooting.

The next Lois picture that Fox released after *Behind That Curtain* was *Words and Music*, the Movietone sound film that the studio had assembled from material it had deemed too worthwhile to be featured in the short subject *Movietone Follies*. Directed by James Tinling and produced by Chandler Sprague, who would play a part in several of Lois's upcoming films, *Words and Music* consisted largely of three spectacular musical production numbers framed in a flimsy plot that concerned a collegiate music contest and starred Lois as a coed named Mary Brown. Featured with Lois were Tom Patricola, David Percy, Helen Twelvetrees, Frank Albertson, and an uncredited Frances Dee in her first film. Also of note in the cast was one Duke Morrison, appearing in his first credited screen role, a virile young actor who would soon change his name to John Wayne. The picture was well received, *Variety* praising its "pictorial magnificence," and it is likely that because it so ostentatiously showcased Lois's musical and dancing talents, it was instrumental in her winning the stage role of Mary Turner in *Of Thee I Sing* two years later.

At the time she made *Words and Music*, Lois took time to write a revealing entry in her journal about what she had come to feel about Hollywood. She was in pessimistic spirits about her career in general, and such depression was bound to have surfaced in her writing, but she also made some cogent observations. The entry is dated December 11, 1929:

> I have been intending for a long-while to hold forth on Hollywood, old diary, so here goes—
>
> First of all, it is a small town, not in size (My God, no!), but in characteristics. Every inhabitant's business is the business of every other inhabitant, some of the girls are very pretty and the town is usually closed up by eleven. All the residents are possessed of the idea that their city is the only one worth living in (of course, the inhabitants of Kalamazoo probably say the same), but somehow people are terribly emphatic about it out here—The climate *is* wonderful. I grant them that. *But* the mental stagnation is colossal. Perhaps with the advent of talking pictures, and therefore the migration of numerous literary and musical luminaries to this fair coast, the intellectual situation will be less pathetic. The denizens of the motion picture world are like sweet children, adorable, carefree, silly, kind-hearted, and intellectually nil—How on God's earth are we expected to turn out masterpieces of art with such material? Of course there are the inevitable exceptions and they are the upholders of whatever desire they have to something [*sic*] really beautiful—
>
> The others are so very dear, just like a lot of cute little puppies enraptured with a glorious, lovely life—They move about through a maze of beautiful houses, cars, clothes, perfumes—Still in a dream—Life seems really perfect to them—But then, in the dreamy beautiful muddle that is their life they begin to want everything, they shift husbands, wives, lovers, continuously. They really seem to me in a sense, very innocent about it all. It's done in such a careless, non

begrudging way—Thought means nothing to them—Why bother to think? Life is too exquisite, too fast-moving.

Utilizing the analytical skills Steichen taught her, Lois made other specific mention of her acting peers in 1929:

There are so painfully few good actors or actresses. Louise Dresser is an actress worthy of the name, Janet Gaynor can do one type of portrayal beautifully, Greta Garbo is very fine and a great personality, Norma Shearer is always competent but never great, Clara Bow might be great if she had intelligence, Dolores Costello is luscious looking and possessed of great charm but as to acting is nil, Lillian Gish was great in three pictures, *Way Down East, The White Sister,* and *Broken Blossoms,* but her technique is too obvious and she does not really live, she is always the same, Mae Marsh and Nazimova were the nearest to *artists* we have ever had in pictures—It's such a pity they dropped out.... Charlie Farrell has great talent in certain parts, those where he can play himself, a masculine Gaynor as it were, [Emil] Jannings is fine but always the same, Richard Barthelmess is splendid but not possessed of enough intelligence, Paul Muni most approaches the great actor—and, of course [John] Barrymore could be if he so wished.

Erich von Stroheim and F. W. Murnau were among the directors Lois most respected, although she viewed each with reservations. "Von Stroheim missed terribly on *The Wedding March*," she wrote, referencing his 1928 drama in which he had starred with Fay Wray. "He shouldn't write his own stories if they are going to prove as uninteresting as that one. But his previous films have been splendid." In an observation about Murnau, she rather bitterly alluded having missed out on playing the lead role in *Sunrise*:

Murnau is great in certain respects but lacks certain qualities.... Perhaps it is because everything has not been quite fitted—if you catch my meaning. Many elements enter in to a perfect thing. First the story, then the director, actors, etc. I should like to see him direct a great story with fine actors with plenty of character, not the weak, putty-like people he so often has, people that he can mould well, but *cannot* inject *life* into—That vital, glorious something is nearly always missing in his actors.

The irony of Lois's criticisms of her fellow film actors' work is that her own pictures at this time, which from here on were all talkies, were not much better. *A Song of Kentucky* followed *Words and Music* at the box office, but it was a less impressive film. Produced by Chandler Sprague and directed by Lewis Seiler, this picture was an odd mix of romance, crime, horse racing, and mediocre songs. Lois plays Lee Coleman, a racehorse owner who is engaged to one man, played by Douglas Gilmore, but who falls in love with another, played by Joseph Wagstaff. Intrigue ensues, with Gilmore framing Wagstaff for a crime, but by the end Lois and Wagstaff have overcome the odds, and all ends happily. Based on a book by Con Conrad, Sidney Mitchell, and Archie Gottler, the film was slight, but Lois, outfitted by her *Stella Dallas* costumer Sophie Wachner, looked sparkling. Dorothy Burgess, the actress Fay Bainter's niece, who appeared in many films throughout the 1930s and 1940s, and Hedda Hopper, who would again appear with Lois in *West of Broadway* two years later and who would eventually achieve fame as a Hollywood gossip columnist, were also in the cast.

In 1930, Fox loaned Lois out to Warner Brothers, a studio at which she had never worked, for a substantial opportunity, the female lead in a much-heralded upcoming Al Jolson picture, *Mammy*. At the time, Jolson was a huge and powerful star. Zelda Fitzgerald once remarked, long before the advent of the Beatles, that he was more popular than Jesus. Lois believed that appearing in a film with him would do wonders for her career. What she did not count on, however, was that the size of Jolson's ego matched the magnitude of his fame, and that he would make certain that the finished picture was edited to showcase him and him alone. Indeed, one watching the film today has a hard time of it if not a Jolson devotee.

Directed by Michael Curtiz, *Mammy* did not deviate from Jolson's proven success formula. A heavy drama was liberally punctuated with songs delivered by him in bravura, vaudevillian style. Based on a play entitled *Mr. Bones*, by James Gleason and Irving Berlin, the film concerned the goings-on at a traveling minstrel show, including murder, and featured several songs by Berlin. Lois played the film's love interest, Nora Meadows, and in a few scenes was quite lovely, especially in one sequence in which Jolson sings "Across the Breakfast Table" to her while she looks down at him from a landing, but otherwise she was almost totally wasted in the film. Every potential opportunity she had to develop her character was discarded as the film relentlessly refocused the story upon him. Other stars in the film, including Lowell Sherman and Louise Dresser, suffered similar fates.

Commercially, such inequities hardly mattered, because the film was a great success, affording Lois the most exposure she had had in many months. In a review of the film after its posh New York premier at the Warner's New York, *Variety* reported that after the screening Jolson appeared before the audience and remarked, in response to wild applause, "I hope you're not kidding me; that you really like this picture, although I suppose in the morning I will read where some cuckoo says it's lousy." Such "cuckoos" did exist, as they still do, but it cannot be disputed that the film stands out as an important cultural phenomenon of its day.

It is unfortunate, however, that Lois was used to such ill advantage in *Mammy*. In its original review, *Variety* put it most succinctly when it observed of Lois's performance, "Miss Moran looked oke, with little to do," but, because it was a film Jolson made at the peak of his fame, it remains one of her best-remembered pictures. Lois perhaps best expressed her own attitude toward such films in a 1928 journal entry in which she targeted films that were box-office successes but artistic disappointments. "If you ask me," she wrote, "all pictures aimed *directly* at the old b.o. are usually the biggest failures."

Back at Fox, Lois next appeared in *Not Damaged*. Released approximately a month after *Mammy*, this film did not give her improved acting opportunities and, at that, did much poorer business at the box office. In it, she played Gwen Stewart, an idealistic girl who dreams of being married in a church ceremony and who is intent upon remaining a virgin ("not damaged") until her wedding night. Working in a music store and rooming with a flamboyant clairvoyant (Inez Courtney), she has a devil of a time maintaining her purity, however. At one point she has a dream of herself walking nude down a street, an image her roommate tells her suggests that true love will come to her. Eventually, she does meet her dream lover (Walter Byron) at a party, falls in love with him, and at last enjoys the wedding of her dreams, her purity intact and unsullied. *Variety* believed that the film, which Chandler Sprague directed, was "a good program picture that holds interest throughout," but disliked the "unexpected sugary sentimental ending."

Byron would again appear with Lois in her next film, *The Dancers*. In theory, *The Dancers* would have been a refreshingly robust film for Lois. Written by Sir Gerald du Maurier and Viola Tree, it had proven a showy stage triumph for Tallulah Bankhead in 1923. In reality, it did not make an effective transition to the screen in 1930. On celluloid a syrupy romance set in a mountain lumber camp, this film featured English characters behaving much too politely for the setting. Lois played the role of Diana, a standard love interest that did little to further her career and of which *Variety* commented, "It's doubtful if any actress short of an inspired Bernhardt could have made much of this stereotyped fictional figure." Chandler Sprague, who had produced *Words and Music* and *A Song of Kentucky* and who was fresh from his work on *Not Damaged*, directed *The Dancers*, and the film costarred Phillips Holmes, a charismatic youth who is today best remembered for *An American Tragedy* (1931) and *Dinner at Eight* (1933); Mrs. Patrick Campbell, the legendary Edwardian stage actress; and Byron. It also featured Mae Clarke, a comely tyro actress who achieved her career zenith the following year with *The Public Enemy*, in which James Cagney famously thrust a grapefruit into her face, and *Frankenstein*. In *Featured Player: An Oral Autobiography of Mae Clarke* (1996), James Curtis quotes Clarke's remembrances of Lois at the time of *The Dancers*: "Goodness knows, at the time, she was very important. She had already made a hit. She was more or less the bigger girl on the Fox lot and I was Johnny-come-lately. I realized I had better behave myself. But she was very nice."

Lois established a friendship with Clarke and in 1954 would arrange for her to make a guest appearance on her television series, *Waterfront*. Additionally, she greatly admired and was perhaps in later years even haunted by the memory of the soulful Phillips Holmes. She was deeply saddened when he was killed in a plane crash during World War II. She was also delighted to be appearing with Campbell, who had become a theatrical legend in plays by George Bernard Shaw, including *Pygmalion*, in which she originated the role of Eliza Doolittle. She had also appeared, far less successfully, in the title role of the short-lived 1924 stage version of *Stella Dallas*. Lois wrote to the Lya de Putti scholar Albert Guérard in 1981 about the experience of working with Campbell on *The Dancers*. "She was about 68, younger than I am now," she said, "but I thought of her as *the* great lady of the English theater—She was great fun. When she saw herself in the rushes for the first time, she was appalled—'Oh, my God, I look like a sack of potatoes tied in the middle.'... She'd tell me 'Always speak in pear-shaped tones, my dear.'" The unique cast notwithstanding, *The Dancers* was poorly received. *Variety* summed up the critical reception: "It's all very tedious."

Lois's following film, *Under Suspicion*, confirmed her fears that she was enmeshed in a losing streak of mostly mediocre pictures. This light musical paired her with J. Harold Murray, a noted vaudeville and Broadway musical performer who had recently appeared in three other musicals at Fox. The plot of the film was slight, tracing the romance between Alice Freil (Lois) and John Smith, a Canadian

Mountie (Murray), but it featured lovely scenery and was in fact the first sound film to be filmed in the Canadian Rockies. The highlight of the picture was a blazing forest fire. Directed by A. F. Erickson, the film did not ignite at the box office.

Shortly after *Under Suspicion* played in theaters, Lois appeared in a full-length stage play, the first time she had done so since *The Wisdom Tooth* in 1925. Increasingly dismayed by the declining quality of her film roles, she reasoned that the stage could offer her fresh opportunities to revitalize her career and to again showcase her abilities as a serious actress. On a brief leave of absence from the studio, she cast her net for a part in a Broadway play and landed a lead role in her friend Robert Sherwood's newest drama, *This Is New York*. Sherwood had admired Lois since he had written his *McCall's* and *Vanity Fair* reviews of her performance in *Stella Dallas* in 1926.

Unfortunately, *This Is New York* was one of Sherwood's least successful undertakings, even if he did originally characterize it, as quoted by John Mason Brown in *The Worlds of Robert E. Sherwood* (1965), as "an out-and-out comedy, almost a farce, and extremely modern." Lois played Emma Krull, a senator's daughter who becomes entangled in the suicide of a bootlegger's moll. Premiering at the Plymouth Theater on November 28, 1930, costarring Geoffrey Kerr and featuring costumes by Hattie Carnegie, the play was unsuccessful, running only fifty-nine performances, and it was not one of Sherwood's better-remembered works. He himself was not particularly fond of it.

At the time Lois appeared in *This Is New York*, other film actors were also appearing in stage plays, but much was particularly made of Lois's venture into Broadway. The finished production, however, turned out to be neither the artistic nor the commercial triumph for which she had hoped. It did provide her with invaluable theatrical experience, though. In an interview she gave to the columnist Mabel Duke at the time, Lois commented on the difficulties she faced as a film star appearing in a Broadway play:

When a new star comes to Broadway in a blaze of glory, folks sit back and say "Show me!" It's the performance and not the name that counts.... Stage and screen audiences are vastly different. Screen fans go to see a favorite player. Stage audiences want a good play, and no matter how talented the star is, if the play is poor it is bound to fail.

Although *This Is New York* was not a hit, Lois garnered good reviews for her work. Brooks Atkinson remarked in the *New York Times*, "Lois Moran, once of the movies, has a modest splendor about her acting," and *Screen Play* noted, "Lois Moran has broken the jinx that trails Hollywood stars who turn to Broadway for a whirl at stage plays. Her first appearance in *This Is New York* was such an outstanding success that she was almost overwhelmed by a deluge of applause, flowers and telegrams from hundreds of admirers." Lois would go on to appear onstage several more times in the course of her career; she starred in another Sherwood play, *The Petrified Forest*, several years later in San Francisco.

After the critical disappointments of her last few films and the commercial failure of *This Is New York*, Lois was pleased that when she returned to the studio in 1931 the next picture assigned to her was a good one, a splashy ocean-liner drama to be directed by William K. Howard entitled *Transatlantic*. It featured a strong ensemble cast that included Edmund Lowe, Jean Hersholt (Lois's friend from the *Stella Dallas* days), Greta Nissen, Myrna Loy, John Halliday, and Earle Foxe (who had played with Lois in *The River Pirate* and *Blindfold* and would again appear with her in *The Spider*). A well-made film, *Transatlantic* benefited from handsome sets that won an early Academy Award for Best Interior Decoration for its art director, Gordon Wiles. Moreover, its plot was an absorbing mix of crime and soap opera, a precursor to many such high-seas dramas to come, and it was all served up with dash and style by a group of beautiful and talented performers. Myrna Loy looked particularly gorgeous in this film and in her 1987 autobiography *Being and Becoming* noted that it was her personal favorite of the films she made while under contract at Fox. The picture did not provide a particularly strong part for Lois, who played the ingénue role Judy Kramer, but overall it was advantageous for her to have appeared in it because it proved popular both critically and financially. The *New York Daily Mirror* observed that the film was "splendidly acted by an unusually interesting cast." The *New York Daily News* agreed, opining that there was "not a dull moment in the film."

In her next picture of 1931, *The Spider*, Lois made her contribution to 1930s film horror. A visually creative thriller directed by William Cameron Menzies and Kenneth MacKenna, the film concerned a murder that takes place in the audience during a magician's performance and the efforts, culminating in a bizarre séance, to apprehend the killer. Edmund Lowe, in his fourth and final film with Lois, played the magician, Chartrand, and Lois played the accused killer's sister, Beverly Lane. The picture was more a showpiece for Lowe than for Lois, and both were overshadowed by the imaginative Art Deco sets, designed by the art director Carli Elinor and moodily photographed by James Wong Howe; but it still sustains suspense and remains one of Lois's most unusual efforts, certainly on a par with *La galerie des monstres* and *The Road to Mandalay* in terms of exoticism. In the 1990s, Hugh Hefner funded a pristine restoration of the film.

The Spider was the last film released under Lois's contract with Fox. She opted not to remain at Fox because she believed that the studio had lost interest in properly guiding her career and in casting her in quality films. As she complained in a *Collier's* magazine interview in 1932, she had grown tired of being "stamped as a fluffy ingénue." She therefore returned to life as a freelance film performer. Freelancing had served her well in most of the films she had made before she signed with Fox, and she hoped that it would now serve her again. She made two pictures as a born-again freelancer. The first, entitled *Men in Her Life*, was shot at Columbia, another studio for which she had never before worked. She was attracted to this project because it was based upon a story by Warner Fabian, the pen name of Samuel

Hopkins Adams, who had written a variety of racy, wildly popular youth-oriented tales in the 1920s. *Men in Her Life* also allowed her to enact a worldlier, more interesting type of character than the bland heroines Fox had been assigning to her.

In this film, she portrayed Julia Cavanaugh, a lady of uncertain virtue who is being blackmailed. Her costar was the intense Charles Bickford, who played the role of a man who comes to her defense and kills the blackmailer. The movie turns into a tense courtroom thriller when Bickford is tried for the homicide, but all ends happily. A compelling drama directed by William Beaudine, who had directed Lois to much less effect in *The Irresistible Lover*, it is today sometimes a featured entry in film retrospectives of hard-boiled dramas of the 1930s. Glamorous and polished, Lois held her own in this powerful film and proved, as she had so many times before, that her range as an actress had again been underestimated. Columbia was the most no-nonsense, hard-edged studio at which she had ever worked, a fact reflected in her performance, which was brittle, cold in its sexuality, and taut, qualities that would have served her well had she continued making films into the film noir era of the 1940s.

Lois was moderately pleased with her role in *Men in Her Life*, certainly the most substantial she had enacted in a while. She continued to be depressed and anxious about her career, however, and still believed that she had yet to regain the prestige she had lost in the wake of her recent mediocre Fox vehicles. She remembered that *Photoplay* magazine once entitled its Letters to the Editor section "Brickbats and Bouquets," and she believed that after the bouquets of *Stella Dallas* and several of her other earlier films, she had now arrived at a plateau in her career in which brickbats were clearly the order of the day. An opportunity arose for her to return to MGM, however, and, remembering the huge success of *The Road to Mandalay*, she readily returned in hopes of achieving another, much-needed hit. She agreed to costar with John Gilbert in a comedy-drama entitled *West of Broadway*, directed by Harry Beaumont and costarring Madge

Evans, Ralph Bellamy, and three other actors with whom she had appeared before: Gwen Lee (*Sharp Shooters*), El Brendel (*The Spider*), and Hedda Hopper (*A Song of Kentucky*).

Lois was intrigued by the idea of appearing with Gilbert because she had admired his work in the films he had made at MGM with Greta Garbo in the 1920s, particularly *A Woman of Affairs* in 1928. She had first met him at the 1927 tea party at which Scott and Zelda Fitzgerald had boiled the guests' wristwatches and jewelry, and in 1948 she recalled to Arthur Mizener that at the time she had found the actor "extremely handsome but drunk." In 1931, she realized that Gilbert, like her, had seen better days in his career. In the silent era an undisputed superstar, he was now an alcoholic suffering a steep career decline because of widespread rumors that his voice was high-pitched and unsuitable to sound pictures. Nevertheless, he was still a star of magnitude and an important marquee name. Lois hoped that appearing with him in a slick MGM production would rescue her from her own career doldrums. She agreed to play Dot, a promiscuous, potty-mouthed gold digger whose life changes when she realizes that she loves a millionaire World War I veteran, played by Gilbert, who has married her in a drunken stupor after a brief one-night stand. Lois could not have chosen a character more against type, and watching the film today one cannot help but be amazed by the astonishing differences between her blasé, secular Dot in this, her last, film, and the naive, ethereal Laurel in *Stella Dallas*. Earlier, in conjunction with the release of *Love Hungry* in 1928, a publicity photograph had appeared of her in modern flapper-era clothing looking with disdain at a childhood picture of herself in a heavy Victorian frame, but that had not been enough. It took something more powerful for Lois to establish a new image. *West of Broadway* gave her that opportunity.

MGM gave her a complete makeover for *West of Broadway*, and as Dot she slithered about in slinky gowns designed by Vivian Baer, wore plenty of garish costume jewelry, and faced the camera with a heavily made up face that transformed her into a glamorous, seductive film siren. This new, flashy, aggressively sexual appearance contrasted jarringly with her earlier look. Lois had begun her physical conversion in *Men in Her Life*, but it was not until *West of Broadway* that the transformation was complete. She had never looked as sensual or alluring in any of her previous screen work, nor had she spoken such sexually frank dialogue or involved herself in such ribald plot machinations. She proved herself a deft comedienne and demonstrated that she could have held her own as a glamorous, modern actress of the 1930s. George Hurrell, the Hollywood studio photographer renowned for the hypnotic, lyrical "Hurrell Touch" with which he crafted many extraordinary celebrity images, took a series of camera portraits of her in costume from this film, and these photos, in which she wears a clingy black gown and large hoop earrings, smokes cigarettes, and aims smoldering looks toward the camera, are among the most ravishing and sensual studies he ever composed of any performer.

Film magazines and newspapers of the day readily reproduced Hurrell's images of Lois, one expressing downright shock in its caption:

> Great heavens! Can this be Lois Moran? Why, says the oldest inhabitant, it was only a few years ago that she was Laurel in *Stella Dallas*, a lovely *child*, not even an ingénue. And now she's of the sophisticated sisterhood. Well, there's no use denying that she has all that it takes, plus brains, but somehow it just isn't right for Lois to grow up with that look in her eyes.

When the *Los Angeles Times* ran one of the photos on the front page of its Sunday film pictorial section in September, 1931, it placed it with a headline reading, "Who Said They're Getting Sweeter?" And Mark A. Vieira's 1997 book *Hurrell's Hollywood Portraits* featured one of these photos on the back of the volume's dust jacket.

In spite of the new opportunities *West of Broadway* gave her, however, Lois did not enjoying making it. She liked Gilbert but in 1963 paid him a rather backhanded compliment in the *San Francisco*

Examiner: "John Gilbert was handsome and smart. He wasn't as bright as Ronnie [Ronald Colman, her *Stella Dallas* costar] but he was very sweet." Otherwise, she was in perpetual bad spirits, in part because of the lingering anger she felt toward Fox executives for having cast her in those poor, ineffectual films during the last half of her tenure at that studio. She was also involved in an automobile accident on the set with Ralph Bellamy when their chauffeur suffered a heart attack while behind the wheel (neither Lois nor Bellamy was injured, but the chauffer died—as late as the 1980s, the *National Enquirer* ran a piece describing this unfortunate event), and as shooting progressed she realized that the film was likely to fail at the box office because the public would almost certainly not take to her radically new image and because Gilbert was at such a low in his career that he literally could do no right. When the film was released, the reviews justified her gloom. *Variety* called it "a totally unconvincing and barely coherent mass of material," remarked that Gilbert "holds little because the plot behind him holds nothing," and noted that Lois was "handicapped from the start by one of the poorest make-up jobs in modern films."

Time has been much kinder to *West of Broadway*, however, and it holds up today as a fresh, quickly paced, entertaining picture that typifies the freewheeling era of early 1930s filmmaking before the Hays Code. Perhaps the best summation of the film's quality has come from Lois's son, Tim Young, who recently saw the film for the first time and exclaimed, "I couldn't take my eyes off it. Who knew that Mother was capable of that kind of acting? I was utterly amazed. I had never seen that side of her before." *West of Broadway*, it was popularly believed at the time, had brought Lois's film career to an end, to quote T. S. Eliot (one of Lois's favorite poets), "not with a bang but a whimper." Time has proven otherwise.

The Gershwins, *Of Thee I Sing*, and Life as a Jubilee

*L*ois emerged from the production of *West of Broadway* exhausted and depressed. She was reading Nietzsche at the time and gave thought to his assertion that if one gazes into an abyss long enough the abyss will begin to gaze back into him. Had Hollywood become an abyss for her? It was now a fount of failure and pain; by devoting so much of her energy to it, was she in turn becoming cheerless and disenchanted? She determined that she needed a respite from filmmaking and spent her leisure time both in Los Angeles, where she now owned a beach house, and in New York, where she maintained an apartment at 277 Park Avenue that overlooked an acre of colorific gardens. It was 1931, and she was now twenty-two. Since she was no longer bound to a film studio by a long-term contract, she was free to do what she pleased with her life. She did not know whether she wanted to return to films, but she did want to pursue stage work again. For the time being, however, she luxuriated in her personal life and tried not to think about her career, which, as she perceived it, was almost in ruins. She wrote in her diary in April 1932 about the emotional difficulties she was experiencing: "I have been a bit emotionally upset, a bit confused, very happy, very sad, but I have come through with colors flying—Methinks I have been quite grown-up about everything."

She attempted to find refuge in her relationship with Douglass Montgomery but was unsure about her feelings for him. "I've sometimes wanted so desperately to belong to him," she wrote in her journal, "and yet always my mind says, 'No—you don't love him—or at least not enough—and you don't really desire an affair.'" She added, "Doug and I don't love each other. We are just extraordinarily congenial both mentally and physically and both slightly impatient and longing for the right one to come along." They did make a handsome couple.

In Los Angeles and New York, Lois lived peacefully. She spent time with friends in her Malibu beach house, which had previously belonged to the Virginia Valli, a popular 1920s screen actress and the wife of Charles Farrell. "I remember that there was a group that always spent time at the beach with Mother and Gladys," recalls Tim Young.

> This included George O'Brien and Edmund Lowe. Others that were frequent guests were John Wayne, who Mother first knew as Duke Morrison, and Ward Bond. They had all yet to be really discovered. I seem to remember that Mother had something to do with getting Wayne a screen test. Robert Montgomery was also in that group.

Lois, who must have looked like Rosemary Hoyt roaming the shore of the French Riviera, was relaxed by the ocean. She socialized, caught up with her reading, and rested at the beach house.

In New York, Lois enjoyed what she referred to in her journal as "very exciting times." She spent her mornings visiting with Gladys and Betty, chatting with friends, or sunbathing and reading Rupert Brooke under what she described as a "D. H. Lawrence sun" on the roof of her apartment building. She also lunched and shopped with Gladys, Betty, and a new friend, the stage actress Sally Floyd, who had not long previously understudied in the first staging of Eugene O'Neill's *Mourning Becomes Electra* in 1931.

During the afternoons, she continued her singing lessons, writing in her journal that "singing is a supreme joy" and establishing herself as a mezzo-soprano. She began studying under the renowned Frank

La Forge, whom she described in her journal as an "amazingly fine person" and whose students had included the American baritone Lawrence Tibbett. She also took acting lessons from Laura Elliot, a respected coach, and under her guidance, she recorded in her journal, "had one ecstatic experience. I suddenly *found* myself one day. Now I know I am truly a great actress (or rather I will be). I have finally succeeded in breaking through my reticence and reserve." Her extroverted friend, the actress Yvonne Printemps, she further recorded, also advised her to put "complete abandon" into her singing and acting. Lois attempted to put such advice into practice and as a result wrote, "I *am* most tremendously happy about my acting."

She devoted her evenings to dining out, dancing, and attending numerous plays and musicals. The bustle, lights, and head-tilting silver skyscrapers of the city at night invigorated her and made her feel especially vivacious, carefree, and sexually adventurous. No longer the child who demurely sipped grenadine with Michael Knox in Paris cafés, she prowled the chrome and smoky glass of New York nightlife, drank champagne, and danced at nightclubs featuring live jazz. She also attended parties given by friends, particularly enjoying herself at one soirée Condé Nast gave at his home for the soprano Grace Moore to celebrate the opening of her film *One Night of Love* in 1934.

Lois soon felt the need to return to work, but, in a break from the pattern of earlier years, she began to make decisions without the help of Gladys. She was pleased that in 1932 Fay Wray had given her a Hollywood nod by telling the press that "Lois Moran's dancing" was among her favorite things; but she decided, on her own, that at present she did not wish to return to the movies. "Up until this time," she told Annabel Damon in a 1950 interview for the *Honolulu Advertiser*, "I'd been only the 'sweet young thing' in a number of movies and decided I was due for a break." Energized by her vocal studies with La Forge, she began looking for a stage role, particularly a musical. Lois, continually exhilarated by New York and increasingly intrigued by the prospect of stage work, resolved that her next career step would be to follow up her work in *This Is New York* by again appearing on Broadway. She contacted an old acquaintance, the producer Arch Lebroyn, who sent her on the rounds in search of stage work. "After a day's tramping around to casting offices," she told Damon, "I came home with about 20 scripts under my arm." The result of her efforts was a tremendous lift for her career.

In knocking on doors at the agencies, she learned that a new George and Ira Gershwin musical entitled *Of Thee I Sing* was being cast. She fondly remembered the afternoon in August 1926 when Henrietta Malkiel, a friend of Ira and his wife, had taken her and Gladys to tea at George's Riverside Drive apartment, where she and George had discussed the possibility of her one day starring in one of his musicals, and more recently she had even amused herself by choreographing her own dances to his 1924 *Rhapsody in Blue*. She was exhilarated by the chance to achieve her dream of appearing in one of the Gershwins' musicals. *Of Thee I Sing* was a satire on the American presidency that included the role of Mary Turner, a simple girl who is chosen to be First Lady because of her ability to prepare delicious corn muffins. Lois saw immediately that the play would be a huge success, just as she determined that Mary would be a perfect role for her because, like so many of her film parts, she was an innocent character thrust into worldly situations. The innocents in her films usually faced compromise by sexuality, but this character was unusual because the threat to her was political.

Lois believed that her singing skills had progressed to the point where she could handle the musical demands of playing Mary, and, although nervous, she auditioned. Many experienced stage singers coveted the part, and one of Lois's principal rivals was her fellow film actress Madge Bellamy, but Lois, perhaps because of her previous meeting with Gershwin and because she had proven her musical talents in *Words and Music*, won the day in the intense, competitive casting process. By landing the role of Mary Turner, Lois commenced a spectacular, if brief, new era in her career. Like that of Laurel in

Stella Dallas some seven years earlier, the role of Mary offered Lois an unusually fine opportunity to excel in a new medium: complex musical satire.

George S. Kaufman, whom Lois wrote to this author in 1987 she "adored," directed the play and cowrote the script with Morrie Ryskind; the Gershwins wrote the score, Ira providing sparkling lyrics to George's music. Starring along with Lois were William Gaxton, a seasoned stage and vaudeville performer who was best known for having starred in shows such as Rodgers and Hart's *A Connecticut Yankee* in 1927 and Cole Porter's *Fifty Million Frenchmen* in 1929 and who had most recently appeared in an unprecedented ten-week vaudeville run at the Palace Theater; and Victor Moore, a popular comedian whose theater work had included the Gershwins' *Oh, Kay!* in 1926 and *Funny Face* in 1927. The Gershwins had earlier tackled social satire in *Strike Up the Band* in 1927 (revised in 1930), which concerned war profiteering, but they mastered the art with *Of Thee I Sing*, which they assembled with panache and which was so merry, witty, and amusing in a Gilbert and Sullivan sort of way that the pointed jabs they were making at American politics went over with smoothness and ease. The play won a Pulitzer Prize for drama for its book, the first time a musical had ever won that award, although George was omitted from the citation because his contribution was deemed musical and not literary. In a 1972 letter to the *San Francisco Chronicle*'s drama critic, Terrence O'Flaugherty, Lois recalled of the show, "The lines were brilliant, the satire beauteous and subtle and enchanting."

Of Thee I Sing's storyline concerned a presidential candidate, John P. Wintergreen (Gaxton), whose advisers deem that he should run on a platform of "Love" and devise a beauty contest in order to select his wife. They choose the glamorous Diana Devereaux (Grace Brinkley), but he instead falls in love with a secretary to one of his advisers, Mary Turner (Lois), who can bake corn muffins, and refuses to marry Diana. He and Mary successfully campaign together, and on the day he is sworn in as president he marries her. The jilted Diana makes trouble, however, and such a furor arises that he is almost impeached. He is saved when Mary announces that she is pregnant. She goes on to give birth to twins, and Diana is married off to the vice president, Alexander Throttlebottom (Moore). The scintillating score included such numbers as "Wintergreen for President," "Love Is Sweeping the Country," "A Kiss for Cinderella," "Who Cares?," and the title song. "Who Cares?" was one of the most popular songs in the show, a romantic duet between Gaxton and Lois in which both proclaim that nothing really matters because they have each other and because life is, after all, "one long jubilee."

Opening during the Christmas season of 1931 at the Music Box Theater, *Of Thee I Sing* was a colossal hit, running a phenomenal 441 performances over four years. George Jean Nathan called *Of Thee I Sing* "a landmark in American satirical musical comedy," and George Gershwin himself, as quoted by Edward Jablonski in his 1987 biography *Gershwin*, remarked that it was "one of those rare shows in which everything clicked... [it is the] one show that I'm more proud of than any I have written." Lois garnered pristine reviews for her portrayal of Mary. In his *New York Times* review of the play, Brooks Atkinson summed up her critical reception: "Lois Moran is a charming President's bride." She triumphed as Mary Turner, and her Broadway success did much to assuage the forlorn hope that continued to haunt her over her dismal last months in Hollywood. As she had hoped, the future now really was golden; life was indeed a jubilee.

Lois wrote in her journal that she took great pleasure in being the "belle of the ball" in the glittering New York theater world and reveling in the "marvelous business" that the show was doing. In one journal entry, she described her life as a Broadway star. "Back to Broadway at night," she wrote. "Packed houses, laughter, dirty jokes from Billy [probably William Gaxton], moments of deepest pride when I sing well, despair when I don't, pleasure in working, in improvement, comradeship, nice friendly electricians, stage-hands, applause—swelling music—and home to a quiet house."

Lois's cousin Betsy Blair went to see *Of Thee I Sing* when she was a young girl and was highly impressed. "[Lois] was a shining figure in my childhood during the Second World War and also in my imagination always," she wrote to this author in 2004. She also wrote in her autobiography *The Memory of All That: Love and Politics in New York, Hollywood, and Paris* that in 1950, she asked George S. Kaufman if he recalled Lois at the time of the play. "He said she was a miracle: she sang like a bird, was a good dancer, a true beauty, and quietly very intelligent," Blair recounted. "He remembered her at Sardi's after every matinee eating alone and reading a book. In fact, he couldn't recall ever seeing her without a book."

Lois took joy in being a part of the New York theatrical scene at the time she starred in *Of Thee I Sing*. "Lucky me," she wrote to this author in 1988. "Was in New York at just the right time (the early '30s) when everybody was fresh and bright. They were all young when I knew them, though I was the youngest. [Paul] Robeson, Marion Anderson, [Geraldine] Farrar, Lily Pons, George G. was writing something for her when I was in *Sing* [Gershwin composed *For Lily Pons Melody No. 79* in 1933]." She also knew the torch singer Libby Holman, the writer Joseph Hergesheimer, and the novelist Michael Arlen. She maintained, however, "I was far too young then to appreciate all the wits around me." One of Lois's fondest memories of the *Of Thee I Sing* experience included Oscar Levant, whom Gladys did not like. A witty bon vivant, composer, and gifted pianist who for a time seemed inseparable from the Gershwins, Levant, according to Lois, helped Gershwin write another of his classic musicals, *Porgy and Bess* (1935): "George wrote a lot of *Porgy and Bess* when I was sitting on the floor between the two grands as he and Oscar Levant played (wonder I didn't lose my hearing). This was after the show in his apartment on Riverside Drive."

Levant made a vivid impression upon Lois. She had known him in Hollywood years earlier. Gladys did not like him because, while she acknowledged his talent, she also considered him arrogant and rude. Lois, on the other hand, got along with him, admired his quick mind, and was mesmerized when watching his fingers dance as he played the piano. She wrote to this author in 1988:

> He'd written a song named "Lady, Play Your Mandolin"... so he was quite the rage in Hollywood. Met him someplace, he used to come to play my piano, along with Sam Behrman, author of *Biography* and other plays. Oscar drank gallons and gallons of coffee (he didn't drink hard liquor), played all of *Bohème* (strangely enough, his favorite opera), with me singing the women's parts, he the men (couldn't sing worth a damn). Brilliant guy.... He, as I recall, knew *everything* about baseball, dates, names and players.

In 1955, Stanford University staged a student production of *Of Thee I Sing*, and Lois, then an artist-in-residence at the school, baked corn muffins for the girl who played Mary and gave an interview to the campus newspaper, the *Stanford Daily*, in which she recalled other details about the show's original production. In the course of the run, she recalled, she wore out three bridal gowns, but, she added, "I never got tired of playing it. The music always gave me a lift." Disaster once almost struck onstage when Lois was beset by a winter cold. "As I made my entrance down the stairs in the wedding scene," she said, "I opened my mouth to sing and not a word would come out. Two big tears started down my cheeks when suddenly Billy Gaxton, the original John P. Wintergreen, started singing my part. So... from then on we just started passing the parts around according to who had colds."

Lois also recollected that there was a scene in the play in which Gaxton and Moore tossed jokes back and forth for eight minutes. They began improvising, however, and eventually that scene turned into half an hour. "It was a wonderful scene," she explained, "but finally George Kaufman, author and director, had to stop them because the show ran so late." Later still, in a 1963 *San Francisco Examiner* article, she recalled more about *Of Thee I Sing*, referencing earlier composers as well as a popular Rodgers and Hammerstein Broadway musical of more recent vintage. "It was really an amazing show," she commented. "It was the Gilbert and Sullivan of its day, the *South Pacific* of its day."

Of Thee I Sing toured in the East, and Kaufman, Ryskind, and the Gershwins wrote a sequel entitled *Let 'Em Eat Cake* that opened on October 21, 1933, at the Imperial Theater in New York. Lois, Gaxton, and Moore again assumed the lead roles of Mary, Wintergreen, and Throttlebottom. This play, however, was darker and more complex, and it delivered its satire with a heavy hand rather than with the confectioner's delicacy that had characterized *Of Thee I Sing*. It featured songs such as "Come the Revolution," "Climb Up the Social Ladder," and "Hanging Throttlebottom in the Morning," titles indicative of its more serious and politically challenging tone. It opens as Wintergreen is campaigning for reelection, Mary at his side, but he is defeated. He and Mary then set up shop selling blue shirts that Mary makes (a parody of Hitler's brown shirts). Wintergreen comes up with the idea of overthrowing the government and to win the support of the army promises it the war debt. He is successful and becomes a kind of dictator (hence the play's title). However, few of the nations wish to repay their war debt, and Wintergreen and Throttlebottom are overthrown and sentenced to the guillotine. On the day of their execution, Mary tells the crowd that if the new regime is installed the women would not be able to wear the latest fashions, whereas if they keep Wintergreen they would be able to wear anything they like. Her appeal works, and power is restored to Wintergreen. He, however, wishes only to set up a clothing store. Throttlebottom assumes the presidency.

Lois liked *Let 'Em Eat Cake* better than *Of Thee I Sing*, but critics were generally unkind. Gilbert W. Gabriel summed up the uneasy critical attitude when he wrote that the show was "immensely, occasionally magnificently funny" but was "apt to make you chew your fingernails, apologize for living and wonder whether you yourself don't belong up there on the stage below the guillotine's wit-edged blade." Moreover, *Time* magazine, in an unsigned review, complained:

> When the opening scene of this musicomedy began with the familiar martial strains of "Wintergreen for President," Manhattan first-nighters applauded happily. They recalled what a fine show *Of Thee I Sing* had been, leaned back in their seats to enjoy its sequel. But when the curtain fell on *Let 'Em Eat Cake* there was an embarrassing dearth of applause.

In keeping with what the *Time* reporter had observed, audiences almost uniformly disliked the play, and it flopped, running for only eighty-nine performances.

Lois was aware that *Let 'Em Eat Cake*'s more somber political tone would make it less of a crowd pleaser than *Of Thee I Sing*, and she was not surprised by its negative reception. She had worked even harder on it, though, than she had on *Of Thee I Sing* because it made greater demands of her vocally: her part had been expanded, and she was required to lead complicated production numbers. The grand romantic ballad between Mary and Wintergreen in this production was entitled "Mine," an intoxicating, show-stopping duet that was difficult to perform because it was sung in counterpart to a chorus. In spite of her efforts, the weak box-office receipts could not be overcome, and the show, as Lois put it, "quietly died." She did receive encouraging personal reviews for her reprisal of Mary, however. Brooks Atkinson observed in the *New York Times*, "[She] contributes an unassertive charm that is . . . a blessing."

After *Let 'Em Eat Cake* closed in 1934, Lois, exhausted after starring in two consecutive Broadway shows, vacationed for a month in Palm Beach, Florida, a rainbow-hued city that was new to her. There, as she wrote in her journal, she enjoyed "an elegant, frivolous time" and "became a complete play-girl." She continued to practice singing, but otherwise life became a carnival of "too many parties, too many men, too many cigarettes, too many cocktails," echoing Fitzgerald's summation of his own lifestyle in 1927 as "one thousand parties and no work." When her vacation there was over, after she had gorged herself with sex, jazz, and cocktails, she realized that something was missing, that life for her had to consist of more than a perpetual holiday. "I *am* depressed," she wrote in her journal in March 1934. "Methinks I need a good love affair or a husband. Men upset me too much—It would be much simpler if I were a man—But you're not, Lois, so make the best of it." She set about making the best of her life at the time in three ways: she resumed seeking out new career opportunities; she spent time with Gladys and Betty; and she remained vigilant in her search for the ideal mate.

Lois at last believed, without reservation, that she no longer had to prove her talents as an actress. She was also financially secure. In consequence, she was in no hurry to return either to films or to the stage, although she would have preferred Broadway to Hollywood—in her journal, she still referred to herself as "stage-struck." Curiously, she did appear at the time in a two-reel comedy for Columbia, *Ladies Not Allowed*, an entry in the studio's short-lived *Lamb's Gambols* series. Created for merriment by professional actors, the *Lamb's Gambols* were loosely constructed burlesques of old-time melodramas. *Ladies Not Allowed* lampooned the success of *Of Thee I Sing* and featured the three stars, Lois, Gaxton, and Moore.

After *Ladies Not Allowed*, Lois and Gladys calculated that the next logical medium for her to consider would be radio, which appealed to her now because it paid well, would allow her to make use of her finely trained voice, and would keep her name before the public while she was sorting out how she wanted to proceed with her career. She worked on the radio angle and hoped to obtain permanent work on the air. She went to an audition in April 1934, but nothing substantive came of her efforts. She would not again attempt radio until after World War II.

Lois was excited when an offer came in for her to return to the stage to play the lead in John van Druten's play *There's Always Juliet*, but the project fell through. Given the weak immediate possibilities of quality radio and stage work coming her way anytime soon, she gradually began to think of returning to Hollywood, where she was assured of finding work. Memories of those unpleasant last days on the set of *West of Broadway* drifted back to her, however, and she procrastinated, determining instead to deal for the moment with other matters.

Lois continued to consider Gladys and Betty the center of her personal life and doted on them. She never wavered in holding her mother in the highest esteem, and her adoration only strengthened with the passing of time. "God, how I love that woman," she wrote in her journal in 1932. With Betty, Lois enjoyed being an older sister, and she additionally appreciated the dynamic the girl brought to the family. Since the Wall Street crash in 1929, Gladys had been increasingly absorbed by the stock market. The headaches from which she had always suffered worsened, and she became tense and apprehensive. She had invested conservatively, so the depression reduced the Moran finances but did not level them, but the market still consumed Gladys to the point of obsession. Launching Betty's career gave her another focus in life, and Lois could not have been happier.

To Lois, family was of paramount importance. When life was going well for Gladys and Betty, she felt secure and happy in a way that went far deeper than the good feelings she experienced when her career was succeeding. Increasingly anxious to add to that joy, she was always in search of the perfect man to marry and with whom she could create a family. That search was no easier for her, a stage and screen celebrity, than it has ever been for anyone else, and she alternated between despair and high hopes in her quest for a mate. In the autumn of 1934, however, her dreams began to materialize when she and Gladys attended a dinner party in New York and she found that a distinguished pioneer of aviation, Colonel Clarence M. Young, was present. She had known him briefly in previous years but had erroneously believed that he was engaged to one of her friends. Now

Gladys and Lois, adorned in a chic leopard's paw coat, pose for the press, ca. 1927.

Carrying books, a film script, and a traveling case that Samuel Goldwyn and Henry King presented to her at the end of the filming of *Stella Dallas*, Lois is glimpsed at a train station in a 1929 press photo.

Lois having fun with her adopted sister, Betty Evans, ca. 1926.

With Phillips Holmes in *The Dancers*, 1930.

As posed by Alfred Cheney Johnston, the official photographer for *The Ziegfeld Follies*, for *The Music Master*, 1926.

Edmund Lowe, Lois's most frequent co-star, poses with her in *Making the Grade*, 1929.

Clad in fur, ankles fashionably cocked, and surrounded by Art Deco trappings, Lois poses for Max Munn Autrey, who frequently photographed her, in 1928.

The modern Miss Louise Bowen (Lois) encounters the prudish Henry Willoughby (Neil Hamilton) in *Don't Marry*, 1928.

The cast and crew of *Publicity Madness*, 1928, relax between takes. *From left to right*: Director Albert Ray, Lois, the terrier that nearly stole the film, and Edmund Lowe.

Jean Hersholt, Edmund Lowe, and Lois aboard ship in *Transatlantic*, 1931.

The affection Lois felt for co-star George O'Brien on and off the set is evident in this still from *True Heaven*, 1929.

Lois with Mrs. Patrick Campbell in *The Dancers*, 1930. Campbell complained of looking overweight in the film.

The Belle of Samoa, a 1929 Fox Movietone short subject and the first film in which Lois spoke, paired her with the veteran comedy team Clark and McCullough.

The atmospheric thriller *The Spider*, 1931, marked Lois's lone foray into the 1930s horror genre.

In *Mammy*, with Al Jolson, 1930.

As the romantic Lorette in *Sharp Shooters*, 1928.

A not-so-subtle publicity pose for the murder thriller *Behind That Curtain*, 1929, with Warner Baxter, who had enacted the screen's first Jay Gatsby in the 1926 version of Fitzgerald's novel.

West of Broadway, 1931, her final film, gave Lois the opportunity to work with John Gilbert.

Lois on the town with Douglass Montgomery in the early 1930s. She briefly considered marrying him.

By the time this still with Lawrence Gray was taken for *Love Hungry*, 1928, Lois was becoming increasingly serious about cultivating a more glamorous image.

Hurrell's thunderous affirmation of the fact that Lois was capable of achieving sex goddess status. This is one of the photos he composed of her in 1931 in conjunction with *West of Broadway*.

Lois in one of the many wedding gowns she went through playing Mary Turner in the long run of *Of Thee I Sing*.

William Gaxton and Lois in a publicity still for *Of Thee I Sing*, 1931.

Above: The *Of Thee I Sing* stars in Baltimore, out of costume, ca. 1933. *From left to right*: Gaxton, Lois, and Victor Moore.

Left: At a promotional event for *Of Thee I Sing*.

Mr. and Mrs. Clarence Young in Palm Beach, Florida, shortly after their marriage in 1935.

Lois and her young son, Tim, boarding Pan Am's China Clipper at Treasure Island, California, ca. 1941.

Lois and Dr. George Altman during rehearsals of *Twelfth Night* in June 1941.

Lois, Preston Foster, and the adolescent Tim Young, who was visiting the set, pose for a photograph during a break in filming an episode of *Waterfront*, 1954.

Lois working at a blood drive for the Red Cross during World War II. Her efforts were so successful that she was dubbed "Bloody Mary."

Souvenir program for *Kitty Doone*, 1950.

Bottom left: This is how photographer William Mortensen, in a photograph taken in conjunction with his 1927 *Vanity Fair* spread "The Seven Ages of Lois Moran," envisioned Lois would appear when she became old. Lon Chaney praised the makeup effects Mortensen achieved.

Bottom right: The real aged Lois Moran, in the 1980s at her home in Sedona, Arizona, tending her houseplants and enjoying life.

disabused of that false belief and consumed by the prospect of marriage and the reality of what she considered her advancing age (for, like Fitzgerald, she considered youth fleeting), she was attracted to Young in a way she had not been before. Lois implored Gladys to pull some strings with the party's hostess in order to be seated next to him.

An intense, brooding man with thick, moderately curly black hair and piercing blue eyes that turned green when he was angry, the nearly six-foot-tall Young, whose friends called him "Dutch," stood out in any gathering. Successful, conservatively dressed in the Brooks Brothers fashion with vest, bow tie, and hat, somewhat in the style of Fitzgerald, and possessed of ebony-strength diction in a baritone that could be both authoritative and tender, he was forty-six, over twenty years older than Lois, and possessed a breadth of experience that impressed many, including the editors of *Time* magazine, who had featured him on their cover in 1932.

A graduate of Yale, Young briefly practiced law before World War I called him into service. During the war he became fascinated by flying. He flew bombers from 1917 to 1919 and spent five months as a prisoner of war in Austria. In 1925, he was appointed director of aeronautics of the United States Department of Commerce and served in the Republican Hoover administration as assistant secretary for aeronautics from 1929 to 1933. Young was the recipient of the second official pilot's license ever issued, knew Orville Wright, and assigned the pilot's license to Charles Lindbergh that allowed him to make his celebrated nonstop flight to Paris in 1927. Young had known Lindbergh years before that historic flight and remained a close friend.

In 1931, Young came under fire when in his government position he grounded more than thirty planes of the type that had carried Knute Rockne, the renowned Notre Dame football coach, to his death earlier that year. By grounding the planes, Young virtually paralyzed the nation's burgeoning commercial airline business. Congress denounced him, and the plane manufacturer complained that he was costing them many thousands of dollars, to which he replied, "How much is a life worth?" His vigilance on the issue resulted in increased airline safety measures. When Franklin Roosevelt took office in 1933, Young moved on, prompting the actor and humorist Will Rogers to tell the *Washington Times*, "This fellow Clarence Young, the head of commercial aviation, has done more for it than anybody since the Wright Brothers. I don't know anything about his going to be removed for Democratic purposes, but it will require twelve Democrats to replace him adequately." Young became the Pacific Alaska division manager for Pan American Airlines, a position that required him to pioneer flight routes across the Pacific. Confident, disciplined, and directed, he excelled in his position and was at the forefront of creating overseas air travel. "In my mind and many others'," explains Tim Young, "my father was one of the true pioneers of aviation and the development of commercial aviation in the United States and in the world. He never gained Lindbergh's name recognition, but he was responsible for much of how airlines are run today, from the towers to air traffic control and beyond."

In later years, Lois often described her first meeting with Young as "love at first sight." He certainly met her criteria and was, according to Tim Young, "a pretty powerful character when Mother met him." Evaluating the situation with Steichen's elements of understanding, love, observation, and imagination, she quickly determined that this was a man she wanted to know better. She was successful in her bid to sit next to him at that dinner party and by dessert realized that strong chemistry sparked between them. They began dating. Lois claimed never to have noticed the twenty-year age difference between them.

"I like my dear C.M.Y.," she wrote in her journal in November 1934, referring to him by initials because he loathed his given name. As their courtship progressed, Young began paying her visits at her home. He would arrive after she had concluded the singing lessons that she continued to take, and they would usually sip cocktails, see a film, or visit friends. Shortly before Christmas, she confessed in her journal, "I'm quite foolish about him. I love to do things for him, silly domestic things—I want to mend his socks, sew on his buttons, give him presents, mother him." She basked in "above all, happiness in each other!" In later years, she remembered being so smitten with Clarence at the time that one evening she almost fell out of her apartment window in New York when she saw him crossing the street.

The idea of marrying him began to preoccupy her. Late in life, she generally claimed that she knew she wanted to marry him the moment she laid eyes on him, but this is not accurate. She loved him but in truth did have significant reservations about marriage, in spite of her long-held desire to wed. She was now a famous and sophisticated woman of the world, a position she had worked long and hard to achieve. In New York, she lived in an elegant apartment, possessed a vast personal wardrobe, and socialized with many prominent celebrities and intellectuals of the day. She was, she knew, at the peak of her beauty, intellect, and creativity, and she worried that marriage might diminish her luster and limit the potential of the future of her career. She was also beset by the common anxiety of being committed to one person.

"Goodness knows I'd like to be a good wife to him," she wrote in her journal that December, "but somehow I just can't be tied to one person—What is wrong with me, dear God? I just must be free and alone." A couple of days later came another entry: "I love C. very much, but not enough—We are so happy together and he is content because he has seen and done everything, but I am not! I have *so much* to do before I can be content—I probably never will be, as a matter of fact." Her indecision on the matter consumed her.

Clarence, who loved Lois and appears to have had marriage as the goal from the start, was aware of Lois's hesitations and attempted to work with her to resolve them, as reflected in another entry Lois wrote at the time. "C. has been trying to persuade me to go to California with him," she said, "but I just can't. I'd love it so, still I *won't* be tied to anyone. He is so sweet, says I can leave when I please, go anywhere I want, pursue my 'godam career' as he calls it, as much as I desire."

Still, she had doubts. The first Christmas they spent together resulted in her falling even more deeply in love with him, however.

By late January 1935 Lois had come to the sobering realization that if she married Clarence she would have to give up her career. He assured her that this was not the case and that she would be free to pursue her acting work after they were wed, but Lois recognized in him strong traditional values that would make such a compromise improbable at best. She also sensed that if married she herself would gradually lose sight of her career as she slipped into her future role as a wife and mother rather than as an actress. "Dear C.M.Y.," she nervously scribbled in her journal on January 26, "You're driving me crazy—What am I going to do about you? You and 'career' upset me no end—I hate and love you both! Goodnight and to hell with you!!!! (both!)!" On February 10, 1935, she capitulated. Wishing to avoid fanfare and publicity, she and Young were married in a simple civil ceremony. They drove from New York to Baltimore, where they persuaded the clerk of the court to issue them a spur-of-the-moment license, and then had the ceremony performed by a Baltimore minister. The weeks that followed were among the happiest of her life.

"Here I am, dear diary," she wrote approximately a month later, "an old married lady! We've been married almost a month—Hurray!" Eventually, however, she came to find that Clarence was given to bad moods, probably as the result of the stress of his profession, and was often ill tempered and brusque with others, including herself. This kink concerned her, but she was determined to make her marriage work and tackled the matter with the same verve and imagination with which she would have infused one of her film characters. She had married Clarence for love, but it is also possible, in those days when practicality was more frequently taken into account in choosing spouses than it is now, that he also appealed to her because he was a successful, strong man who could offer her financial and, she believed, emotional security. Clarence's work necessitated that he and his new wife move to San Francisco—the airline's headquarters were located at Treasure

Island, halfway between the city and Oakland. En route to the City by the Bay, the newlyweds visited Los Angeles, where Clarence met some of Lois's friends, including Douglass Montgomery, who owned a house in the Hollywood Hills. Not surprisingly, he disliked the former object of Lois's affections, although Lois observed in her journal that it was Montgomery's "actorish manner" that really disturbed him. Clarence's reaction to the actor was typical of his opinions of many of Lois's film and theater friends. Lois did not give such social considerations much thought, however, and instead concentrated on finding a home in San Francisco.

After a good deal of searching, the Youngs moved into a spacious penthouse apartment at 1940 Vallejo Street. Once settled, Clarence devoted most his energies to his work, and Lois began to think of ways she could incorporate her career into her new life. Living in San Francisco made it difficult for her to make movies in Hollywood, but she and Clarence had worked out a plan: he would maintain an office in Los Angeles, and she could periodically travel there for film work, returning home after production had concluded. Lois was comfortable with the scheme, but in the early days of her marriage she wanted to remain as close to Clarence as possible. She continued to practice singing, recording the keys of various songs in her journal, but otherwise devoted her life to him and to cultivating new friends in the Bay Area.

Lois noted repeatedly in her journal that she was deliriously happy, but in the final entry, dated September 9, 1935, she noted that Clarence had alarmed her with one of his "down" periods, during which he was overtaken by fatigue and back pain. She realized that being a good wife to him meant that going forward with her career would not be easy. The dilemma of marriage versus career befell many of Lois's colleagues, of course, and it has been well documented that many of them, including Bette Davis, Myrna Loy, and Joan Crawford, chose to divorce rather than give up their work. Lois, on the other hand, was determined to make her marriage work and was anxious to become pregnant.

Accordingly, she reasoned that the best course to take would be to look for stage work in San Francisco so that she could continue to act while at the same time remaining close to home. In marriage, Clarence was not as supportive of Lois's "godam career" as he had been during their courtship, but in the days when a husband's word was law he allowed her to appear with Conrad Nagel in a West Coast production of Robert Sherwood's *The Petrified Forest* at the Geary Theater in San Francisco. Lois played Gabrielle, a dreamy waitress in an Arizona diner that is taken over by gangsters. Gabrielle, like Lois herself, was a bookworm who read poetry and cherished dreams of bettering herself. Lois related strongly to the part. Alas, even though the play was suitable for Lois, this mounting was short lived, as the Warner Brothers' screen version starring Bette Davis as Gabrielle was soon to appear. It was during the brief run of the play, however, that she received news she had waited her life to hear. After six months of marriage, she was pregnant.

Lindbergh and Wartime San Francisco, the Cruise of the *Cheryl Ann*, and an Eagle Soars above Coffee Pot Mountain

"Dad broke into a cold sweat the day I was born," recalls Tim Young. "My head came out looking pointed and he was terrified something had gone wrong. He was normally reserved, but he ran all over the hospital frantically trying to get someone to assess his new son's pointed head. Mother was beside herself. Finally, the doctors calmed them both down and reassured them that nothing was wrong, that it sometimes takes babies' heads time to settle."

With this mishap, Mr. and Mrs. Clarence Young welcomed their son, Timothy Marshall, into the world on October 6, 1936. Lois had at last achieved her dream: she was married and had begun a family. Gladys, a proud grandmother, was at her side; and, as she had done the evening *Stella Dallas* had opened at the Apollo Theater in New York over a decade earlier, she reassured her daughter that the future was nothing short of radiant. Lois held her baby close to her, gazed around the hospital room at the loving faces of Clarence and her mother, as well as at the wealth of roses and autumn chrysanthemums that had been sent to her, and was overcome by the safest, most secure feeling she had ever experienced.

The Youngs returned to the Vallejo Street apartment to begin life as a family. Lois had given up the New York apartment, and Gladys continued to live in the home in Beverly Hills. Of paramount importance to Clarence was establishing a solid family with his new wife and son. He was aware that he and Lois had agreed that she could continue working after their marriage, but he believed it was best for the time being for her to remain at home with Tim. Lois, who loved her new husband and doted madly on their new child, agreed and decided to put her career on hold, at least for a time.

Tim's infancy was a blissful time for Lois, and she relished mother-hood. She had adjusted to marriage, mastered how to handle Clarence's intensity and mood swings, and in general thought little of return-ing to her career. She enjoyed taking her son for walks with Charles Lindbergh through Golden Gate Park, and at the age of one the child learned how to swim in Cecil B. De Mille's ornate, San Simeon–style Greek-columned swimming pool. In 1941, however, when Tim was not quite five years old, she again experienced that familiar thespian longing. By that time, Tim had a governess and Clarence was increas-ingly absorbed in his work at Pan Am, so she concluded that the time had come for her to start acting again.

She resolved to appear on stage in a classic, and her "beloved Shakespeare," as she called the great Elizabethan, came quickly to mind. Clarence, still aware of his agreement with Lois and cognizant of Tim's stability, reluctantly gave his blessing to her searching out such a part, as long as it was to be staged locally. As it happened, the Berkeley Diamond Jubilee theatrical festival was planning a production of the bard's 1600 comedy *Twelfth Night* at the Hearst Greek Theater in Berkeley. The production's director, George Altman, a former asso-ciate of the German stage and film director Max Reinhardt, knew of Lois's previous achievements and cast her in the play as Viola, a merry role that required her to masquerade as a man as well as to sing. Lois, elated to return to the stage, devoted herself to rehearsals and went on to give a sparkling, well-received interpretation of the character in a lavishly costumed staging of the play that was presented on Sunday, June 8, 1941. She was particularly overjoyed when Tim ran out onto the stage afterward to greet her. Her notices were complimentary, and a new Shakespearean play was planned for each season. Then World War II intervened.

The war also impacted her next venture when, later that year, she set about making another of her dreams come true: starring in an opera. She had devoted years to voice lessons, many of which had prepared her to sing classically, and believed that her voice was as polished as it would ever be. When she learned that a local production was being planned of one of Mozart's lesser-known operas, *Bastien and Bastienne*, to be performed in English at the Palace of the Legion of Honor Museum, she honed in on that work with excitement and eagerness. A rarely performed work that Mozart composed in 1768, when he was only twelve, *Bastien and Bastienne* incorporated dialogue in addition to the music; hence, in a way, it resembled the popular musical comedies in which she was accustomed to performing. Its plot concerned Bastienne, a shepherdess who fears that her boyfriend, Bastien, has abandoned her for another pretty face. Lois set out to play Bastien, the male role. In *Twelfth Night*, she had portrayed a woman posing as a man. In *Bastien and Bastienne*, she *was* a woman posing as a man.

The timing of *Bastien and Bastienne* could not have been more unfortunate. In the midst of rehearsals, on December 7, 1941, the Japanese bombed Pearl Harbor. Lois and the small company did go on to present the opera, but very few saw it, and virtually no mention was made of it in the press.

The bombing of Pearl Harbor and the entry of the United States into World War II, of course, affected many, and the Youngs were no exception. Because of his high-level position in aeronautics, Clarence played an important part in the conflict: the American government often sought his expertise and even held at least one top-secret meeting at his home. Lois was eager to do her part, as well, and was drawn to the Red Cross. As a tireless organizer of blood drives, she achieved noteworthy results, earning her the sobriquet—this time a great compliment—of "Bloody Mary." In a 1963 *San Francisco Examiner* interview with the sculptor Beniamino Bufano, who was at the time planning to design a statue for the prison at Alcatraz Island, Lois recounted an amusing anecdote about her "Bloody Mary" tenure. "I was over there [at Alcatraz] during the war," she explained. "I was collecting blood for the Red Cross [and] I took my son Tim. He was about eight and at the age when he wore a cowboy suit—with two guns on his hips. And do you know, they took his guns away?"

In addition to the work she did for the Red Cross, Lois took part in another wartime event, an extraordinary one whose story has never before been told. "We were never sure we'd ever be able to talk about it," says Tim Young, "but I think enough years have passed that it is safe to make public." In February or March of 1942, he explains, a top-secret meeting was held at the Youngs' Vallejo Street apartment in San Francisco to discuss whether Japan should be taken by air power alone or in conjunction with ground forces. "Dad was head of Pan Am at the time and a key to the Pacific," Young explains, "and Mother was one of the top people in the American Red Cross in San Francisco, so it makes sense that they would have hosted the meeting at their home. San Francisco was considered the next port of entry for the Japanese into this country after Pearl Harbor." Those present at the clandestine conference included some of the most important figures of the Allied cause: President Franklin D. Roosevelt; Harry Hopkins, his secretary of state and confidant; Fleet Admiral Chester Nimitz; Charles Lindbergh; and various generals of the army and marines.

The whole of Vallejo Street was closed off by the police and Secret Service; and, as San Francisco was under air-raid alert after Pearl Harbor, the apartment had been equipped with large blackout screens in the main windows and double-thick blackout curtains in other rooms. "Dad and Lindbergh wanted to immediately establish air superiority," Young remembers. "They wanted stronger air power to go directly into Japan instead of taking the Pacific island by island on land." For security reasons, Lois never spoke of the wartime conference at her Vallejo Street penthouse. She did become great friends with Lindbergh, however, and often mentioned him. She enjoyed recalling those walks she and Lindbergh sometimes took Tim on through Golden Gate Park. She also liked telling a story about one evening during the war when she and Lindbergh had gone to dinner in downtown San Francisco. Afterward, in the darkened streets, she had forgotten where she had parked and could not find her car. "It was my most embarrassing moment," she recalled in her 1970s autobiographical working notes. Lindbergh had found Paris in his famous 1927 flight, however, and he had no trouble now finding Lois's lost vehicle in the murky roadways of the City by the Bay.

Not long after the end of the war, Clarence again went to work for Pan Am and relocated the family to Atherton, a suburb of San Francisco. The Youngs bought a property there at 172 Elena Avenue, an extensive gated estate with a spacious living room facing gardens, much as Lois's New York apartment had done in the 1920s and 1930s. "Mother had her grand piano in that living room, always with a large flower arrangement," Young recalls. "She would play every once in a while."

In Atherton in the mid- to late 1940s, Lois devoted herself to a substantial amount of postwar volunteer work with veterans, in both San Francisco and Los Angeles. She helped to organize the Brentwood and Sawtelle Veterans' Hospitals in Los Angeles, then worked tirelessly to make life more pleasant for the veterans housed in these facilities as well as in others in the Bay Area. She also drew upon her radio experience, limited as it was, to devise a local veterans' radio show that ran three times a week; it eventually developed formal dramatic productions with the help of some hospitalized Seabees and the radio station staff. She was also instrumental in creating a liberal-minded series of radio plays aimed at veterans and entitled *We Are Many People* that took aim at bigotry and intolerance.

Lois was justly proud of her volunteer efforts with war veterans. This work gave her the personal fulfillment she had first experienced in 1926, when she and Richard Barthelmess had visited the boys' orphanage and the Tonsil Hospital in New York. By 1949, though, postwar America was fast becoming more settled, and she believed that the time was now right for her to move on a bit from her volunteer work and resume acting. She had not been onstage since 1941, and her thespian urges were again asserting themselves. She resolved to return to the stage. Clarence, never happy about Lois's resuming her career, went along with her desires because a play would have a limited run and relatively predictable working hours. She thought it best to find a vehicle that would not make stringent demands upon her as an actress so that she could focus her energies upon readjusting to the theatrical experience in general. Such a project did materialize for her in a San Francisco community theater production of *Mother Is a Freshman*, a light, if not improbable, comedy by Raphael David Blau and Christopher Sergel about a mother who returns to college. Loretta Young's film version of the play appeared the same year, and the small stage version featuring Lois was quickly forgotten.

After *Mother Is a Freshman*, a trenchant, more substantial play by Aben Kandel entitled *Kitty Doone* came her way in 1950. It was a project she badly wanted to do: it would give her the opportunity to enact the meaty title role, which, while not at all likable, would give her some powerful dramatic opportunities. Clarence, who had to admit he was pleased to see Lois looking so happy, gave his approval, and she agreed to star in a production to be staged at the Pasadena Playhouse. The plot concerned a glamorous but aging film actress, Kitty, who has seen better days but is obsessed with staying at the top.

A fictional blending of such high-voltage stars as Bette Davis, Joan Crawford, and Tallulah Bankhead, *Kitty Doone* presented Lois with a variety of acting hurdles that, according to the reviews she received, she met successfully. Lois "makes the character as hard as granite," wrote Patterson Greene in the *Los Angeles Examiner*. Katharine Von Blon observed in the *Los Angeles Times*, "Lois Moran still retains her fresh charm and beauty, and offers a colorful rendition of the devastating Kitty." Lois enjoyed playing a bitch and was pleased with her work in it.

Lois and Clarence had for over twenty years been friends with Don Tressider, the president of Stanford University in Palo Alto, not far from Atherton. Tressider and his wife, Mary, had respected Lois as a film actress and had known of her work in *Twelfth Night* and *Bastien and Bastienne*. As her friend, fan, and neighbor, he invited her to become an artist-in-residence at Stanford in 1950. She soon became a presence at the campus, teaching dance and drama and appearing in plays there. In 1950 she enacted her first play as an artist-in-residence: Aeschylus's *The Oresteia*, in which she played Athena. It was perhaps as a result of her work for the school that *Of Thee I Sing* was staged there in 1955.

The best-received of the campus plays in which Lois appeared was a 1951 production of *Biography*, a witty 1932 comedy by S. N. Behrman, whom she had known in the 1930s. Considered by many to be the American Oscar Wilde, he had impressed Lois with his intelligence, and years later she welcomed the opportunity of appearing in one of his most celebrated plays. She enacted the role of Marion Froude, a playgirl who is given a chance to write her autobiography but finds trouble along the way. Lois took pride in the finished production.

Lois was also pleased at this time to cultivate a friendship with Bette Davis and Gary Merrill, who were then, in 1952, married and fresh from successful film pairings in the movies *All About Eve*, *Phone Call from a Stranger*, and *Another Man's Poison*, and who came to San Francisco that year to perform her touring theatrical show, Charles Sherman's musical *Two's Company*. "Dad and Mother loved Merrill," Young recalls, but what is most intriguing is Lois's relationship with the notoriously mercurial, temperamental Davis. "Bette was Bette," Young says. "She smoked like a chimney, drank and cursed like a sailor, and she was already pretty wrinkled." He continues, "Bette was never all that fond of other actresses, but she liked Mother. Marriage and family were on Bette's mind back then, and I think she secretly admired Mother for having had the guts to leave a promising career for the sake of establishing a family."

Lois was further elated in January 1953 when *Collier's* magazine published a piece by Herb Caen entitled "San Francisco's Most Glamorous Women" and included her. Caen, a columnist for the *San Francisco Examiner*, was fond of Lois and selected her to be part of the group of twelve, which consisted otherwise largely of socialites. He wrote a brief article that accompanied a large color photograph of the chosen ladies posed elegantly in a group setting. Lois had sat for many such group photos on movie sets in her youth, and her experience was evident. As in those earlier pictures, she stood out, even though she was the most modestly attired. The other women in the photograph donned plenty of satin, lace, floral accents, and ostentatious jewelry. Lois, on the other hand, wore a simple, elegant white dress accentuated with a pearl choker and earrings—quintessential Fragile Cameo.

In contrast to Caen's article, Lois's home life at the time was not particularly glamorous. Clarence, back to work running Pan Am, was absorbed in his career, and Tim was involved in his studies. Her work for the Red Cross was tapering off; she could not devote all of her time to her artist-in-residency at Stanford; and while she had scores of friends, they could not provide her the emotional affirmation she needed. Her resumption of acting had also caused her to begin missing her career, and she seriously contemplated the ramifications of what she had forfeited by giving up her work.

To make matters worse, Clarence and Gladys did not get along. Gladys had liked him well enough at the beginning, but over the years these two strong-willed people, who were approximately the same age, clashed regularly and quarreled about any number of issues, including Tim's upbringing and Lois's career. Clarence, a strict disciplinarian, believed that Tim's childhood should be highly structured and sent him to rigid military and college prep schools, whereas Gladys had hoped the boy would be better exposed to the liberal arts, as had been Lois. She was ignored on this point, and Tim, like his father, disliked her. Additionally, she was in favor of Lois's returning to acting on a more frequent basis, and in expressing this opinion, which she did often, she infuriated Clarence.

All this strife made Lois increasingly depressed. Wandering the large house in Atherton, often alone, she felt lonely, ignored, and incalculably old. Twenty years earlier, she had been a movie and theatrical star as well as an inspiration to one of America's most famous writers. Now the glitter of her youth had passed her by, and she found herself a disillusioned middle-aged housewife. She felt trapped and unappreciated. For solace, she turned to what was readily at hand. Like her onetime lover Fitzgerald, she began drinking heavily. She became a functioning alcoholic, tippling at all hours, hiding liquor bottles throughout the house, and proving that even naive child wonders could grow older and overwhelmed by sadness and regret. (Ironically, it was at this time that she was corresponding with Arthur Mizener on the subject of Fitzgerald's alcoholism.) Clarence noticed the problem before Gladys and Tim became aware of it, but all concerned ultimately believed that it was a situation best handled by simply ignoring it. Happily, new acting work soon came Lois's way. It did not remedy her alcoholism but at least placed it, for a time, in the background.

By 1954, her drinking had quietly worsened, but the roots of that problem—loneliness, familial tension, remorse over the loss of her acting career—were the catalysts that drove her to seek work again, and she believed that the challenge of making a film comeback was within her grasp. She pragmatically concluded that she was no longer a movie star and instead focused her attentions upon television. In its infancy in the early 1950s, television was uncharted territory that needed acting talent. Lois decided that the new medium was sure to offer her promising opportunities.

Clarence viewed the matter with distaste, but he realized that his wife was unhappy, and he worried about her worsening alcoholism. In spite of his reservations, then, he reasoned that a return to acting might alleviate Lois's surreptitious boozing. He therefore agreed to it, but only if she could find work that would allow her to film in Hollywood half-time so she could still be a presence in their Atherton home. To everyone's surprise, she was offered a part in a new television series entitled *Waterfront* that would be filmed every other two weeks and would not even require her to appear in every episode, thus more than meeting Clarence's residency condition. She was overjoyed. "I think Mother was still missing the spotlights," Young says. "Getting the part in *Waterfront* was good for her."

An action series with a family-themed subplot, *Waterfront* starred Preston Foster, a veteran of Hollywood he-man action films of the 1930s and 1940s, as John Herrick, the captain of the tugboat *Cheryl Ann*, and revolved around his adventures in and around the San Pedro Harbor. Lois played his wife, May Herrick. *Waterfront*'s family-oriented episodes, which were the ones in which Lois usually appeared, made it clear that a wife's unquestioning devotion to her husband was expected; but if this Eisenhower-era thinking rankled Lois, who at heart was still a feminist ahead of her time, she did not show it. On the contrary, she enacted May with just a dash of sly, tongue-in-cheek humor that showed she did not take any of it too seriously.

A humorous example of her approach to the character can be glimpsed in the "Christmas at the Harbor" episode from 1954. In one scene, in an apparently unscripted moment, a glass ornament falls from the Herrick Christmas tree and shatters on the floor, whereupon May, in a single fluid, lightning-fast motion, is instantly present both with a twinkle in her eye and a portable floor sweeper in her arms, eager to the point of mania to clean up the mess. Cleaning up messes is what television women did best in the 1950s, but in this scene Lois seems to be telling us with humorous exaggeration that nothing is ever as it seems.

"Mother brought years of experience to that series," Young explains, "and it shows in the details." Appearing in *Waterfront* did not cause her drinking to abate, however. "I began to see some of what her drinking was doing to her," he says. "I excused it, because Dad did so as well. I was still too young to understand the full impact of the problem. Hidden bottles all over the place. There's the slightest slur to some of her dialogue if you listen hard enough."

Her alcoholism aside, the *Waterfront* period was one of the happiest in Lois's life. *Variety* praised the show in general as well as her "excellent support" as May Herrick. Tim once visited the set, and she was further elated when Mae Clarke, her friend and costar from the Fox days, made a guest appearance in one episode. In a 1954 letter to the critic Terrence O'Flaugherty, she related a description of her return to the cameras that is startlingly reminiscent of a classic scene in the 1950 Billy Wilder film, *Sunset Boulevard*, in which the aging silent-film star Norma Desmond, played by Gloria Swanson, returns to a film set, also after twenty years of retirement, and revels in being recognized by members of the crew with whom she once worked. At the time, Lois seldom went out to the movies, in contrast to her younger years, and, as Tim Young points out, most probably had not seen the film.

Lois was not a deranged recluse like Norma Desmond—in fact, the only post-stardom attribute she had in common with that character was chronic drinking—but her retelling of the event could have been taken directly from the script of Wilder's film. She found the reunion with old coworkers pleasant, but it was not the intense emotional experience for her that it was for Norma Desmond in the film. "It is great fun acting professionally again," she wrote to O'Flaugherty.

> Worked with at least half of the crew years ago—so felt right at home—Dave, the head gaffer (electrician to you—and a very important guy) nudged me the first day, as he was setting the lights—saying "Remember *Transatlantic* at Fox?" I sure did. Dave and I did four or five pictures at Fox together—Wm. K. Howard, director of the film, died just a few weeks ago.... Then came a yell from on high— "Lois, remember the old days at MGM?" That was "Hollywood"— We'd worked together on Jack Gilbert's last film before he died—

I think it was called *West of Broadway*. Well, this went on all day—Found more and more old friends and they all treated me as if I were still a little girl—So, naturally, I felt warm and protected and happy. How lucky can a woman be?

After *Waterfront*, Lois, for the most part, retired from public life. Her battle with drinking was no doubt one of the primary reasons she opted for seclusion from the spotlight, but now, in her forties, she believed also that she was no longer youthful enough to continue to seek singing and acting roles. In 1955, she spoke briefly about Fitzgerald on the NBC radio series *Biography in Sound* and was spotted dancing with Ray Bradbury at a soirée but otherwise kept a low public profile. Throughout the rest of the 1950s, she and Clarence traveled extensively, often with Tim, and she enjoyed seeing the world and let go, once and for all, of thoughts of returning to her career. She continued to drink, but as the years went on she did so more out of physical addiction than as a result of mental anguish.

Lois's friend at the time, the fellow film actress Marian Marsh, did not recognize any outward signs of Lois's alcoholism, however. Marsh, a retired star of the 1930s who had acted in pictures with high-profile actors such as John Barrymore, Peter Lorre, and Boris Karloff, socialized sporadically with Lois during the early 1950s, particularly at the time of *Waterfront*. Around that time Lois and Clarence spent time in Palm Springs, where Marsh lived, because her husband, Clifford W. Henderson, was a renowned aviator—among other accomplishments, he was the founder and managing director of the National Air Races—who knew Clarence. She recalled to this author in 2004:

> Lois Moran was a name that wasn't used very often when I knew her in the 1950s, but I thought it was an exceptional name. I knew of her long before I started my own film career. I was very young then, and I remember her name foreboding something very big. She was ending her career roughly about the time that I was beginning mine. We used to meet from time to time, as our husbands were both flyers and we both had been in the movies, and I can today say only

the nicest things about her. I didn't know her well, but the association was certainly there. I remember her fondly. We had enjoyable conversations, and I never noticed a trace of alcoholism. She was always a charming, well-spoken person.

Another of Lois's contemporaries, the silent-film and early-talkie actress Anita Page, had similar memories of Lois at this time. Page was an emotive MGM dramatic star who had made her name in films such as *Our Dancing Daughters* in 1928 and *The Broadway Melody* in 1929. The Italian dictator Benito Mussolini, who for a time was said to be obsessed with her, had once proposed. She married Retired Admiral Hershel A. House, retired from films, and for over forty years lived in Coronado, California, where she often gave cocktail parties at her home. Clarence, who as a distinguished aviator was a good friend of House, and Lois frequently attended these parties. Page remembered Lois to this author in 2004 as a fellow actress who at the time had become "matronly, had gained a bit of weight, had grown quite settled, and loved her cocktails and made no pretense about it." She concluded that she found Lois to be "the loveliest person." Page also remarked that she and other actresses often wondered why Lois had abandoned a promising career, but they apparently were not aware of the complex dynamics of Lois's marriage to Clarence that had prevented her from returning to her career full-force.

In February 1963, Lois appeared publicly again, looking fatigued and a bit heavier, by taking part in the showy closing ceremonies for the Fox Theater in San Francisco, which was being torn down to make room for an office building. Because it had featured location scenes shot in San Francisco, *Behind That Curtain* had been the first film screened at the theater when it opened on the evening of June 28, 1929, and Lois's presence at its closing now was thus a much-heralded event. The farewell program included onstage appearances by celebrities such as Jane Russell, Kay Starr, and Jane Wyman. Guests of honor included Lois, Hedda Hopper, Gary Merrill, and Shirley Temple

Black. Witnessing the closure of the spectacular theater, one of the greatest of the awe-inspiring Art Deco film palaces of the past, saddened Lois; the movie house conjured pleasurable memories of the days when such cinemas played a big part in her life. The theater was padlocked immediately after the conclusion of the ceremonies and felled by a wrecking ball a short time later.

Where had the years gone, Lois wondered that evening as she was chauffeured back to her home in Atherton after the festivities. It seemed only a short while ago that she had filmed *Behind That Curtain*, but when a clip of it was shown during the ceremonies it looked antique to her. Pulling her fur collar close to her throat and gazing out of the limousine's window at the glistening city lights as they flickered by, she allowed her mind to wander a bit. Did anyone remember Trefilova and Kiki de Montparnasse, two of her more exotic acquaintances from Paris in the 1920s? Both were now dead. Did Warner Baxter, her costar in *Behind That Curtain*, still have his once-huge army of fans? He had died after undergoing a lobotomy in 1951. And what had become of Edmund Lowe, another of her costars? He had appeared with her four films, more than had any of her other leading men, and had recently taken ill during the production of *Heller in Pink Tights* in 1960 (this proved to be his last film; he died in 1971). What was George O'Brien doing nowadays? She had made three films with him and even been infatuated with him for a time. She loved Clarence, but my oh my, had George caused her heart to race. He had fought, she knew, during World War II and had made films during the Korean conflict (he died in 1985). What would have become of Lya de Putti had she not choked to death on that chicken bone? Lois remembered her jet-black hair and the long fingers she had described in her journal as claws.

As the limousine cruised along the highway, Lois's mind began to throb with even more questions. What would Scott Fitzgerald have gone on to write? Would she still have been featured in his works? Was Carl Van Vechten, who was alive and living in New York, still snapping his photographs? Did George Jean Nathan ever achieve his dream of becoming great? Would John Wayne fans ever remember him as the Duke Morrison she had known in *Words and Music*? Was anyone still familiar with the great film and stage work done by Belle Bennett and, at that, did anyone realize that she had died of throat cancer in the early 1930s? Did anyone still know the once famous names of Louise Dresser, Phillips Holmes, and Jean Hersholt? For that matter, did anyone remember that person called Lois Moran for anything other than *Stella Dallas* and her association with Fitzgerald? What would *she* have gone on to accomplish had she not retired when she did? Her thoughts were abruptly interrupted as the limousine stopped and the chauffeur opened the door. She was back home now, back to life today, entrenched again in reality. She wanted to live squarely in the present, she reminded herself as she stepped out of the car and glanced up at the stars. "We are all in the gutter, but some of us are looking at the stars," one of the writers she admired, Oscar Wilde, had once remarked. Every now and then it was fun to look at the sky, as she had done at Fitzgerald's party at Ellerslie, and allow herself the luxury of revisiting the faces and events of her youth.

At the time the Fox San Francisco closed, Lois and Clarence had come to realize that their home in Atherton was too large for them, especially as Tim now had a home of his own on the water in Tiburon, across the bay from San Francisco. He had graduated from Stanford in 1958 and joined the army to become an Airborne Ranger. Following in his father's footsteps, he now held a high-level position at Pan Am. On a suggestion from Tressider, she and Clarence moved into an apartment near the Stanford campus. However, when Clarence, who had for years smoked four packs of Camel cigarettes a day, was diagnosed with emphysema, they sought a drier climate and moved to Phoenix, Arizona. Finding Phoenix too hot, in 1968 they bought a home in nearby Sedona, a cooler, scenic art colony said to possess restorative powers; Clarence found the area especially attractive because he had taken up landscape painting. The Sedona house featured attractive scenic views of Sedona's famous red rock formations, including the Coffee Pot Mountain, so called because of its shape.

By the time Lois moved to Sedona, she and Betty had become absorbed in their own families and were no longer as close as they once had been. They did keep in touch, however. In the late 1930s, Betty had embarked upon her own film career, but she was not as successful as Lois had been. She landed supporting roles in a few films and appeared on Broadway, most notably in the 1942 Cole Porter musical *Let's Face It!* Like Lois, she placed marriage and family above her career and retired when she married. Lois spoke fondly of her in later years. "She's a real fine actress," she wrote to a film researcher in 1984. "Her loss to us, professionally, is her family's gain." The two had otherwise grown apart, however, and, just as Betty seldom mentioned Lois, Lois rarely brought up the subject of her adopted sister. Nor was Lois in contact with her cousin, Betsy Blair.

In 1973, Lois suffered two devastating setbacks when both Clarence and Gladys passed away. Her world shattered as her two greatest sources of strength left her. Clarence succumbed first, to the emphysema. In accordance with his wishes, he was cremated, and Tim Young scattered his ashes over Sedona. Lois had been married to Clarence for nearly forty years and described her late husband at the time as "a noble man, a gentle man, a loving and wise and witty man." He was mourned as one of the undisputed founding fathers of aviation. Gladys died of old age a short time later. The iron maiden who had once so forcibly dictated the course of her daughter's life had mellowed with age and, like Edith Darlington Dowling, had become a quiet, home-loving woman who devoted her time not to the stock market but to hobbies and to reminiscing with friends and relatives. Because of the very difficult year Lois was experiencing, Betty took care of her funeral arrangements.

"That was a horrible year for both myself and Mother," remembers Tim. "We both hit the bottle pretty hard at that time." Lois, who, as Young explains, always liked to be taken care of, was now more alone than she had ever been. At the age of sixty-four, amidst the beautiful red rocks of Sedona, she had hit, she believed, rock bottom. What she had not counted upon was her life's way of rejuvenating itself in times of sorrow. She had lost her husband and her mother, but much remained in her life. She and Tim would become closer than they had ever been, and she would find in Sedona a sense of community that comforted and energized her throughout her remaining years.

By the mid-1970s, Lois had begun to again enjoy life, but there remained that one demon left for her to conquer, her alcoholism. She took pleasure in being part of the Church of the Red Rocks choir and enjoyed working with its director, a tenor named Joe Barclay. However, her drinking had become even worse since the passing of Clarence and Gladys. She was involved in multiple drunk driving incidents, and it was not unusual for her to show up tipsy to choir rehearsals. "She was deteriorating as the drinking took a stronger and stronger hold of her," Tim Young explains. As is true of many alcoholics, Lois denied that a problem existed. She was therefore stunned when Barclay asked her to leave the choir. "That shocked Mother," Young says.

The expulsion from the choir jolted Lois into admitting her addiction, and, with her son's help, she checked herself into St. Luke's Hospital in Phoenix, one of the best-known alcohol and drug rehabilitation facilities at the time. "She became sober and never drank anything but iced tea after that," Young explains, "but I believe damage had been done to her body by that time." Now a model of sobriety, Lois was reinstated in the choir and resumed life as normal.

In addition to the choir, the Sedona Arts Center was fast becoming one of the driving forces of her life. When she first came to Sedona, she had helped to found an art and theatrical complex, the Sedona Arts Center, which originally had been a barn, and over the years she became increasingly involved with it. Her main work for the center was writing a weekly newspaper column about it for the local *Red Rock News* entitled "Down at the Barn." The column became a regular feature of the paper, and she wrote it to the very end of her life.

Lois did not dwell on the past during the Sedona years, which spanned 1968 to her passing in 1990, but she was usually willing to discuss her younger days. She believed acting had been a profession that had done much to shape her character and sensibilities. She always maintained that she had made the correct decision in leaving her career when she did, and in Sedona she kept her focus squarely upon the here and now. As her 1920s contemporary Diana Serra Cary, known then as the child star Baby Peggy, pointed out in a 1995 letter to this author,

> It is always nice to hear about some early star who managed to walk away proudly and happily into another world after Hollywood and Broadway. There are so many Norma Desmonds whose intellectual ignorance of their real selves permits their egos to lock them inside the gilded cage of their aging screen images. Lois seemed to be a very level-headed and "normal" movie star.

In Sedona, Lois did often speak of writing her memoirs, which she planned to entitle, referring to herself and Clarence, *The Actress and the Flyer*, but her passion for the present negated the fascination with the past she would have needed in order to write such a book. It is possible that she lacked appreciation for what considerable accomplishments her life and career had been, probably because prosperity in the world Carl Van Vechten had described in *Vanity Fair* in 1927 as "Fabulous Hollywood" had come too easily for her to have recognized its brilliance in later years. She had never had to struggle, never had to toil in the lower ranks of stardom, because success had come to her swiftly, luminously, and when she was very young.

She did keep in touch with many of the friends of her past. She wrote, for example, to Jack Mulhall, her costar in *God Gave Me Twenty Cents*, when she learned in the 1980s that he was a nursing home. In the 1970s and 1980s, she exchanged Christmas cards each year with Frank La Forge's widow. She made a point of entertaining Colleen Moore when she visited Sedona in the 1970s. "She was an elegant person, no matter what Scott said about her," she observed in a letter to this author in 1987, referring to Fitzgerald's famous description of himself having been the spark that ignited the Jazz Age and Colleen Moore the flame. She encountered Fitzgerald's daughter Scottie at an event in Washington in the 1970s and remembered her as "a talented girl, a real nice person," and she made the acquaintance of Frances Kroll Ring, who had been Fitzgerald's secretary at the end of his life, when she did the interview for the Canadian Fitzgerald documentary in the 1980s. "I [had] lunch with Lois Moran at the Ambassador Hotel before it was totally shut down in, I think, the early 1980s," Ring recalled in a letter to this author in 2004.

> I don't remember how or why. I think it was arranged by a public relations person. [Lois] was petite, charming, and aged. . . . Her life was totally removed from Hollywood, but she was ever interested in the arts and wrote a newspaper column of which she was proud. She was totally unpretentious and was interested in how Fitzgerald was at the premature end of his life. It was inspiring to see how in control of her life she was with no affectation of having been a star.

Arrangement for Lois's lunching with Ring at the Ambassador was exceedingly shrewd, as that was the hotel where Fitzgerald was staying when he met Lois in 1927. In addition to the likes of Scottie and Frances, some of Lois's friends in Sedona had links to old Hollywood, as well, such as Lorraine Bendix and Earl Sennett, the nephew of Mack Sennett, who taught drama and staged plays there. She also knew Jane Russell and Ann Miller, both of whom lived in Sedona at various times.

Laurel Dallas, Mary Turner, and Rosemary Hoyt had grown old graciously and contentedly in Sedona. Lois had long ago shed the extra pounds she had gained in the late 1950s. A physically small woman, she wore a fresh flower in her hair every day in her old age, perhaps as a sign of her joy to be alive and as an indicator that the brickbats she believed had plagued her at the end of her Hollywood career had given way once again to a life of bouquets. She and Tim often took trips to a vacation home they maintained in Big Bear, California, and she looked forward to spending Christmases there. She kept two pet cats in Sedona that she doted upon and named Nero and Caesar, and she filled her home with plants and flowers. One of the last photographs taken of her was a 1989 snapshot of her at the Sedona Arts Center. There she was, in Fitzgerald's words, flashing luminous blue eyes and donning a white carnation in her hair. Looking far younger than she was, she smiled and danced with a maraca clutched festively in her outstretched hand.

Lois turned eighty in March 1989. She had long held a belief that she would not live long after this age, and, almost as if on cue, she became depressed and her body began to decline. In that winter, she was diagnosed with breast cancer, and her doctor strongly recommended an immediate course of radiation treatment in Flagstaff. Tim Young was against it because he thought it would do more harm than good, but the doctor prevailed. "I think going for the chemo everyday was unduly traumatic for her," he asserts, "and I don't think it did all that much to prolong her life."

Indeed, no sooner had the radiation therapy concluded than she began to suffer a series of small strokes called transient ischemic attacks, or TIAs. These began to take their toll as she became weaker, more exhausted, and increasingly unable to find her words when she spoke. To make matters worse, in 1990, she fell at her home in Sedona and broke her hip. "Fortunately, I bounce, not break, and am recuperating rapidly," she declared in the last letter she wrote to this author, in 1990, but the fall was more serious than she let on and Young decided she needed full-time care. Reasoning that perhaps it would be best for her to spend some time in a nursing home, where she could be properly cared for and recuperate, he approached his mother. "I said, 'Mother, do you think you might want to try it for a while and see how it works out?' She agreed that it was worth a try. She was very tired by that time." Young happened to be on the board of directors of a new, state-of-the-art convalescent home in Sedona called the Kachina Rest Home. "It is a beautiful facility," he says, "and we got her a room with a magnificent view of the red rocks of Sedona."

Lois's time at Kachina was by all indications a pleasant experience for her, considering the circumstances. "They treated her just like the star she was," Young says. Both the staff and the residents of the home realized that they had an old-time film celebrity in their midst, and they accorded Lois a reverence that must have comforted her. Wednesday and Friday evenings were particularly gratifying to her, for on those nights some of her films were shown on a large-screen television in the recreation room. "I think we had *Stella Dallas*, *Mammy*, and *Transatlantic*," Young recalls. "Everyone got a huge kick out of seeing these movies." Lois had her own table there on movie nights, and, just as Princeton undergraduates had queued to dance with her in the 1920s, the gentlemen residents would line up for the honor of dining with her. "It was like the Great White Way in Sedona," Young explains. "Mother was holding court. In her mind, it must have been like the days when she was belle of the ball during *Of Thee I Sing*. There was love all around her. I can't think of a more beautiful way for her to have spent her last days."

Lois never became well enough to return home. Fitzgerald had famously described Rosemary Hoyt's "strong young pump" of a heart, but while a literary character could live forever, Lois could not. She died at Kachina at the age of eighty-one at 2:30 A.M. on Friday, July 13, 1990. Astonishingly, in 1934 she had written in her journal, "Friday the thirteenth is always lucky for Mother and me." During the final night of her life, Young and his wife at the time were with her. "I was on one side of the bed, my wife was on the other, and we were each holding one of her hands," he explains. "Mother was very pale, very weak. She was fading, and we all sensed that the end was near." He was at a loss as to what he should say or do at such a time, but suddenly nature took its course. "A breeze swept through the room," he remembers.

> Mother clenched, and I could feel her hand grasp mine tighter. Then the light flickered, and we all felt a presence in the room. I am sure this was my father, come to take Mother away. It's as if he were there, right next to us, saying to Mother, "Lois, it's time to go. Come with me. Let's let the kids live their lives." I firmly believe that was Dad's soul making its appearance to us. Then it was very quiet and Mother quietly passed away.

In keeping with her wishes, her remains were cremated, and Young, as he had done with his father, flew over Sedona and spread her ashes over the red rocks she had loved so much.

Young organized an elegant memorial service at a church in Sedona at which he and her friends paid tribute to her as a beloved wife, mother, friend, and performer who at the height of her career had achieved the rare distinction of having gone from Goldwyn to Gershwin, with a dash of Scott Fitzgerald in between. Many mourners who had known her attended, and the church was filled to capacity. A startling thing happened while Young was delivering his eulogy, which he entitled "Of Thee I Sing, Mother."

> I noticed that everyone was looking toward a window on the side of the church. I quickly turned my head in the same direction, just in time to see a glorious eagle fly by right in front of the window and then soar away into the distance. This was a small church and a low window, so everyone was absolutely flabbergasted that just as I was speaking about my mother, an eagle, of all things, a proud and beautiful creature, would most unexpectedly fly right in front of it. Everyone let out an audible gasp.

Young felt the eagle was Lois's soul taking flight. "Mother was saying good-bye, in her own inimitable way," he says, "and I'm certain she was headed for one last view of Coffee Pot, the mountain that she loved so much in life that she could see from the house. Everyone present that day believes this, and they were a group of pretty sophisticated people." He concludes, "Mother was like that. She did everything in style."

Acting Chronologies

Characters Enacted by Lois Moran

Production Title	Character
La galerie des monstres (1924)	Ralda
Feu Mathias Pascal (aka *The Living Dead Man* and *The Late Mathias Pascal*) (1924)	Adrienne Paleari
The Wisdom Tooth (play, 1925)	Lalita
Stella Dallas (1925)	Laurel Dallas
Just Suppose (1926)	Linda Lee Stafford
The Reckless Lady (1926)	Sylvia Fleming
Padlocked (1926)	Edith Gilbert
The Road to Mandalay (1926)	Rosemary
The Prince of Tempters (1926)	Monica
God Gave Me Twenty Cents (1926)	Mary
The Music Master (1926)	Helene Stanton
Camille (four-reel home movie by Ralph Barton, 1926)	Kitty
The Irresistible Lover (1927)	Betty Kennedy
The Whirlwind of Youth (1927)	Nancy Hawthorne
Publicity Madness (1927)	Violet
U.S.A. (play, 1927)	[Not known]
Sharp Shooters (1928)	Lorette
Love Hungry (1928)	Joan Robinson
Don't Marry (1928)	Louise and Priscilla Bowen (dual role)
The River Pirate (1928)	Marjorie Cullen
Blindfold (1928)	Mary Brower

Production Title	Character
True Heaven (1929)	Judith
The Belle of Samoa (1929, short subject)	[Not known]
Making the Grade (1929)	Lettie Ewing
Joy Street (1929)	Marie Colman (aka Mimi)
Behind That Curtain (1929)	Eve Mannering
Words and Music (1929)	Mary Brown
A Song of Kentucky (1929)	Lee Coleman
Mammy (1930)	Nora Meadows
Not Damaged (1930)	Gwen Stewart
The Dancers (1930)	Diana
Under Suspicion (1930)	Alice Freil
This Is New York (stage, 1931)	Emma Krull
Transatlantic (1931)	Judy Kramer
The Spider (1931)	Beverly Lane
Men in Her Life (1931)	Julia Cavanaugh
West of Broadway (1931)	Dot
Of Thee I Sing (stage musical, 1931–33)	Mary Turner
Ladies Not Allowed (1932, two-reel short subject, part of *Lamb's Gambols* series)	[Unknown; possibly herself]
Let 'Em Eat Cake (stage musical, 1933–34)	Mary Turner
The Petrified Forest (play, 1935)	Gabrielle
Twelfth Night (play, 1941)	Viola
Bastien and Bastienne (stage opera, 1941)	Bastien
We Are Many People (radio series, 1946)	[Various]
Mother Is a Freshman (play, 1949)	Abigail Fortitude Abbott
Kitty Doone (play, 1950)	Kitty Doone
The Oresteia (play, 1950)	Athena
Biography (play, 1950)	Marion Froude
Waterfront (television series, 1954–55)	May Herrick

Film Appearances

La galerie des monstres (1924, filmed in Spain and France)

Consorcio Internacional de Explotaciones Cinematográficas (por Contratación Comercial). Dir. Marcel L'Herbier. Also known as *La barraca de los monstruos* (Spain) and *Gallery of Monsters* (America and United Kingdom). Silent. Cast: Lois Moran, Jaque Catelain, Michel Simon, Claire Prelia, Jean Murat, Lili Samuel, Kiki, Michel Duran.

Feu Mathias Pascal (1924, filmed in France)

Films Albatros. Dir. Marcel L'Herbier. Also known as *The Living Dead Man* and *The Late Mathias Pascal*. Silent. Cast: Lois Moran, Ivan Mosjoukine, Michel Simon, Marcelle Pradot, Irma Perrot, Marthe Mellot, Solange Sicard, Isaure Douvan.

Stella Dallas (1925)

Goldwyn–United Artists. Dir. Henry King. Silent. Cast: Lois Moran, Belle Bennett, Ronald Colman, Alice Joyce, Jean Hersholt, Douglas Fairbanks Jr., Vera Lewis.

Just Suppose (1926)

First National. Dir. Kenneth Webb. Silent. Cast: Lois Moran, Richard Barthelmess, Geoffrey Kerr, Henry Vibart, Bijou Fernandez.

The Reckless Lady (1926)

First National. Dir. Howard Higgin. Silent. Cast: Lois Moran, Belle Bennett, James Kirkwood, Lowell Sherman, Ben Lyon, Charles Murray.

Padlocked (1926)

Famous Players–Lasky. Dir. Allan Dwan. Silent. Cast: Lois Moran, Noah Beery, Helen Jerome Eddy, Louise Dresser, Florence Turner, Allan Simpson, Charles Lane, Charlotte Bird, Richard Arlen, Douglas Fairbanks Jr.

The Road to Mandalay (1926)

Metro-Goldwyn-Mayer. Dir. Tod Browning. Silent. Cast: Lois Moran, Lon Chaney, Henry B. Walthall, Owen Moore, Kamiyama Sojin.

The Prince of Tempters (1926)

First National. Dir. Lothar Mendes. Silent. Cast: Lois Moran, Ben Lyon, Lya de Putti, Ian Keith, Mary Brian, Henry Vibart, Sam Hardy, Olive Tell.

God Gave Me Twenty Cents (1926)

Famous Players–Lasky. Dir. Herbert Brenon. Silent. Cast: Lois Moran, Jack Mulhall, Lya de Putti, William Collier Jr., Adrienne D'Ambricourt, Thelma Todd (uncredited).

Camille (1926)

Dir: Ralph Barton. Four-reel home movie produced by Ralph Barton. Silent. Cast: Lois Moran, Charles Chaplin, Anita Loos, Charles Green Shaw, Paul Robeson, Theodore Dreiser, John Emerson, Roland Young, W. Somerset Maugham, George Jean Nathan, H. L. Mencken, Sinclair Lewis, Joseph Hergesheimer, Alfred A. Knopf, Ethel Barrymore, Rex Ingram, Aileen Pringle, Dorothy Gish, Carmel Myers, Richard Barthelmess, Patsy Ruth Miller, James Rennie, Sherwood Anderson, Clarence Darrow, Sacha Guitry, Yvonne Printemps, Max Reinhardt.

The Music Master (1927)

Fox. Dir. Allan Dwan. Silent. Cast: Lois Moran, Alec B. Francis, Neil Hamilton, William T. Tilden, Helen Chandler, Norman Trevor.

The Irresistible Lover (1927)

Universal-Jewel. Dir. William Beaudine. Silent. Cast: Lois Moran, Norman Kerry, Lee Moran, Gertrude Astor, Arthur Lake.

The Whirlwind of Youth (1927)

Paramount. Dir. Rowland V. Lee. Silent. Cast: Lois Moran, Donald Keith, Vera Veronina, Alyce Mills, Larry Kent, Charles Lane.

Publicity Madness (1927)

Fox. Dir. Albert Ray. Silent. Cast: Lois Moran, Edmund Lowe, James Gordon, E. J. Ratcliffe, Arthur Housman.

Sharp Shooters (1928)

Fox. Dir. John G. Blystone. Silent. Cast: Lois Moran, George O'Brien, Tom Dugan, Noah Young, William Demarest, Gwen Lee, Randolph Scott (uncredited), Boris Karloff (uncredited).

Love Hungry (1928)

Fox. Dir. Victor Heerman. Silent. Cast: Lois Moran, Lawrence Gray, Marjorie Beebe, James Neill, Edythe Chapman.

Don't Marry (1928)

Fox. Dir. James Tinling. Silent. Cast: Lois Moran, Neil Hamilton, Henry Kolker, Claire McDowell.

The River Pirate (1928)

Fox. Dir. William K. Howard. Silent with sound effects and limited dialogue. Cast: Lois Moran, Victor McLaglen, Nick Stuart, Earle Foxe, Donald Crisp.

Blindfold (1928)

Fox. Dir. Charles Klein. Silent. Cast: Lois Moran, George O'Brien, Earle Foxe, Maria Alba, Fritz Feld, Andy Clyde.

True Heaven (1929)

Fox. Dir. James Tinling. Silent with sound effects. Cast: Lois Moran, George O'Brien, Phillips Smalley, Duke Martin.

The Belle of Samoa (1929)

Fox. Dir. Marcel Silver. Sound short subject. Cast: Lois Moran (first all-talking picture), Bobby Clark, Paul McCullough.

Making the Grade (1929)

Fox. Dir. Alfred E. Green. Silent with sound effects. Cast: Lois Moran, Edmund Lowe, Lucien Littlefield, Albert Hart, John Alden.

Joy Street (1929)

Fox. Dir. Raymond Cannon. Silent with sound effects and music. Cast: Lois Moran, Nick Stuart, José Crespo, Rex Bell, Sally Phipps, Maria Alba, John Breeden, Lupita Tovar (uncredited; her first film).

Behind That Curtain (1929)

Fox. Dir. Irving Cummings. Sound. Cast: Lois Moran, Warner Baxter, Claude King, Gilbert Emery, Philip Strange, Boris Karloff, E. L. Park.

Words and Music (1929)

Fox. Dir. James Tinling. Sound; also released in silent version. Cast: Lois Moran, David Percy, Helen Twelvetrees, Duke Morrison (later known as John Wayne), Tom Patricola, Frank Albertson, Frances Dee (uncredited; her first film).

A Song of Kentucky (1929)

Fox. Dir. Lewis Seiler. Sound. Cast: Lois Moran, Joseph Wagstaff, Dorothy Burgess, Hedda Hopper, Douglas Gilmore.

Mammy (1930)

Warner Brothers. Dir. Michael Curtiz. Sound; original version included Technicolor sequence. Cast: Lois Moran, Al Jolson, Louise Dresser, Lowell Sherman, Hobart Bosworth, Tully Marshall, Noah Beery (uncredited), Lee Moran (uncredited).

Not Damaged (1930)

Fox. Dir. Chandler Sprague. Sound. Cast: Lois Moran, Walter Byron, Inez Courtney, Robert Ames.

The Dancers (1930)

Fox. Dir. Chandler Sprague. Sound. Cast: Lois Moran, Phillips Holmes, Mae Clarke, Walter Byron, Mrs. Patrick Campbell.

Under Suspicion (1930)

Fox. Dir. A. F. Erickson. Sound. Cast: Lois Moran, J. Harold Murray, George Brent, J. M. Kerrigan, Marie Saxon.

Transatlantic (1931)

Fox. Dir. William K. Howard. Sound. Cast: Lois Moran, Edmund Lowe, Myrna Loy, Greta Nissen, Jean Hersholt, Earle Foxe, John Halliday.

The Spider (1931)

Fox. Dirs. Kenneth MacKenna and William Cameron Menzies. Sound. Cast: Lois Moran, Edmund Lowe, Howard Phillips, El Brendel, Earle Foxe, Ruth Donnelly.

Men in Her Life (1931)

Columbia. Dir. William Beaudine. Sound. Cast: Lois Moran, Charles Bickford, Victor Varconi, Adrienne D'Ambricourt.

West of Broadway (1931)

Metro-Goldwyn-Mayer. Dir. Harry Beaumont. Sound. Cast: Lois Moran, John Gilbert, Madge Evans, Ralph Bellamy, El Brendel, Gwen Lee, Frank Conroy, Hedda Hopper.

Ladies Not Allowed (1932)

Columbia. Entry in *Lamb's Gambols* comedic two-reel short-subject series. Dir. Joseph Santley. Sound. Music by Victor Herbert and Percy Wenrich. Cast: Lois Moran, William Gaxton, Victor Moore, Otto Kruger, Charles King, DeWolf Hopper, Harrison Brockbank.

Note:
Alice in the Cities, a 1974 West German film, featured another actress by the name of Lois Moran.

Stage Appearances

The Wisdom Tooth (1925)

By Marc Connelly. Produced by Martin Beck. Tryouts in Atlantic City and Baltimore; this production did not reach Broadway. Cast: Lois Moran,

Thomas Mitchell, Marion Ballou, Malcolm Williams, Kate Mayhew, William Wadsworth, Lloyd Neil, Mary Philips, William Randall.

U.S.A. (1927)

A "playlet" produced by the Writers' Club in Los Angeles. Limited run. Cast: Lois Moran, Belle Bennett, Bryant Washburn.

This Is New York (1931)

By Robert Emmet Sherwood. Produced by Arthur Hopkins. Plymouth Theater, New York, opened November 28, 1930; 59 performances. Cast: Lois Moran, Geoffrey Kerr, Allen Atwell, Henrietta Ravenell, Sam Wren, Robert T. Haines. Gowns by Hattie Carnegie.

Of Thee I Sing (1931–33)

Music by George Gershwin; book by George S. Kaufman and Morrie Ryskind; lyrics by Ira Gershwin. Produced by Sam H. Harris. Music Box Theater, New York, opened December 26; 441 performances. Cast: Lois Moran, William Gaxton, George Murphy, Victor Moore, Grace Brinkley.

Let 'Em Eat Cake (1933–34)

Music by George Gershwin; book by George S. Kaufman and Morrie Ryskind; lyrics by Ira Gershwin. Produced by Sam H. Harris. Imperial Theater, New York, opened October 21; 89 performances. Cast: Lois Moran, William Gaxton, Victor Moore.

The Petrified Forest (1935)

By Robert Emmet Sherwood. Limited local run at the Geary Theater, San Francisco, in advance of the release of the Warner Brothers film featuring Bette Davis and Humphrey Bogart. Cast: Lois Moran, Conrad Nagel.

Twelfth Night (1941)

By William Shakespeare. One performance on June 8 at Hearst Greek Theater, Berkeley, California. Dir. Dr. George Altman. Cast: Lois Moran, Gilmor Brown.

Bastien and Bastienne (December 1941)

By W. A. Mozart (opera). Limited run at Palace of the Legion of Honor Museum, San Francisco. Cast: Lois Moran. A more extensive cast listing has not been located.

Mother Is a Freshman (1949)

By Raphael David Blau and Christopher Sergel. San Francisco community theater production in advance of the Twentieth Century–Fox film featuring Loretta Young. Cast: Lois Moran. A more extensive cast listing has not been located.

Kitty Doone (1950)

By Aben Kandel. Pasadena Playhouse. Dir. George Phelps. Motion picture sequence featured in scene 2 dir. Morris Ankrum. A producer was not credited, although Gilmor Brown, who had acted with Lois in *Twelfth Night*, was identified as "Supervising Director." Cast: Lois Moran, Gordon Sears, King Donovan, Betty Flint, Raul Chavez, Jack Bryan, Douglas McEachin, Lois Kimbrell, William Leslie, Michael Concannon, Ed Kemmer. Note: Lois Moran's friend Constance Bennett appeared in a television version of the play in January 1954.

The Oresteia (1951)

By Aeschylus. Production at Stanford University as an Artist in Residence. Cast: Lois Moran. A more extensive cast listing has not been found.

Biography (1951)

By S. N. Behrman. Production at Stanford University as an Artist in Residence. Dir. F. Cowles Strickland. Cast: Lois Moran, Richard Cox, Celeste Ashley, David Kaplan, John Dodds.

Note:
To promote her early films, especially *Stella Dallas* and *Just Suppose*, Lois Moran often made stage appearances in person at movie houses throughout the country. Sometimes she gave brief speeches at such events; at other times, she simply curtsied and exited the stage.

In her later years, in the 1970s and 1980s, Lois Moran gave talks from time to time in Sedona, Arizona, about her life and career.

Television Appearances

Waterfront (1954–55)

Television series. Roland Reed Productions, filmed at Hal Roach Studios for First-Run Syndication. Guy V. Thayer Jr., executive producer; M. Bernard Fox, creator and producer. Filmed on location in San Pedro–Los Angeles Harbor. 1954: seventy-eight episodes, thirty minutes each. With Preston Foster, Lois Moran, Harry Lauter, Douglas Dick, Pinky Tomlin. Lois Moran appeared in thirty-one episodes of this series:

- "The Skipper's Day"
- "Sunken Treasure of San Pedro"
- "A New Whistle for the *Cheryl Ann*"
- "Cap'n Long John"
- "Term Paper"
- "Cap'n John's Dilemma"
- "Family Problems"
- "Sea Bells"
- "Tug O'War"
- "Tailor-Made"
- "Troubled Waters"
- "The Rift"
- "Fog Bound" (featuring guest actress Mae Clarke)
- "Cap'n Christopher"
- "Backwash"
- "Portia of the Sea"
- "Driftwood"
- "The White Ducks"
- "F.O.B. Vera Cruz"
- "Live Bait"
- "Oil Island"
- "Christmas at the Harbor"
- "Fisherman's Fiesta"
- "The Reluctant Guest"
- "Farnum's Folly"

- "Skipper, Beware"
- "The Artful Horse"
- "The Semi-Private Room"
- "Double Exposure"
- "Mike"
- "Beached"

Note:
Lois Moran traveled from Sedona to Los Angeles in the mid-1980s to be interviewed for a Canadian television documentary about F. Scott Fitzgerald. Displeased with the line of questioning, she cut her interviews short and was glimpsed only briefly in the finished production.

Radio Appearances

[Miscellaneous, 1926]

At the Hotel Astor in New York, Lois Moran participated in a banquet at which a live radio performance was given of the plot of First National's new picture *Too Much Money*. Lois was one of a group of actors, none of whom had appeared in the film, who assumed the parts that on screen had included Lewis Stone and Anna Q. Nilsson and who enacted dialogue that had been created to convey the essence of the silent film. The performers spoke in another room, their voices piped into the dining area through a loudspeaker. This event predated a format that would become commonplace in the 1930s: radio dramatizations of films.

[Miscellaneous, late 1945 and 1946]

At the conclusion of World War II, Lois Moran appeared in a series of impromptu radio productions created with the Seabees to foster support for blood drives and military hospitals. Little is known about these productions.

Barbara Tate for Golden State (April 3, 1946)

Interview for local radio station in which Lois Moran ruminated upon her career.

We Are Many People (1946)

The Council for Civil Unity of San Francisco inaugurated thirteen syndicated fifteen-minute episodes, collectively described as "great radio recordings on democratic themes," which Lois Moran and Carol Levene produced to address social issues confronting postwar America. Lois Moran appeared in several of the episodes. Following is a list of the productions and their plot descriptions as set forth in a promotional brochure of the time:

- "Bend with the Wind." Blinky, a schoolteacher, nearly tumbled into a pitfall, but is saved by a pupil.
- "How Far Is Fifty Feet?" What would you do if Filipinos moved in next door to your house?
- "The Other Side of the Coin." There was an unusual story behind the million dollar grant for World War II veterans.
- "The Barrier." Red-headed Marcia had a deep down feeling of hate until she visited Mexico.
- "The Pixie and Mr. Bixby." Maxie was a pixie who really saw a man, but no pixie could believe that such an irrational creature could exist.
- "Let My People Go." A great Negro actress played Juliet and reluctantly went on tour.
- "Radio Is a Wonderful Thing." A secret meeting made Sam mad because he knew that "prosperity means everyone."
- "For Some of the Many People." A blind woman was able to see clearly in a world of discord.
- "We, the Children." Sam Collier never knew that his son had helped him write his greatest banquet speech.
- "City of Tomorrow." A baby's cry helped defeat the Ku Klux Klan.
- "Paper Children." A reporter discovered the profound democratic faith of a shipload of displaced persons.
- "The Pen Is Mightier." A famous mystery writer learned her lesson when she became the victim of her own vicious stereotypes.
- "And Then There Was One." John developed the surprising power of sending people back where they came from.

Biography in Sound (1955)

NBC biographical series. Lois Moran spoke briefly in an episode about F. Scott Fitzgerald.

F. Scott Fitzgerald

Works Featuring Characters Based upon Lois Moran

Short Works

All are short stories except "Princeton," an essay.

Title	Character
"Jacob's Ladder" (*Saturday Evening Post,* August 20, 1927)	Jenny Delehanty (aka Jenny Prince)
"The Love Boat" (*Saturday Evening Post,* October 8, 1927)	Mae Purley
"Princeton" (*College Humor,* December 1927)	[Herself]
"The Bowl" (*Saturday Evening Post,* January 21, 1928)	Daisy Cary
"Magnetism" (*Saturday Evening Post,* March 3, 1928)	Helen Avery
"The Rough Crossing" (*Saturday Evening Post,* June 8, 1929)	Elizabeth "Betsy" D'Amido
"At Your Age" (*Saturday Evening Post,* August 17, 1929)	Annie Lorry
"The Swimmers" (*Saturday Evening Post,* October 19, 1929)	[Not named]
"A Freeze-Out" (*Saturday Evening Post,* December 19, 1931)	Alida Rikker

Novels

Tender Is the Night (Charles Scribner's Sons, 1934)	Rosemary Hoyt
The Last Tycoon (uncompleted; Charles Scribner's Sons, 1941)	[Not named]

Works Consulted

Allatini, Eric. *La barraca de los monstruos: Puesta en escena e interpretada por Jaque Catelain.* [Spanish novella of *La galerie des monstres.*] Barcelona: J. Horta, 1924.

Allen, Frederick Lewis. *Only Yesterday: An Informal History of the 1920s.* New York: Harper & Row, 1964.

Amory, Cleveland, and Frederick Bradlee, eds. *Vanity Fair: A Cavalcade of the 1920's and 1930's.* New York: Viking Press, 1960.

Anderson, Robert G. *Faces, Forms, Films: The Artistry of Lon Chaney.* New York: Castle, 1971.

Ankerich, Michael G. *Broken Silence: Conversations with Twenty-Three Silent Film Stars.* Jefferson, N.C.: McFarland, 1993.

Barrie, James M. *Peter Pan.* London: Puffin, 1986.

Barrymore, Diana, and Gerold Frank. *Too Much, Too Soon.* New York: Signet Books, 1958.

Behrman, S. N. *Biography.* New York: Samuel French, 1963.

Bellamy, Madge. *A Darling of the Twenties: Madge Bellamy.* Vestal, N.Y.: Vestal Press, 1989.

Bellamy, Ralph. *When the Smoke Hit the Fan.* New York: Doubleday, 1979.

Berg, A. Scott. *Goldwyn: A Biography.* New York: Ballantine Books, 1990.

Biggers, Earl Derr. *Behind That Curtain: With Illustrations from the William Fox "All Talking" Photoplay.* New York: Grosset & Dunlap, 1929.

Blair, Betsy. *The Memory of All That: Love and Politics in New York, Hollywood, and Paris.* New York: Alfred A. Knopf, 2003.

Blake, Michael F. *A Thousand Faces: Lon Chaney's Unique Artistry in Motion Pictures.* Manchester: Hudson Hills Press, 1995.

Bogdanovich, Peter. *Allan Dwan: The Last Pioneer.* London: Studio Vista, 1971.

Boylan, Clare. *Al Jolson.* London: Abacus, 1975.

Brooks, Louise. *Lulu in Hollywood.* New York: Alfred A. Knopf, 1983.

Brown, John Mason. *The Worlds of Robert E. Sherwood: Mirror to His Times 1896–1939.* New York: Harper & Row, 1965.

[Browning, Tod, Herman J. Mankiewicz, and Elliott Clawson.] "The Road to Mandalay" [continuity script dated June 10, 1926]. Culver City: Metro-Goldwyn-Mayer.

Brownlow, Kevin. *The Parade's Gone By...* Berkeley: University of California Press, 1968.

———. *Hollywood: The Pioneers.* New York: Alfred A. Knopf, 1979.

Bruccoli, Matthew J. *The Romantic Egoists: A Pictorial Autobiography from the Scrapbooks and Albums of F. Scott and Zelda Fitzgerald.* New York: Charles Scribner's Sons, 1974.

———. *The Notebooks of F. Scott Fitzgerald.* New York: Harcourt Brace Jovanovich/Bruccoli Clark, 1978.

———. *Scott and Ernest: The Authority of Failure and the Authority of Success.* Carbondale: Southern Illinois University Press, 1978.

———. *Some Sort of Epic Grandeur: The Life of F. Scott Fitzgerald.* New York: Carroll & Graf, 1991.

———, ed. *F. Scott Fitzgerald: A Life in Letters.* New York: Charles Scribner's Sons, 1994.

Bruccoli, Matthew J., and Jackson R. Bryer, eds. *F. Scott Fitzgerald in His Own Time.* New York: Popular Library, 1971.

Bruccoli, Matthew J., and Richard Layman, eds. *Fitzgerald/Hemingway Annual 1978.* Detroit: Gale Research, 1979.

Bryer, Jackson R., ed. *The Short Stories of F. Scott Fitzgerald: New Approaches in Criticism.* Madison: University of Wisconsin Press, 1982.

Buller, Richard P. "Lois Moran: Charming Fragile Cameo of the Movies." *Hollywood Studio Magazine,* June 1989, pp. 30–32.

———. "Lois Moran: From Goldwyn to Gershwin." *Films of the Golden Age,* Summer 1995, pp. 34–44.

Burch, Noel and Ben Brewster. *In and Out of Synch: The Awakening of a Cine-dreamer.* Brookfield, VT: Scolar Press, 1991.

✓ Burk, Margaret T. *Are the Stars Out Tonight? The Story of the Famous Ambassador and Cocoanut Grove...Hollywood's Hotel.* Los Angeles: Margaret Burk, 1980.

Card, James. *Seductive Cinema: The Art of Silent Film.* New York: Alfred A. Knopf, 1994.

Carey, Gary. *Anita Loos.* New York: Alfred A. Knopf, 1988.

Cary, Diana Serra. *Whatever Happened to Baby Peggy? The Autobiography of Hollywood's Pioneer Child Star.* New York: St. Martin's Press, 1996.

Coe, Charles Francis. *The River Pirate: Illustrated with Scenes from the Photoplay, a William Fox Production.* New York: Grosset & Dunlap, 1928.

———. *The River Pirate: Illustrated with Scenes from the Photo Play.* London: Readers Library, 1928.

Connelly, Marc. *Voices Offstage: A Book of Memoirs.* Chicago: Holt, Rinehart & Winston, 1968.

Cooke, Alistair. *Six Men: Charlie Chaplin, Edward VIII, H. L. Mencken, Humphrey Bogart, Adlai Stevenson, Bertrand Russell.* New York: Arcade, 1995.

Cowley, Malcolm, and Robert Cowley, eds. *Fitzgerald and the Jazz Age.* New York: Charles Scribner's Sons, 1966.

Curtis, James, ed. *Featured Player: An Oral Autobiography of Mae Clarke.* Lanham, Md.: Scarecrow Press, 1996.

Donaldson, Scott. *Fool for Love: A Biography of F. Scott Fitzgerald.* New York: Delta, 1989.

Donnelly, Honoria Murphy. *Sara and Gerald: Villa America and After.* New York: Times Books, 1982.

Dos Passos, John. *The Fourteenth Chronicle: Letters and Diaries of John Dos Passos.* Edited by Townsend Ludington. Boston: Gambit, 1973.

Dreiser, Theodore. *An American Tragedy.* New York: New American Library, 1964.

Drew, William M. *Speaking of Silents: First Ladies of the Screen.* Vestal, N.Y.: Vestal Press, 1989.

———. *At the Center of the Frame: Leading Ladies of the Twenties and Thirties.* Lanham, Md.: Vestal Press, 1999.

Eames, John D. *The MGM Story: The Complete History of Fifty Roaring Years.* New York: Crown, 1977.

———. *The Paramount Story: The Complete History of the Studio and Its 2,805 Films.* New York: Octopus, 1985.

Easton, Carol. *The Search for Sam Goldwyn.* New York: Morrow, 1976.

Elder, Donald. *Ring Lardner.* New York: Doubleday, 1956.

Ewen, David. *The Story of George Gershwin.* New York: Holt, 1959.

Fabian, Warner. *The Men in Her Life: Illustrated with Scenes from the Columbia Picture.* New York: Grosset & Dunlap, 1930.

Fairbanks, Douglas, Jr. *The Salad Days.* New York: Doubleday, 1988.

Fitzgerald, F. Scott. *The Stories of F. Scott Fitzgerald.* New York: Charles Scribner's Sons, 1951.

————. *F. Scott Fitzgerald's Ledger: A Facsimile.* Washington, D.C.: Microcard Editions, 1972.

————. *The Great Gatsby.* New York: Simon & Schuster, 1979. (Orig. pub. 1925.)

————. *Correspondence of F. Scott Fitzgerald.* Edited by Matthew J. Bruccoli and Margaret M. Dugan. New York: Random House, 1980.

————. *The Price Was High: The Last Uncollected Stories of F. Scott Fitzgerald.* Edited by Matthew J. Bruccoli. San Diego: Harcourt Trade, 1981.

————. *Tender Is the Night.* New York: Charles Scribner's Sons, 1986. (Orig. pub. 1934.)

√ ————. *Afternoon of an Author.* New York: Charles Scribner's Sons, 1987. (Orig. pub. 1957.)

————. *Flappers and Philosophers.* Old Tappan, N.J.: Macmillan, 1987. (Orig. pub. 1920.)

————. *The Short Stories of F. Scott Fitzgerald: A New Collection.* Edited by Matthew J. Bruccoli. New York: Charles Scribner's Sons, 1989.

————. *F. Scott Fitzgerald: A Life in Letters.* Edited by Matthew J. Bruccoli and Judith S. Baughman. New York: Simon & Schuster, 1995.

————. *The Last Tycoon.* New York: Simon & Schuster, 1995. (Orig. pub. 1941.)

————. *This Side of Paradise.* New York: Simon & Schuster, 1995 (Orig. pub. 1920.)

Fitzgerald, F. Scott, and Zelda Fitzgerald. *Bits of Paradise.* New York: Charles Scribner's Sons, 1973.

Fitzgerald, Zelda. *Save Me the Waltz.* Carbondale: Southern Illinois University Press, 1967.

———. *The Collected Writings.* Edited by Matthew J. Bruccoli. New York: Simon & Schuster, 1992.

Flanner, Janet. *Paris Was Yesterday.* New York: Viking Press, 1972.

Fountain, Leatrice Gilbert. *Dark Star: The Untold Story of the Meteoric Rise and Fall of the Legendary John Gilbert.* New York: St. Martin's Press, 1984.

Fowler, Gene. *Good Night, Sweet Prince: The Life and Times of John Barrymore.* New York: Viking Press, 1944.

Frank, Waldo. *Our America.* New York: Boni & Liveright, 1919.

Franklin, Joe. *Classics of the Silent Screen.* Secaucus, N.J.: Citadel Press, 1972.

Freedland, Michael. *Jolson: The Story of Al Jolson; The Original Biography.* London: Virgin, 1995.

Gale, Robert L. *An F. Scott Fitzgerald Encyclopedia.* Westport: Greenwood, 1998.

Gibbs, Philip. *The Reckless Lady: Illustrated with Scenes from the Photoplay, a First National Picture with an All Star Cast.* New York: Grosset & Dunlap, 1925.

Gish, Lillian. *The Movies, Mr. Griffith, and Me.* New York: Prentice-Hall, 1969.

Graham, Sheilah. *College of One.* New York: Viking, 1967.

———. *The Real F. Scott Fitzgerald: Thirty-Five Years Later.* New York: Grosset & Dunlap, 1976.

Graham, Sheilah, and Gerold Frank. *Beloved Infidel.* New York: Grosset & Dunlap, 1976.

Hack, Richard. *Hughes: The Private Diaries, Memos and Letters.* Beverly Hills: New Millennium Entertainment, 2001.

✓ Harris, Radie. *Radie's World: The Memoirs of Radie Harris.* New York: G. P. Putnam's Sons, 1975.

Hemingway, Ernest. *A Moveable Feast.* New York: Charles Scribner's Sons, 1964.

Herzog, Peter, and Romano Tozzi. *Lya de Putti: Loving Life and Not Fearing Death.* New York: Corvin, 1993.

Hirschhorn, Clive. *The Universal Story: The Complete History of the Studio and Its 2,641 Films.* New York: Octopus, 1987.

"Les impudiques." *Le film complet du samedi.* [Paris, French novella of *Joy Street.*] January 31, 1931.

Israel, Lee. *Miss Tallulah Bankhead.* New York: G. P. Putnam's Sons, 1972.

Jablonski, Edward, and Lawrence D. Stewart. *The Gershwin Years.* New York: Doubleday, 1958.

Jablonski, Edward. *Gershwin: A Biography.* London: Simon & Schuster, 1987.

Kandel, Aben. *Kitty Doone.* New York: Samuel French, 1950.

Katz, Ephraim. *The Film Encyclopedia.* New York: Harper & Row, 1990.

Kaufman, George S., Morrie Ryskind, and Ira Gershwin. *Of Thee I Sing: A Musical Play.* New York: Alfred A. Knopf, 1932.

————. *Let 'Em Eat Cake: A Sequel to Of Thee I Sing, a Musical Play.* New York: Alfred A. Knopf, 1933.

Kellner, Bruce. *Carl Van Vechten and the Irreverent Decades.* Norman: University of Oklahoma Press, 1968.

✓ ————. *The Last Dandy, Ralph Barton: American Artist, 1891–1931.* Columbia: University of Missouri Press, 1991.

Klein, Charles. *The Music Master: Novelized from the Play as Produced by David Belasco; Illustrated with Scenes from the Photoplay, a William Fox Production.* New York: Grosset & Dunlap, 1928.

Kobal, John, ed. *Great Film Stills of the German Silent Era.* New York: Dover, 1981.

Kobler, John. *Damned in Paradise: The Life of John Barrymore.* New York: Atheneum, 1977.

Kohner, Frederick. *Kiki of Montparnasse.* New York: Stein & Day, 1967.

Lamparski, Richard. *Whatever Became Of...?* 10th ed. New York: Crown, 1986.

Lanahan, Eleanor, ed. *Zelda, An Illustrated Life: The Private World of Zelda Fitzgerald.* New York: Harry N. Abrams, 1996.

Latham, Aaron. *Crazy Sundays: F. Scott Fitzgerald in Hollywood.* New York: Viking Press, 1971.

LeVot, Andre. *F. Scott Fitzgerald.* New York: Doubleday, 1983.

Loy, Myrna, and James Kotsilibas-Davis. *Being and Becoming.* New York: Alfred A. Knopf, 1987.

Lueders, Edward. *Carl Van Vechten*. New York: Twayne, 1965.

Marx, Arthur. *Goldwyn: A Biography of the Man Behind the Myth*. New York: W. W. Norton, 1976.

Mayfield, Sara. *Exiles from Paradise: Zelda and Scott Fitzgerald*. New York: Delacorte Press, 1971.

Meade, Marion. *Dorothy Parker: What Fresh Hell Is This?* New York: Penguin, 1989.

Mellow, James R. *Charmed Circle: Gertrude Stein and Company*. New York: Praeger, 1974.

———. *Invented Lives: F. Scott and Zelda Fitzgerald*. Boston: Houghton Mifflin, 1984.

Merkin, Richard. *The Jazz Age as Seen through the Eyes of Ralph Barton, Miguel Covarrubias, and John Held, Jr.* Exhibition catalog, Museum of Art, Rhode Island School of Design, September 25–November 10, 1968. Providence: The Museum, 1968.

Meyers, Jeffrey. *Scott Fitzgerald: A Biography*. New York: HarperCollins, 1994.

Milford, Nancy. *Zelda: A Biography*. New York: Harper & Row, 1970.

Miller, Don. *B Movies*. New York: Ballantine Books, 1988.

Mizener, Arthur. *The Far Side of Paradise: A Biography of F. Scott Fitzgerald*. New York: Vintage Books, 1959.

———. *Scott Fitzgerald and His World*. New York: Putnam, 1972.

Moore, Colleen. *Silent Star*. New York: Doubleday, 1968.

Mortensen, William. *The Seven Ages of Woman: Suggested by William Shakespeare, the Acting and Portraying Being Done by Miss Lois Moran*. Hollywood: Privately printed, 1927.

Nathan, George Jean. "Memories of Fitzgerald, Lewis and Dreiser." *Esquire*, October 1958, pp. 148–49.

Novela Cinematográfica del Hogar: Tras la cortina. [Spanish novella of *Behind That Curtain*.] Barcelona: Ediciones Bistagne, [ca. 1929].

Novela Fox: Mi vida en sus manos. [Spanish novella of *True Heaven*.] Barcelona: Ediciones Bistagne, [ca. 1929].

Novela Fox: Pirata del rio. [Spanish novella of *The River Pirate*.] Barcelona: Ediciones Bistagne, [ca. 1929].

Novela Paramount: El torbellino de la juventud. [Spanish novella of *The Whirlwind of Youth.*] Barcelona: Ediciones Bistagne, [ca. 1929].

Paine, Albert Bigelow. *Life and Lillian Gish.* New York: Macmillan, 1932.

Paris, Barry. *Louise Brooks.* New York: Alfred A. Knopf, 1989.

Peyser, Joan. *The Memory of All That: The Life of George Gershwin.* New York: Simon & Schuster, 1993.

Phillips, Gene D. *Fiction, Film, and F. Scott Fitzgerald.* Chicago: Loyola University Press, 1986.

Prigozy, Ruth. "From Griffith's Girls to *Daddy's Girl*: The Masks of Innocence in *Tender Is the Night.*" *Twentieth Century Literature*, Summer 1980, pp. 189–221.

———. *F. Scott Fitzgerald.* New York: Overlook Press, 2002.

Prouty, Olive Higgins. *Stella Dallas: Illustrated with Scenes from the Photoplay, a Samuel Goldwyn–Henry King Production.* New York: Grosset & Dunlap, 1923.

———. *Pencil Shavings: Memoirs.* Cambridge: Riverside Press, 1961.

Ralston, Esther. *Some Day We'll Laugh: An Autobiography.* Metuchen, N.J.: Scarecrow Press, 1985.

Ring, Frances Kroll. *Against the Current: As I Remember F. Scott Fitzgerald.* Berkeley: Creative Arts Books, 1987.

The Road to Mandalay: A Thrilling Throbbing Romance of Singapore Based on the Motion Picture Story by Tod Browning and Herman J. Mankiewicz. New York: Jacobsen-Hodgkinson, 1926.

Roulston, Robert, and Helen H. Roulston. *The Winding Road to West Egg: The Artistic Development of F. Scott Fitzgerald.* Lewisburg, Pa.: Bucknall University Press, 1995.

Schulberg, Budd. *The Disenchanted.* New York: Random House, 1950.

Sherwood, Robert Emmet. *This Is New York: A Play in Three Acts.* New York: Charles Scribner's Sons, 1931.

———. *The Petrified Forest.* New York: Charles Scribner's Sons, 1935.

Sinclair, Upton. *Upton Sinclair Presents William Fox.* Los Angeles: Privately printed, 1933.

Skal, David J., and Elias Savada. *Dark Carnival: The Secret World of Tod Browning, Hollywood's Master of the Macabre.* New York: Anchor Books, 1995.

Sklar, Robert. *F. Scott Fitzgerald: The Last Laocoön*. New York: Oxford University Press, 1967.

Slide, Anthony. *The Vaudevillians: A Dictionary of Vaudeville Performers*. Westport, Conn.: Arlington House, 1981.

———. *Silent Portraits: Stars of the Silent Screen in Historic Photographs*. Vestal, N.Y.: Vestal Press, 1989.

Stars of the Movies and Featured Players. Hollywood: Hollywood Publicity, 1927.

Stars of the Photoplay. Chicago: Photoplay, 1930.

Stein, Gertrude. *Selected Writings of Gertrude Stein*. Edited by Carl Van Vechten. New York: Random House, 1946.

Stewart, Lawrence D. "The Gershwins: Words upon Music." Program notes to *Ella Fitzgerald Sings the George and Ira Gershwin Song Books*. Verve MG V-4029-5, 1959.

Talmadge, Margaret. *The Talmadge Sisters: Norma, Constance, Natalie; An Intimate Study of the World's Most Famous Screen Family*. Philadelphia: J. B. Lippincot, 1924.

Tate, Mary Jo. *F. Scott Fitzgerald, A to Z: The Essential Reference to His Life and Work*. New York: Checkmark Books, 1998.

Taylor, Kendall. *Sometimes Madness Is Wisdom: Zelda and Scott Fitzgerald, a Marriage*. New York: Ballantine Books, 2003.

Teachout, Terry. *The Skeptic: A Life of H. L. Mencken*. New York: HarperCollins, 2002.

Thompson, Frank, ed. *Henry King, Director: From Silents to 'Scope*. Based upon interviews by David Shepard and Ted Perry. New York: Directors' Guild of America, 1995.

Tilden, William T., Jr. *The Art of Lawn Tennis*. New York: George Duran, 1922.

Toll, Seymour I. *A Judge Uncommon: A Life of John Biggs, Jr*. Philadelphia: Legal Communications, 1993.

Turnbull, Andrew. *Scott Fitzgerald*. New York: Charles Scribner's Sons, 1962.

Vaill, Amanda. *Everybody Was So Young: Gerald and Sara Murphy, a Lost Generation Love Story*. New York: Broadway Books, 1999.

Vermilye, Jerry. *The Films of the Twenties*. New York: Citadel, 1985.

Vieira, Mark A. *Hurrell's Hollywood Portraits.* New York: Abrams, 1997.

Westbrook, Robert. *Intimate Lies: F. Scott Fitzgerald and Sheilah Graham; Her Son's Story.* New York: HarperCollins, 1995.

Wiser, William. *The Crazy Years: Paris in the Twenties.* New York: Atheneum, 1983.

Zeilinger, Johannes. *Lya de Putti: Ein vergessenes Leben.* Vienna: Karolinger, 1991.

Index

Text Permissions and Photograph/Illustration Credits